D0881221

ON LAW AND JUSTICE

Paul A. Freund

ON LAW AND JUSTICE

The Belknap Press of Harvard University Press

1968 CAMBRIDGE, MASSACHUSETTS

Preface

The commodious title of this volume fairly reflects the diversity of its content. Essays such as those collected here are – to adapt a figure of Mr. Justice Holmes – fragments of the author's fleece gathered from the hedgerows through which he has chanced to pass.

Despite the diversity, there will be found, I believe, a unity of outlook. Certain themes recur, and when they do I can only hope that the reader will feel not that he is hearing the same composition but only that he is listening to the same composer. Explicitly or implicitly the essays try to suggest that the processes of law – the procedures and ways of thought of lawyers and judges – may contribute more generally to our thinking, may help us to live with uncertainty and ambiguity, may teach us to cope with the great antinomies of our aspirations: liberty and order; privacy and knowledge; stability and change; security and responsibility. Above all, we may discern through the law that the profoundest reality and the most demanding morality lie not in particular judgments or results but in the process of moving toward them.

No effort has been made to obliterate the occasional nature of some of the essays, which shows through in their style and scope. "Social Justice and the Law," for example, which might be expected to offer a program for the more equitable distribution of goods and services, is in fact an attempt to probe the meaning of justice with the benefit of the lawyer's distinctive experience in pursuing it; this theme was dictated by the nature of the occasion, a symposium on the meaning of justice, in which the other participants were drawn from philosophy, political science, and economics. Despite temptation, second thoughts have not been allowed to substitute for what originally appeared in the essays, but where the turn of events has made a statement erroneous, a footnote marked by an asterisk or a bracketed addition to an original footnote has been inserted to note the development.

Responsibility for this volume must be shared by my generous and seductive friend Thomas J. Wilson, Director of the Harvard University Press, whose gentle but persistent prodding brought on a suspension of my critical faculties for just the necessary time.

P.A.F.

Cambridge, Massachusetts
September 1967

Contents

I   THE COURT AND THE CONSTITUTION

1 New Vistas in Constitutional Law

Anniversaries are a time for retrospect and prospect, looking into the murky past and peering into the misty future. In 1889, to mark the centennial of the Constitution, a celebration was held at the University of Michigan. One of the speakers, Professor Charles A. Kent, speaking on constitutional development since 1864, took a backward and forward look at the due process clause of the fourteenth amendment.[1] Pointing out that a large number of cases had reached the Supreme Court on this ground, he quoted the impatient remark of Justice Miller in 1877, in *Davidson v. New Orleans*, that "the docket of this court is crowded with cases in which we are asked to hold that State courts and State legislatures have deprived their own citizens of life, liberty, or property without due process of law," and that "the clause under consideration is looked upon as a means of bringing to the test of the decision of this court the abstract opinions of every unsuccessful litigant in a State court of the justice of the decision against him..."[2] The speaker reviewed the efforts, all of them futile, to induce the Supreme Court to set aside state laws prohibiting the sale of intoxicating liquors and of oleomargarine, laws fixing maximum rates and

The Owen J. Roberts Memorial Lecture, delivered November 7, 1963, at the University of Pennsylvania Law School; reprinted from 112 U. Pa. L. Rev. 631 (1964), copyright the University of Pennsylvania Law Review.

[1] Kent, *Constitutional Development in the United States, as Influenced by Decisions of the Supreme Court Since 1864*, in Michigan University, constitutional History of the United States as Seen in the Development of American Law (1889).

[2] *Id.* at 231-32, quoting Davidson v. New Orleans, 96 U.S. 97, 104 (1877).

charges for railroads and storage elevators, and laws dispensing with the petty jury or the grand jury in state courts. The
speaker concluded:

These and other decisions show that for the protection of all the
ordinary rights of life, liberty, and property, each individual must rely
mainly on the constitution, statutes, and judiciary of his own State,
and that the jurisdiction of the Supreme Court of the United States
can be successfully invoked, at present, only in extreme cases. Still,
the jurisdiction exists in all this class of cases, and the time may come
when that court, with a changed membership and changed tendencies,
may set aside State laws deemed most important for the proper
administration of justice.[3]

Within a year of that address, the Supreme Court decided the
case of *Chicago, M. & St. P. Ry. v. Minnesota*,[4] holding that the
due process clause was violated by a state law making the findings of a state commission conclusive on the subject of equal and
reasonable charges for railroad transportation. The case can be
seen as one of those bridge decisions that open up new terrain
by connecting it with familiar ground. The deprivation of
property, it was insisted, must be the result in the end of a
judicial determination as a matter of due procedure in the
strict sense, and the judicial function must ultimately include a
decision on the reason of the law and the order. From that
decision, wrote Judge Hough in 1919, "I date the flood."[5]

At almost the same time as the Michigan celebration, the
Harvard Law School Association was awarding a prize for the
best essay by a member of the graduating class. The award
went to Charles E. Shattuck for his paper entitled "The True
Meaning of the Term 'Liberty' in Those Clauses in the Federal
and State Constitutions Which Protect 'Life, Liberty, and
Property.' "[6] The prize-winning author noted the tendency of

---

[3] *Id.* at 233.
[4] 134 U.S. 418 (1890).
[5] Hough, *Due Process of Law — To-day,* 32 HARV. L. REV. 218, 228 (1919).
[6] 4 HARV. L. REV. 265 (1891).

state courts to give the term "liberty" a meaning considerably broader than physical freedom of the person, and specifically to include the right to follow any ordinary calling. Setting himself against this latitude of meaning and protection, the author concluded:

One is obliged to ask why it should include thus much and no more. If it includes the right to pursue any lawful trade, why should it not include the right to worship in any lawful manner, to print or speak in any lawful manner? Possibly, if the point should arise, it would be held to include all the above liberties, although the writer has not found any statements in the books to that effect. The reasons for supposing that the term should not be so interpreted have already been set forth.[7]

Mr. Shattuck had to wait a little longer than Professor Kent to find that his rhetorical question was not so rhetorical after all. Here the progression was from property to proprietary liberties—liberty to pursue a lawful calling, to make contracts, and to manage one's business—and so at length to liberty of the mind and in the forum of ideas. The judicial bridgework was constructed of questions, of concessions for the sake of argument, and finally of solid holdings. The story is familiar enough, but it may be worth recalling briefly at a time when we are inclined to account liberties of the mind and forum as the starting point and to ask in turn whether these may not imply parallel liberties of a proprietary kind. In 1907, Justice Holmes could say, in a case on contempt of a state court by a newspaper publication, "We leave undecided the question whether there is to be found in the Fourteenth Amendment a prohibition similar to that in the First."[8] In 1922, answering a contention that a state law requiring employers to give a letter to an employee upon discharge or termination of service describing the cause of his leaving was an infringement of a right of the corporation derived from the guarantee of freedom of

---

[7] *Id.* at 392.
[8] Patterson v. Colorado, 205 U.S. 454, 462 (1907).

speech, the Court observed that "neither the Fourteenth Amendment nor any other provision of the Constitution of the United States imposes upon the States any restrictions about 'freedom of speech' or the 'liberty of silence'; nor, we may add, does it confer any right of privacy upon either persons or corporations."[9] Meanwhile, questions began to be raised. In his dissenting opinion in *Gilbert v. Minnesota,* Justice Brandeis concluded with a sharp confrontation: "I cannot believe that the liberty guaranteed by the Fourteenth Amendment includes only liberty to acquire and to enjoy property."[10] In *Gitlow v. New York,* argued and reargued in 1923 and decided in 1925, Justice Holmes, joined by Justice Brandeis, introduced his dissenting opinion with the flat assertion:

The general principle of free speech, it seems to me, must be taken to be included in the Fourteenth Amendment, in view of the scope that has been given to the word "liberty" as there used, although perhaps it may be accepted with a somewhat larger latitude of interpretation than is allowed to Congress by the sweeping language that governs or ought to govern the laws of the United States.[11]

The majority in that case were impelled to make an assumption which proved in the long run more significant than the decision: "For present purposes we may and do assume that freedom of speech and of the press—which are protected by the First Amendment from abridgment by Congress—are among the fundamental personal rights and 'liberties' protected by the due process clause of the Fourteenth Amendment from impairment by the States."[12]

The rest of the story is well known, and it is one in which Justice Roberts played a significant role. The chief justiceship of Charles Evans Hughes was the watershed. Beginning with *Near v. Minnesota* in 1931,[13] in which Justice Roberts was an

[9] Prudential Ins. Co. of America v. Cheek, 259 U.S. 530, 543 (1922).
[10] 254 U.S. 325, 343 (1920).
[11] 268 U.S. 652, 672 (1925).
[12] *Id.* at 666.
[13] 283 U.S. 697 (1931).

indispensable member of the majority of five, liberty of the press was firmly assimilated to the other liberties that had received shelter under the fourteenth amendment. Freedom of religious belief and exercise was established in an opinion by Justice Roberts himself in *Cantwell v. Connecticut*,[14] and the foundation for liberty of association was laid in *DeJonge v. Oregon*.[15] In the same period the guarantees in favor of defendants in criminal cases were given new vitality, notably in the right to counsel,[16] the exclusion of coerced confessions,[17] and the scrutiny of jury lists for evidence of racial discrimination;[18] and the separate but equal doctrine began to be eroded in decisions on state provision of higher education.[19]

All of this movement and ferment, so obscure to the vision of 1889, reflected a sensitivity to values that had emerged in the society and that were sharpened by visible and powerful threats here and abroad. It is no accident, after all, that during the tenure of Justice Roberts, which coincided with the rise of totalitarian dictatorships, the Court found occasion to set aside the action of Mayor Hague of Jersey City in handpicking the speakers permitted to use the public square, the action of a Huey Long-dominated legislature of Louisiana levying an oppressive tax on the big-city press, and the action of Governor Sterling of Texas in declaring martial law in defiance of a federal court order.[20]

Today we are in the centennial year of the Emancipation Proclamation and are approaching the hundredth anniversary of the fourteenth amendment itself. For all of the warnings posted by the examples of anniversary prophecies, the temptation is nevertheless strong to cast an eye on the vistas opened

[14] 310 U.S. 296 (1940).

[15] 299 U.S. 353 (1937).

[16] Powell v. Alabama, 287 U.S. 45 (1932).

[17] Brown v. Mississippi, 297 U.S. 278 (1936).

[18] Norris v. Alabama, 294 U.S. 587 (1935).

[19] Missouri *ex rel.* Gaines v. Canada, 305 U.S. 337 (1938).

[20] Hague v. C.I.O., 307 U.S. 496 (1939); Grosjean v. American Press Co., 297 U.S. 233 (1936); Sterling v. Constantin, 287 U.S. 378 (1932).

by recent developments. But before venturing on that hazardous course, a few words ought to be said about the process of deriving meaning from, or infusing meaning into, the noble and spacious clauses of the amendment. I have said that the process obscured to the vision of 1889 reflected a heightened sense of values in the contemporary world. To say this is to raise the perennial and nagging question of objectivity in constitutional law.

It is no disparagement of a work of art or of its interpreters that it takes on new relevance, yields new insights, answers to new concerns, as the generations pass. Nor is it a reproach to a Constitution "intended to endure for ages to come, and to meet the various crises in human affairs" or to its interpreters that it too responds to changing concerns of the society to which it ministers. As *Hamlet* has at one time or another been seen as a story of revenge, a study of the borderland of sanity, a search for rational instead of spectral modes of evidence, an analysis of mother-fixation or a death-wish, and as none of these can be said to be wrong, each having some relevance and some validity, so it need not be cause for despair that to one generation the Constitution was primarily a means of cementing the Union, to another a safeguard of property, to another a shield of access to political participation and equality before the law.

In a recent essay, Professor Stuart Hughes has set out his view of the problem of objectivity for the historian:

I remember that at one time I really believed that the writer or teacher of history could and should attain to a sublime detachment. As the French put it, he should be above the mêlée of human events, delivering with sovereign confidence the "verdict of posterity." Since then, an intense exposure to the ideas of Benedetto Croce has cured me of such notions: I have learned that the result of the historian's efforts to be detached has usually been the very opposite of what anyone would call great history. It has been bloodless history, with no clear focus, arising from antiquarian curiosity rather than from deep personal concern, and shot through with metaphysical and moral assumptions that are all the more insidious for being artfully concealed.

This does not mean that I—and others like me—have learned from Croce to write partisan history with a good conscience. Far from it: we detest mere polemic, and we certainly know how to distinguish between fine historical writing and writing designed to serve a cause. We recognize that historians have been right in striving for serenity and the world-embracing view. But we understand this aspiration in rather a different sense from the way in which it used to be taught to us. What we have learned from Croce and his like is that "objectivity" is to be valued only if it is hard-won—only if it is the end result of a desperate *and conscious* battle to rise above partisan passion. The man who does not feel issues deeply cannot write great history about them. Unaware of his own prejudices, he cannot bring them to full consciousness and thus transcend them, nor will his prose be infused with that quality of tension and excitement that comes from strong emotion just barely under control. Only after he has mastered his own limitations can the historian begin to make constructive use of them. "Man's capacity to rise above his social and historical situation," as Carr puts it, "seems to be conditioned by the sensitivity with which he recognizes the extent of his involvement in it." [21]

I venture to think that even Chief Justice Hughes, without making allowance for grandfatherly pride, would have found that portrayal of the historian's art to be a fair statement, *mutatis mutandis,* of the constitutional jurist's as well.

I wish to consider three recent developments in the law of the fourteenth amendment: first, the extension of the idea of due process in criminal cases; second, the new concept of equal protection in the reapportionment cases; third, the expanding notion of state action or, better, state responsibility. Obviously a rounded treatment of all these thorny issues is not possible. What I shall try to explore is the extent to which these developments open up straight, unclouded vistas or disclose curtained patches of haze that may call for circumspection in the judicial passage.

The extension of the idea of due process in criminal cases is

[21] Hughes, *Is Contemporary History Real History?,* 32 THE AMERICAN SCHOLAR 516, 520 (1963).

symbolized by *Mapp v. Ohio*,[22] ruling that the products of an unconstitutional search and seizure must be excluded from evidence in a state no less than a federal criminal trial. This development was in fact foreseen by Justice Roberts, though with no enthusiasm. In his Holmes lectures at Harvard in 1951, he pointed out that the concept of due process was being extended by assumptions for the sake of argument — "We are led to speculate when the Court will hold that the Fourteenth has absorbed the Fifth and Eighth Amendments" (compare the evolution of the guarantees of speech) — while the logical result of that extension, the reversal of state convictions, was being withheld. It was an uneasy compromise — "a strange medley," he called it, "of federal and state law" — that could not, in his judgment, endure.[23]

Now that the compromise has been abandoned and the exclusionary rule of evidence made mandatory, will there be a reexamination of the federal substantive rules of search and seizure themselves to determine more precisely than was necessary heretofore just what rules may be ascribed to the Constitution and what to the supervisory power over the federal, as distinct from the state, courts? We have already seen an equal division of the Court on this issue: whether the requirement of self-identification of the officers at the door is indeed a constitutional command for all or only the better practice demanded of federal officers.[24] Since the common law did not impose an exclusionary consequence on illegal searches and seizures, an absolute equation of common-law rules of official conduct with the new demands of the fourteenth amendment is, from a functional or operational point of view,misleading. To enlarge the consequences of violating the rules is tantamount to redefining the rules themselves. It does not require a tongue of prophecy to predict that some reexami-

[22] 367 U.S. 643 (1961).
[23] ROBERTS, THE COURT AND THE CONSTITUTION 87-89 (1951).
[24] Ker v. California, 374 U.S. 23 (1963).

nation at the fringes of constitutional standards will be undertaken, and that there may be some latitude left for state variations.

A related problem is the temporal, rather than the territorial, reach of the *Mapp* case — the issue of retrospective application to prisoners seeking release or a new trial through habeas corpus. Since the new evidentiary rule goes not to the intrinsic fairness of a trial already held but to an effective sanction for the enforcement of rules of police conduct, and since that sanction will operate prospectively, the compulsion to apply the exclusionary policy retrospectively is relatively weak; latitude here too may well be left for local option.* A more difficult question of retrospective application is posed by the rule requiring the appointment of counsel for indigent defendants in state cases involving serious charges. The answer may well turn on a question of the relation of the recent *Gideon v. Wainwright* decision[25] to the predecessor doctrine deriving from the opinion of Justice Roberts in *Betts v. Brady.*[26] In overruling that case, did the Court mean to lay it down that a trial without counsel is necessarily unfair, or only that the effort to apply *Betts v. Brady* on a case-by-case basis, looking for aggregate unfairness in the conviction under review, proved to be weariness of flesh and spirit and ought to be superseded by a flat rule of judicial administration in the state courts, a rule, moreover, that experience with *Betts v. Brady* might well have moved them to adopt for themselves in the interim? Here the mode of opinion-writing in overruling is more than a matter of style or manners; it has operative implications for an important class of cases. Perhaps the style of the *Gideon* opinion was meant deliberately to foreclose this question in favor of a retrospective command; but the Court has chosen not to say so, electing to put the question in the first instance to a state

---

* The Court has held that the exlusionary rule need not be applied retrospectively. Linkletter v. Walker, 381 U.S. 618 (1965).

[25] 372 U.S. 335 (1963).

[26] 316 U.S. 455 (1942).

court.[27] Whatever the outcome in particular classes of cases, it would be regrettable if a supposed necessity to conform the criteria on habeas corpus to evolving standards of judicial administration and review in criminal trials should in the future prove to be a dogma reflexively inhibiting the Court in the evolution of those standards themselves.

If the reapportionment case[28] — to turn to the new vista of equal protection of the laws — was an extraordinary decision, it was a response to an extraordinary problem. The obstacles in the way of federal judicial review were formidable. The standing of the complainants ought to be linked to their substantive rights as voters, and since it begs the question to say that they had a right to absolute fractional equality with voters in other districts choosing among other candidates, and since principles of representation have long been a matter of diversity — resting on population, or area, or other interests, or a combination of these — a formulation of the complainants' legal rights may ultimately have to probe deep into the foundations of political philosophy. The issue seems more aptly one of a republican form of government than of personal rights of individual voters. Moreover, the problem of equity jurisdiction, the shaping and enforcement of a decree, was no less formidable, given the awkward solution of an election at large with no proportionality through districting, and the risk of inaction or stalemate in the lawmaking branches of state government.

But the case before the Court was a particularly insistent one. The state constitution itself had resolved the issue of the basis of political representation in favor of the principle of numbers; the actual apportionment was not the product of any

[27] Pickelseimer v. Wainwright, 375 U.S. 2 (1963); see Daegele v. Kansas, 375 U.S. 1, 89 (1963), *remanded for consideration in light of* Douglas v. California, 372 U.S. 353 (1963). [Subsequently the Court did make clear that the rule concerning counsel was to be applied retrospectively. See Johnson v. New Jersey, 384 U.S. 719, 727 (1966).]

[28] Baker v. Carr, 369 U.S. 186 (1962). For some of the complexities in a theory of democratic representation see BUCHANAN & TULLOCH, THE CALCULUS OF CONSENT (1962).

considered legislative policy but of legislative inaction for sixty years; and no popular procedure like the initiative and referendum, independent of the legislature, was available under state law. It is sometimes said that when legislatures and executives cannot be moved to advance the cause of liberalism, the opportunity and responsibility devolve on the courts. Stated thus baldly, the counsel is surely a dangerous invitation, dangerous to the standing of the Court and false to the liberalism in whose name it is propounded. But in the context of the Tennessee apportionment case the default of the lawmaking machinery had special relevance, for the very structure and processes that are presupposed in representative government had become distorted.

The future will test the Court's resourcefulness in defining the rational bounds of patterns of representation without resorting to a simplistic criterion of one man, one vote — a criterion meaningful in an election for a single state-wide office or for a particular representative but question-begging in the case of a collegial body to be chosen with a view to balanced representation. This is the kind of challenge that even a John Marshall did not always succeed in meeting satisfactorily. That the power to tax involves the power to destroy — pronounced to strike down a state tax discriminating against the United States Bank[29] — that the power over commerce among the states is exclusively lodged in Congress — asserted in order to set aside a state-granted monopoly[30] — these were doctrines going beyond the necessities of the case or the problem, doctrines which plagued constitutional law for a long time, because they could not contain the counterpressures from state interests that had been slighted in the formulas. The general direction of Marshall was characteristically wise, but the momentum of doctrine shot beyond its mark, and other generations were obliged to retrace some giant steps in order to follow a viable course. The problem for the courts in reapportionment, I suggest, is

[29] McCulloch v. Maryland, 18 U.S. (4 Wheat.) 316 (1819).
[30] Gibbons v. Ogden, 22 U.S. (9 Wheat.) 1 (1824).

similar: to maintain direction while avoiding the confounding of the rational with the doctrinaire.*

The unfolding concept of state action, or state responsibility, has made a strong appeal to those students of our society who see in the modern corporation, the labor union, and other forms of association a microcosm of the state itself. In strength, in importance, in their impact on their members and on the community, some at least of these organizations do appear to rival and resemble formal governmental units. What more natural, then, than that they should be "constitutionalized," subjected to the restraints which have been leveled by the Constitution at government itself?

The decisions which have thus far brought certain "private" action under the restrictions of the fourteenth amendment have taken us a long way beyond a formalistic view of the responsibility which that amendment attaches to deprivations by the "State." The Court has shown a sense of realism in this development, but has so far declined to take the step of unhinging the amendment from close state involvement, and to overrule the Civil Rights Cases. Where the state has delegated certain governmental functions to private groups, the groups are held to constitutional duties in carrying them out, as in the conduct of party primaries, which are an integral part of the political electoral process,[31] and the normally governmental

---

* The Court has extended the doctrine of numerical equality to districting of the second house of a state legislature, Lucas v. Forty-Fourth General Assembly of Colorado, 377 U.S. 713 (1964). But other decisions have declined to upset a system containing some multi-member districts, where some voters find themselves in a minority because of the larger size of the district, although an invidious plan to that end would be treated differently. Fortson v. Dorsey, 379 U.S. 433 (1965). And the doctrine of voting weight has not served to invalidate a run-off election for governor in a malapportioned state legislature, Fortson v. Morris, 385 U.S. 231 (1966), or to interfere with certain forms of local governmental bodies chosen on bases other than equal weight to individual voters in the constituency. Sailors v. Kent County Bd. of Educ., 387 U.S. 105 (1967).

[31] Smith v. Allwright, 321 U.S. 649 (1944).

conduct of a company-owned town.[32] The latter case is of special interest because it concerns rights of public assembly and religious exercise, illustrating the reach of the amendment beyond acts of discrimination. Another class includes cases where the state may fairly be held responsible for the private conduct, by granting an exclusive or near-exclusive franchise, or by providing special facilities to carry out the private plan.[33] A further group includes cases where state-owned facilities are involved, through lease or similar arrangement.[34] The decision in *Shelley v. Kraemer*,[35] holding unconstitutional the judicial enforcement of a racially restrictive housing covenant, is susceptible of various interpretations, but the reiteration in the opinion that there were a willing seller and a willing buyer suggests that the state court was in those circumstances regarded as the effective cause of the discrimination. Or the decision may be rationalized by assimilating the enforcement of a neighborhood covenant, binding on all successors in interest, to a municipal zoning ordinance binding on all neighborhood property owners when a certain majority of them have approved a racial restriction.

The further vista of an overruling of the Civil Rights Cases has been opened to some eyes by the public-accommodations bill and the controversy over its proper constitutional basis — the commerce clause or the fourteenth amendement. The immediate purpose of the fourteenth amendment was to validate the Civil Rights Act of 1866, which was directed to acts under color of state law. When in 1875 Congress undertook to prohibit not acts under color of state law, but discriminatory practices by public carriers, inns, and theaters, the statute was held to exceed the authority conferred by the amendment.[36]

[32] Marsh v. Alabama, 326 U.S. 501 (1946).
[33] Pennsylvania v. Board of Directors of City Trusts, 353 U.S. 230 (1957); Steele v. Louisville & N.R.R., 323 U.S. 192 (1944); *cf.* Pennsylvania v. Board of Directors of City Trusts, 357 U.S. 570 (1958).
[34] Burton v. Wilmington Parking Authority, 365 U.S. 715 (1961).
[35] 334 U.S. 1 (1948).
[36] Civil Rights Cases, 109 U.S. 3 (1883).

When it is asked why the Civil Rights Cases have not been overruled, and what the prospects of overruling are, the best clue to an answer lies in the cloudiness of the meaning of the question—"overruling" the decision. It is easy enough to state the principle on which the cases were decided: that only acts for which the state is in some meaningful way responsible are comprehended by the amendment. But to state the principle that would underlie an overruling is far from easy. The dissent of Justice Harlan is itself not wholly clear, but at all events he did not take the position that all private action permitted by state law could be reached by Congress because all such action is philosophically a delegation of sovereign power. What would be involved is not simply an *ad hoc* determination, or an appeal to moral sentiment, or a problem of choice between the slogan of property rights and the slogan of public responsibility of public enterprises. Because the fourteenth amendment is spacious in its guarantees and is cast largely in terms of prohibitions that are self-executing (by way at least of injunctive relief and defenses to legal claims, without enforcement legislation), any decision "overruling" the Civil Rights Cases has implications for judicial power and duty that transcend the immediate controversy. Such a decision would have a momentum of principle that might carry it far beyond the issue of racial discrimination or public accommodations. The point is not that the step must therefore be rejected; it is that if the step is taken, it should be done with clear awareness of its larger implications. In this respect it differs qualitatively from a step taken under the commerce clause, for that is primarily a grant of legislative power to Congress, which can be exercised in large or small measure, flexibly, pragmatically, tentatively, progressively, while the recognition of guaranteed rights, if they are declared to be conferred by the Constitution, is not to be granted or withheld in fragments. Therefore, it is necessary to arrive at some conception of the range of rights which an overruling of the Civil Rights Cases would create for the courts and the Congress to enforce.

Equal protection and due process are the guarantees of the amendment which have been most intensively applied against official state action. In considering their possible applications following an overruling of the Civil Rights Cases, three levels of questions are raised: to what *enterprises,* to what *activities* of those enterprises, and by what *standards* shall the applications be made?

If the extension were limited to public utilities in the strict sense, those enterprises having a duty, under the common law or statutes of the state which created them, to serve the public generally, there might be no problem, for the state itself would be discriminating in its law if its courts would enforce this duty on behalf of all except members of a particular race or religion. But public utilities in this sense are a narrow class of enterprises — public carriers and inns for lodging — and it would have to be shown (as it was not in the Civil Rights Cases) that the state practiced discrimination in enforcement of the general legal duty to serve imposed under its own law.

It has been suggested that a right be recognized against all establishments licensed by the state; the license would be the nexus between state and private responsibility. Licensing varies in scope and function from state to state, and from city to city. It may signify only that an establishment has paid a tax, or satisfies sanitary or safety standards, or is operated by qualified persons. To make the constitutional right to be served turn on the presence or absence of a license would thus produce some anomalous results, substituting a new formalism in the movement away from an older one. Moreover, as a practical matter, a local government would not find it difficult to dispense with the requirement of a license while retaining control over sanitary, safety, and similar conditions as well as over tax liability. The standards imposed on an establishment in these respects could be enforced by injunction or civil and criminal penalties, without the device of a license.

There is one type of license which stands on a different footing — a certificate of convenience and necessity, conferring a monopoly or near-monopoly. When the state grants such a franchise, it forecloses potential competitors from operating on a possibly nondiscriminatory basis, and so in a special sense the state may be regarded as contributing to the discriminatory policy followed by its franchise holder. This penumbra of the fourteenth amendment has already been recognized without legislation, in connection with the duties of a union holding an exclusive bargaining position under law and a private bus line holding a franchise.[37]

If licensing by itself were regarded as a basis for application of the fourteenth amendment, the question would arise whether private schools and colleges licensed by a state, or lawyers, or indeed all corporations operating under state charter, could properly be omitted from the coverage. Similarly, if licensing gives rise to constitutional duties and corresponding rights, it is hard to see how any exemptions could be made on the basis of size, any more than other constitutional rights, like that of freedom from censorship, can be made to turn on the size of an establishment.

An alternative basis for identifying certain enterprises with the state for purposes of the fourteenth amendment is the concept of businesses affected with a public interest, a category that for many years was used to signify those enterprises that could be subjected to state control over prices and rates. But even for this permissive purpose, the classification proved unsatisfactory and artificial, and when in 1934 this criterion was frankly abandoned by the Court in an opinion by Justice Roberts, the decision was generally welcomed as clearing the constitutional atmosphere.[38] Mr. Justice Roberts said:

It is clear that there is no closed category of businesses affected with a public interest. . . . In several of the decisions of this court wherein the expressions "affected with a public interest," and "clothed with a

---

[37] Steele v. Louisville & N.R.R., 323 U.S. 192 (1944); Boman v. Birmingham Transit Co., 280 F.2d 531 (5th Cir. 1960).
[38] Nebbia v. New York, 291 U.S. 502 (1934).

public use," have been brought forward as the criteria of the validity of price control, it has been admitted that they are not susceptible of definition and form an unsatisfactory test of the constitutionality of legislation directed at business practices or prices.[39]

If agreement were reached on a definition of establishments subject to the fourteenth amendment, the further question would be faced of the activities or practices that are encompassed. Is discrimination in employment included equally with discrimination in service? If one is covered and the other is not, is Congress or the Court restricting thereby the bounds of constitutional guarantees, since injunctive remedies would normally be open even apart from statute to restrain threatened infringements of constitutional rights? Since the amendment relates to many practices besides discrimination, since indeed it now absorbs the basic guarantees of the Bill of Rights, questions will arise over the applicability of these to the establishments that are assimilated to the state: whether, for example, such an establishment could make preferential contributions to a church, and whether its intracorporate procedures must satisfy standards of due process of law.

If the private licensee takes on to some extent the constitutional duties of the public licensor, there is the further problem of the standards for defining those duties. If an official licensor gave preference to the sons of licensees, a serious issue would be raised under the equal-protection clause.[40] If the licensee himself followed a policy of nepotism in his business, would a similar constitutional issue be raised? In all likelihood a new set of constitutional standards would have to be formulated for private practices covered by the amendment—a set conforming neither to the legal-ethical codes for purely private conduct nor to the constitutional code for governments and their agencies.

The combination of these uncertainties—the class of establishments, the kinds of practices, and the standards to be

---

[39] *Id.* at 536.
[40] Kotch v. Board of Pilot Comm'rs, 330 U.S. 552 (1947).

set—may well account for the Court's adherence to the basic principle of the Civil Rights Cases. It is not a matter of lack of sympathy for the moral claims asserted; the real problem is an *institutional* one, whether at the national level those claims are to be vindicated, in private relations, through processes of legislation under a congeries of powers (commerce, defense, spending), or whether they are to open up new areas of direct constitutional relationships which will call for judicial creativity and innovation on a formidable scale.*

It is ironic that some of the sentiment in Congress for a public-accommodations bill based on the fourteenth amendment rather than the commerce clause came from legislators who were concerned that the commerce clause is too expansive and would put business to the hazard of too pervasive national regulation, while the fourteenth amendment was thought to be the safe and natural vehicle for the securing of Negro rights. It is an ironic tribute to the incantation of slogans.

I have said enough to make it plain that the new vistas in constitutional law are not, in my judgment, boundless, that they are not free of shadows and even treacherous turns. What I am saying is perhaps simply, as others have been saying, that there are no absolutes in constitutional law.

* A majority of the Court has indicated in dictum that the fourteenth amendment may itself be given a somewhat flexible scope through the enforcement power of Congress; that Congress may determine what is necessary and appropriate to carry out at least the guarantee of equal protection of the laws. United States v. Guest, 383 U.S. 745, 761, 774 (1966) (opinions of Clark, J., and Brennan, J., for six members of the Court). The context was the question of the power to reach a private conspiracy to deprive Negroes of equal access to public facilities. Though such private interferences may be reached (and quite possibly, by similar reasoning, private racial discrimination in housing, contributing to inequality in public services), a connection with state activity or responsibility is still requisite. Compare also Katzenbach v. Morgan, 384 U.S. 641 (1966), upholding an act of Congress that overrode New York's voting requirement of literacy in English as applied to Spanish-speaking Puerto-Rican educated citizens. That Congress might go further in defining unequal protection of the laws than the Court might be prepared to go unaided is the moral of the decision; but there was no problem of state action in the case.

But I would wish to dissociate myself from those who instance the school prayer decisions[41] as a yielding to absolutes. In the result the decisions do not, as is often loosely asserted, ban prayer and Bible-reading from the public schools. They ban prescribed public prayer and devotional Bible-reading—a rather different thing. The difference between such prayer and a period of meditation during which each student may recite silently what his spirit or training prompts is a considerable constitutional difference but hardly a drastic one in practice; to regard it as drastic for religion is to exalt the words of the mouth over the meditations of the heart in a way repugnant to the great religious traditions and to exalt official conformity over religious voluntarism in a way offensive to the American political tradition.

Not only in result but in legal foundation as well the prayer decisions hardly deserve to be condemned as absolutist. They would so deserve if they were based on a supposed principle forbidding any and all public aid to religion. Such a principle would presumably prohibit the use of public parks for religious causes (assuming them to be available for secular causes), to say nothing of chaplains in the armed services, military exemption for conscientious objectors, statutory dispensation from Sunday laws for sabbatarians, and a host of other legislative supports given on account of religion. Obviously any sweeping proscription would raise a painful dilemma when the claims of free exercise were met by so absolute a conception of establishment. But in the prayer cases the two guarantees, so far from colliding, supplement each other. In saying this, I put more central emphasis than the opinions did on the special circumstance of the psychological coercion on children toward conformity in the atmosphere of a schoolroom, and the consequent pressure on freedom of religious conscience—in sharper terms, the official pressure to yield to what is worship for most and

[41] Abington School Dist. v. Schempp, 374 U.S. 203 (1963); Engel v. Vitale, 370 U.S. 421 (1962).

may be idolatry for some. If it be suggested that this argument ignores the right of free exercise by the majority, or that it will be time enough to ban the ceremonies when they reach the stage of sectarian worship (meanwhile affording the nonconformists the privilege of nonparticipation, as in the flag-salute case), the answer is the same: that to vest school boards and courts with the task of drawing lines between sectarian and nonsectarian forms of a concededly religious activity would only compound the objection by vesting essentially theological disputes in secular hands and so impinging on the nonestablishment guarantee. The problem resembles that in the *Miracle* case,[42] where in order to escape from the vagueness of the criterion of "sacrilege" as a standard for censorship it would be necessary to vest in secular agencies the role of defining this theological concept and thus to become impaled on the horn of establishment. If an escape from absolutism is usually to be found in recognizing and sharpening differences of degree, that course is hardly open when it entails a decision from among competing theological positions.

I have likened the Constitution to a work of art in its capacity to respond through interpretation to changing needs, concerns, and aspirations. In a larger sense all law resembles art, for the mission of each is to impose a measure of order on the disorder of experience without stifling the underlying diversity, spontaneity, and disarray. New vistas open in art as in law. In neither discipline will the craftsman succeed unless he sees that proportion and balance are essential, that order and disorder are both virtues when held in a proper tension. The new vistas give a false light unless there are cross-lights. There are, I am afraid, no absolutes in law or art except intelligence.

---

[42] Joseph Burstyn, Inc. v. Wilson, 343 U.S. 495 (1952).

2. Constitutional Dilemmas

This magnificent building, which exemplifies the creative spirit in architecture, bodies forth in symbol the nature of law itself. For does not law, like art, seek to accommodate change within the framewirk of continuity, to bring heresy and heritage into fruitful tension? As Alfred North Whitehead has observed, a society maintains its civilization by preserving its symbolic code while giving expression to forces that, repressed, could break the society asunder. And so the basic dilemmas of art and law are, in the end, not dissimilar, and in their resolution – the resolution of passion and pattern, of frenzy and form, of convention and revolt, of order and spontaneity – lies the clue to creativity that will endure.

Consequently this building, so silently eloquent in its artistic resolution, makes my speech for me. All I can do is attempt to document this theme by pointing to some constitutional dilemmas and their historic or potential resolution.

Let me begin with three of the oldest American constitutional dilemmas. First and most fundamental of all is the reconciliation of sovereign immunity and the rule of law, two principles that pursued blindly will produce an inevitable collision. You will recall the cycles through which this problem passed: the suability of a state in *Chisholm v. Georgia*,[1] the

The Gaspar G. Bacon Lecture on the Constitution of the United States, delivered at Boston University, October 29, 1964, on the occasion of the dedication of a new Law School building; reprinted from 45 B.U.L. Rev. 13 (1965).
[1] 2 U.S. (2 Dall.) 419 (1793).

overruling of this by adoption of the eleventh amendment, then a formalistic line between suits against a state and suits against officers; and finally (in *Ex parte Young*)[2] an accommodation that permits suits against officers when they are unconstitutionally encroaching on interests of person or property. There is still room for a moving accommodation, in the direction of greater governmental responsibility under a test of undue interference by litigation with the carrying on of government business.

A second long-standing dilemma is the conflict between the national common market and local protectionism. Marshall's exuberant nationalism sought to solve the problem with clear-cut absolutes: the power over commerce among the states is exclusively vested in Congress; the power to tax involves the power to destroy; goods in the original package are immune from local taxation when brought in from a sister state. All of these absolutes have had to be abandoned because they ignored the very real competing interests of local communities in respect of revenue, health, safety, and welfare.

Whitehead used to compare his view of the world with that of his friend Bertrand Russell: "Bertie sees it at noon on a brilliant sunny day; I see it at dawn on a misty morning." John Marshall was, however improbable the spiritual ancestry appears in other respects, the precursor of Bertrand Russell in his view of national and state powers over commerce. Has not a century and a half of experience shown that the Whitehead way was the path of greater wisdom?

This is not to extol fuzziness and confusion as the solution to dilemmas; there is a difference, after all, between a misty dawn and an enveloping London fog in which shapes are lost to view and direction abandoned. The foggy route has unhappily been taken in some of the commerce-power dilemmas, particularly in the field of state taxation.

As late as the 1963 Term the Court found itself at large in

---

[2] 209 U.S. 123 (1908).

the old problem of state gross receipts taxes applied to income from interstate sales by a manufacturing company.[3] The state of Washington applied such a tax to revenues derived by General Motors from sales to retail dealers in that state of cars assembled in Missouri and elsewhere and shipped to the Washington retailers. There was a time when such a tax would have been held invalid as a tax "on" interstate commerce itself, fluctuating as it does directly with the volume of interstate business. Later, under the exigency of the fiscal needs of the states, and by extension from decisions upholding property taxes on goods brought in from sister states and still in the original package, a state was permitted to tax on a nondiscriminatory basis.[4] Meanwhile, however, a formalistic criterion had been established to justify a tax in the state of orgin as well: a tax on manufacture or mining, measured by the value of the goods when ready for shipment.[5] By a curious turn, the automobiles involved in the recent Washington case were manufactured in St. Louis, the very place where the manufacturers' tax had been imposed and sustained and apparently was still assessed.

In these circumstances an opportunity was presented—an obligation would hardly be too strong a word—to review the philosophy of taxability or immunity of interstate gross receipts. Should they be wholly immune from state taxation? Should they be taxable in full both in the state of origin and of destination? Should formal subjects of taxation, like manufacture or assembling, make it easier to countenance essentially multiple taxation of receipts? Should an allocation formula be required, like the so-called Massachusetts formula for corporate net income taxation, setting up a tripartite formula composed of property, payroll, and sales ratios? If so, where should

[3] General Motors Corp. v. Washington, 377 U.S. 436 (1964).
[4] *Compare* Crew Levick Co. v. Pennsylvania, 245 U.S. 292 (1917) *with* Western Live Stock v. Bureau of Revenue, 303 U.S. 250 (1938).
[5] Heisler v. Thomas Colliery Co., 260 U.S. 245 (1922); American Mfg. Co. v. St. Louis, 250 U.S. 459 (1919).

the sales be allocated: for this formula dilutes, but does not solve, the problem of choice between the manufacturing and selling states.[6] (Does the value derive, T. R. Powell used to ask, from the goodness of the goods or the gullibility of the customers?) Questions such as these would be asked in the light of the realistic objections that can be raised against certain, but not all, forms of taxes on interstate business: the risk of discrimination, covert as well as overt, against goods from without the state or destined for other states; the risk of the pyramiding of similar taxes by virtue of the multistate nature of the transactions; and the exploitation by a state of its stategic geographic location, as in the levying of transportation taxes. Against these risks would be set the possible inner political check, protective of the common market, where the burden of the tax is borne by consumers within the taxing state.

The opportunity, unfortunately, to ask the significant questions was not taken, and instead the debate between majority and dissenters turned mainly on an issue that has served to mark a jurisdictional line for sales taxes: whether there was enough local activity by the seller in the market state to warrant such a tax.[7] This criterion, more apt at best for a due-process test than a test under the commerce clause, has produced some artificial distinctions between the power to levy a sales tax and to levy a use tax. To import it into the gross-receipts field is to compound its inaptness. Moreover, in

---

[6] Compare the interesting analysis of allocation formulas for corporate net income taxation in State Taxation of Interstate Commerce, Report of House Comm. on Judiciary, H.R. REP. No. 1480, 88th Cong., 2d Sess. 1 (1964), especially at 560-88. This Report recommends in favor of the state of origin for purposes of assigning sales in an allocation formula, on grounds of administrative convenience and ease of compliance. These considerations weigh more heavily in retail sales, where the multitude of transactions makes record-keeping onerous, than in the ordinary wholesale business. Aside from the element of convenience, the state of market would seem to have the stronger claim, because the burden of the tax is borne there and taxable intrastate competitive sales are made there.

[7] Compare McGoldrick v. Berwind-White Coal Mining Co., 309 U.S. 33 (1940) with McLeod v. Dilworth Co., 322 U.S. 327 (1944).

electing not to consider the bearing and potential validity of the manufacturers' tax in the state of origin, the Court evaded the problem of pyramiding which is central to the philosophy of a common market. In taking the keyhole view the Court has left the taxation of gross receipts in a status similar to the question of multiple escheat of intangibles.[8] For a century now the Court has failed to resolve the dilemma of the principle that interstate commerce cannot be taxed by the states and the countervailing principle that interstate commerce must pay its way. Of the decisions over this long period one can only speak in the terms used to describe John Bunyan's pilgrims: "They go not uprighly, but all awry with their feet; one shoe goes inward, another outward, and their hosen out behind; there a rag and there a rent, to the disparagement of their Lord."

A third historic dilemma is posed by the guarantee against a state's passing a law impairing the obligation of contract and the necessities of social control under the police power. This confrontation occurred as early as 1810, in *Fletcher v. Peck,*[9] and Chief Justice Marshall met it in characteristic fashion, giving a sweeping content to the contract clause. It was left to Justice Johnson, concurring, to discern the dilemma and endeavor to resolve it on principle, which he did in the quaint terminology of the day by distinguishing two kinds of governmental interests, rights of jurisdiction and rights of soil, which can no doubt be translated into the modern terms regulatory and proprietary interests of a state. There is a difference between a minimum wage law made applicable to outstanding contracts and the reduction of state employees' contractual salaries as an economy measure for the state. In the former case, to borrow a favorite phrase of Chief Justice Hughes, parties cannot by "prophetic discernment" fetter the powers of government by making contracts that would foreclose those powers.[10] Where

[8] Western Union Tel. Co. v. Pennsylvania, 368 U.S. 71 (1961). [Clarified in Texas v. New Jersey, 379 U.S. 674 (1965).]

[9] 10 U.S. (6 Cranch) 87 (1810).

[10] See, *e.g.,* Norman v. Baltimore & Ohio R.R., 294 U.S. 240, 310 (1935).

Marshall heard only a single voice emanating from the contract clause, his successors have attuned themselves to stereophonic sound.

To turn to dilemmas of more recent origin, we encounter the conflict between freedom of speech and press and the laws of the states concerning defamation. There are those who insist that the first amendment means what it says: "no law" abridging the freedom of speech means no law. An argument of this sort calls for three observations. In the first place, this kind of literalism is not indulged in with respect to other clauses of the Constitution. The contract clause, for example, prohibits a state from passing "any law" impairing the obligation of contract. Those who give the first amendment an absolutist reading would be the first to reject a similar reading of the contract clause. Second, to meet literalism with literalism, what is to be construed in the case of state regulation is the language of the fourteenth amendment, "liberty" and "due process of law." And finally, in historical perspective, even after the Sedition Act of 1798 produced a libertarian reaction, an uncompromising view of the first amendment was rendered acceptable because there remained the possibility, so far as the Federal Constitution was concerned, of prosecutions for libel under state law. Jefferson himself suggested to the governor of Pennsylvania the desirability of a few well-chosen actions for defamation against the virulent Federalist press.[11]

There is a certain analogy here to an Australian problem under their commerce clause. Commerce and intercourse between the states, the Australian constitution declares, shall be "absolutely free." This kind of constitutional rhetoric is a sure breeder of troubles. If the clause had been given an absolute interpretation and at the same time had been confined to protection against laws on the state level, it would doubtless have proved workable. But in fact a virtually absolute meaning was coupled with its application to state and federal action

[11] See Levy, Jefferson and Civil Liberties: The Darker Side 58-59 (1963).

alike, with results for the government of a modern industrial society that are readily imaginable.[12]

The *New York Times* libel case[13] is a good example of the dilemma of a free press in an open society and the interest of public officials in protecting their reputation against defamatory statements. The latter interest was, to be sure, rather conjectural on the facts; the plaintiffs were not named or identified in the statements, the falsity was in matters of detail, and there was no evidence or special finding of actual harm to support the verdict of $500,000 against the newspaper. Upon the affirmance of the trial judgment the case was no longer one of the law of torts but one of constitutional law for the Supreme Court. There were a number of ways by which the Court could have set limits on the law of defamation, as has been done in the law of obscenity and sedition. The Court might have required in the case of defamation of public officers, that actual damages be proved and that exemplary or punitive damages be excluded. It might have insisted on a more liberal view of what constitutes truth as a defense. It might, as Justices Black, Douglas, and Goldberg argued, have ruled out absolutely any action for defamation arising out of attacks on public officers related to the conduct of their office. The latter solution would have given a go-ahead signal to the worst elements of the press and pressure groups. The majority, rejecting so single-minded a solution yet persuaded that the judgment below was an intolerable deterrent to an energetic and courageous press, found still another line of resolution: liability would be permissible only on a showing of "malice," that the defendant knew the falsity of the statements or made them in reckless disregard of their truth or falsity.

A number of questions remain. Who are public officers within the meaning of the rule? Are candidates for office included along with incumbents? Will the standard of recklessness be

---

[12] See James v. Commonwealth, (1936) 55 C.L.R. 1.
[13] New York Times Co. v. Sullivan, 376 U.S. 254 (1964).

flexible enough to be adaptable to the seriousness of the libel, or the severity of the damage likely to be suffered if the statements are in fact false? Perhaps too the plaintiff should be allowed to request a special verdict if the judgment goes for the defendant and the plaintiff seeks vindication of his reputation even though the defendant is not liable because no malice was proved.

The religious guarantees of the first amendment contain a built-in dilemma. The two clauses—the guarantee of free exercise and the prohibition against laws respecting an establishment—do, to be sure, reinforce each other in many situations. If only Quakers were made eligible for draft exemption, there would be both an establishment and an impingement on the free exercise of religion by other religious objectors. But the two clauses are often in a state of inner tension, as when religious practices generally are given special favoring treatment—for example, in the Sunday-closing cases. From one standpoint the free exercise of religion is thereby upheld, from another an establishment of religion is promoted. Similarly with the question of exemption of sabbatarians from the closing laws. Is such an exemption required for the sake of free exercise of religion, or is it forbidden as an establishment of religion, or does it occupy a middle ground where it is permitted but need not be granted?[14] Or consider the opening up of public parks and buildings for religious ceremonies. Justice Jackson saw a paradox here: a city *must* allow its parks to be so used if they are used for other public functions, but a city *may not* allow its schools to be used for religious exercises.[15] Put in this way the paradox misses the point. The essential difference is that the schoolroom contains a captive audience and so the exercises affect the religious liberty of nonconformist minorities.

It is in this light that the school prayer cases can be best

[14] See Ohio v. Broughton, 171 Ohio St. 261, 168 N.E.2d 744 (1960), *appeal dismissed*, 367 U.S. 905 (1961), sustaining an exemption.

[15] Kunz v. New York, 340 U.S. 290, 311 n.10 (1951) (dissent).

understood. The decisions ought to rest more heavily on the free exercise guarantee than on the question of establishment through public aid to religion. The decisions have been much misunderstood. In particular they have been criticized as outlawing voluntary prayer, when the concept of voluntariness in the context of the schoolroom is a highly artificial one, even though excusal from the exercises be granted. Surely an outright sectarian service could not be justified during school hours by pointing to a provision permitting dissenters to withdraw. Even if a test of nonsectarianism were to be imposed, the secular authorities would have to administer the test and would be drawn into the decision of essentially theological conclusions, thus compounding in another way the mingling of church and state. It is in the light of this analysis that a different expression of humility and reverence in the schoolroom can be judged admissible: a moment of silent meditation, free of the divisive influence that results from vocal prayers in unison.

Another dilemma that is greatly agitating public opinion is the conflict between individual rights and law enforcement, epitomized by the exclusion of illegally obtained evidence as a necessary sanction for the guarantee against unlawful searches and seizures.[16] It is regrettable that some of the energies now being spent in attacking this rule were not expended earlier in devising alternative sanctions for the constitutional guarantee. Provision for a civil action against the local government for redress against searches and seizures might have forestalled the exclusionary rule.

However that may be, two questions remain. The first is whether the exclusion of such evidence shall be given effect retrospectively, or more accurately through postconviction remedies. If the vice in the use of such evidence were that the trial itself is rendered unfair, such a remedy would be in order. But since the essential aim of the exclusionary rule is a collateral one, to deter the police from using unconstitutional methods to

[16] Mapp v. Ohio, 367 U.S. 643 (1961).

obtain reliable evidence, the object can be secured without so broad an application of the exclusionary rule. Direct review and reversal of convictions based on illegally obtained evidence should be adequate to deter, while leaving unaffected prior convictions of a similar kind. A second question relates to the standards that should be applied to determine the lawfulness of a search and seizure by state authorities.[17] Granted that the fourth amendment has been absorbed into the fourteenth, does it necessarily follow that all the detailed rules of search and seizure must be identical in the two systems? Some federal rules which bear a constitutional label may in fact have been the expression of a supervisory power of the federal courts over federal law enforcement at a time when it was not necessary to differentiate between Constitution and supervision. As an example, rules concerning the warning which must be given before opening the door of a house, or concerning the nature of the belief of an arresting officer, do not seem to be beyond the realm of variation and experimentation. There ought still to be room for some variety and empirical testing at the fringes of the fourth amendment. There is no compelling necessity, particularly in the light of the responsibilities of the localities for law enforcement, that the rules imposed on the states be a mirror image of those applicable to federal enforcement officers.

Somewhat similar observations can be made regarding the right to counsel, particularly regarding the point after arrest at which the right to counsel attaches, on pain of excluding a confession obtained in the absence of counsel. Here too a certain latitude would seem to be in order. Certain alternatives to the presence of counsel might be tried at the stage of interrogation. A strictly limited time period, measured in hours rather than days, coupled with a requirement that the arrested person be informed of his privilege not to answer, and that upon making a statement he must be taken at once before a magistrate to confirm the confession, would be one alternative.

[17] *Cf.* Ker. v. California, 374 U.S. 23 (1963).

Another might be a rule which would exclude the confession itself if obtained without the presence of counsel but which would permit the introduction of evidence secured as the fruit of such a confession.*

Another current dilemma is posed by the guarantee of equal protection of the laws and the pressures for inverse or "benign" measures based on race to correct racial imbalances or disadvantages — herein of "color blindness." Can race or color be made the basis of a legislative classification? The most important point to be made in considering this question is that the color-blind test is not a term of art found in the Constitution but a phrase from the first Mr. Justice Harlan's dissenting opinion in *Plessy v. Ferguson*,[18] or more precisely a phrase taken by him from the brief filed in that case by the gifted novelist-lawer Albion Tourgée. The phrase became a liberal rallying cry, like liberty of contract in the early days of free enterprise, and each of them, if pushed to a drily logical extreme, can become the reverse of liberal.

Equal protection, not color blindness, is the constitutional mandate, and the experience with liberty of contract should

---

* The Court has held that a confession must be excluded where the person in custody was not given an opportunity to consult counsel, or counsel was not proffered in case of indigency, and there was no waiver of the right. Miranda v. Arizona, 384 U.S. 486 (1966). But even here the opinion pointed out, in a passage that has not been sufficiently noticed, that the requirements specified are to be met "unless other fully effective means are devised to inform accused persons of their right of silence and to assure a continuous opportunity to exercise it . . ." *Id.* at 444. And again: "We have already pointed out that the Constitution does not require any specific code of procedures for protecting the privilege against self-incrimination during custodial interrogation. Congress and the States are free to develop their own safeguards for the privilege, so long as they are fully as effective as those described above in informing accused persons of their right of silence and in affording a continuous opportunity to exercise it." *Id.* at 490. It is significant that the Court did not rest its decision on the sixth amendment right to counsel, which would have been direct and inflexible, but on the fifth amendment privilege not to be compelled to be a witness against oneself. Thus the role of counsel is instrumental, one means toward the constitutional end of safeguarding against the coercive atmosphere of interrogation in custody.

[18] 163 U.S. 537 (1896).

caution against an absolute legal criterion that ignores practical realities. Measures to correct racial imbalance are like those to correct an imbalance in the bargaining position of labor. At least as transitional measures they may serve to promote, not to deny, the equal protection of the laws. Of course the conclusion is reached more easily if the state itself has contributed to the present disadvantage by past discrimination; but in any case a disadvantage which exists on racial grounds should be correctible by favored treatment. This the state may do, but need not; it rests in the realm of allowable policy, like granting or refusing special treatment for sabbatarians under Sunday closing laws.

A final dilemma is that of civil disobedience and the duty of law observance. By civil disobedience is meant a nonviolent protest which is open and presents an issue of moral censure in an effort to shake the complacency and sear the conscience of the lawmakers and the community. The civil rights movement has turned to a variety of forms of civil disobedience, of which perhaps the most interesting in principle are the school strike and the rent strike. The rent strike in particular brings into focus laws that are frequently outmoded, deriving more from the feudal law of tenure with its obligations resting on occupancy than from the modern law of contract with its conception of mutually interdependent covenants by tenant and landlord.

Even if it is a part of the philosophy of civil dosobedience that pending a change in the law the demonstrators must suffer the penalties of the law, there are a number of points in the legal system where some amelioration can be had. The discretion of the prosecutor whether or not to bring charges, the ultimate power of the jury, the discretion of the judge in sentencing, and the executive pardoning power are all soft points in the law deliberately designed for the hard moral cases.

The clearest case for civil disobedience is the setting in which the demonstrators have no effective voice in government. Fidelity to law is an obligation based on reciprocity, on the right of participation. The mutual covenant, unhistorical as it may be as a ground of political obligation, reflects a long and vital philosophic tradition going back at least to the Old Testament and coming down through the Mayflower Compact. Participation in the political community implies more than the mere right to vote. It implies equality of access to administrative and decision-making posts, including places on the police force, in the probation service, on the judiciary, and generally in those positions through which the community exerts force against recalcitrant members.

The themes I have tried to develop can perhaps be brought together in an encompassing question: Should the Court serve as the "conscience of the country"? Put in this way, as today it often is put, the answer is plain. It would be a morally poor country indeed that was obliged to look to any group of nine wise men for ultimate moral light and leading, much less a group limited to men drawn from one profession, even that of the law.

But there are two narrower senses in which the Court does inevitably serve as a public conscience. The great fundamental guarantees of the Constitution are, after all, moral standards wrapped in legal commands: due process of law, equal protection of the laws, cruel and unusual punishment, free exercise of religion. When claims are raised in lawsuits that invoke these ethical-legal standards, the opinions of the Court are bound to contribute to our more general thinking about social justice and ethical conduct. Some of our most memorable utterances on these themes we owe to the great Justices who have delivered them as part of their judgments in concrete cases: Holmes, Brandeis, Stone, and Hughes, to name only the departed.

There is a second sense in which the Court serves as a public conscience, which paradoxically tends to limit the Court's freedom of utterance on these themes. The Court has warrant to speak only in the decision of specific litigation and then only as the logic of the case requires these issues to be stirred. In this sense the Court becomes a conscience by acting to remind us of limitation on power, even judicial power, and the interrelation of good purposes with good means. Morality is not an end dissociated from means. There is a morality of morality, which respects the limitations of office and the fallibility of the human mind. Justice Brandeis used to remind himself and others that self-limitation is the first mark of the master. That, too, is part of the role of conscience.

The great constitutional issues which come before the Court reflect not so much a clash of right and wrong as a conflict between right and right: effective law enforcement and the integrity of the accused; public order and freedom of speech; freedom of worship and abstention by the state from aiding as well as from impeding religion.

There are several pitfalls in single-minded thinking on these issues, serious risks in grasping — shall I say blowing — only one horn of a constitutional dilemma. In the first place, constitutional decisions which perceive only one set of ideals are likely to be overturned as experience demonstrates their one-sidedness. Not even Chief Justice Marshall could contrive to establish enduring doctrine out of such partial maxims as "the power to tax involves the power to destroy" and "the power of Congress over interstate commerce is exclusive." Unless the Court respects the other horn of the dilemma, it is in the position of the schoolboy who said that he could spell banana but did not know where to stop. Moreover, partial single-minded views will have difficulty holding the respect of the people, with the result that at a time of crisis when the Court's intervention may be most needed, it will not command acceptance and obedience.

In the next place, single-minded decisions suffer from a loss of insights that the cross-lights of competing principles would furnish. Law is an art, and the words of a literary critic about his function are not inapt for the judge: "Surely we have made the best in us the worst when we have either pushed an insight beyond its field or refused when using one insight to acknowledge the pressure of all those insights—those visions of value—with which it is in conflict. If we do not see this, we have lost the feeling of richness, the sense of relation, and the power of judgment..."[19]

And finally, doctrinaire thinking in constitutional law is a poor example of the role the law can play in the resolution of tensions, domestic and international. Precisely in a time of warring ideologies there is an opportunity that ought to be embraced for the law to demonstrate its search for underlying points of agreement and to work out accommodations that will be tolerable because they recognize a core of validity in more than one position of the combatants.

Fortunately the Supreme Court has on the whole been alert to the risks and pitfalls of absolutist doctrine. Freedom of the press has not been construed as absolute license to engage in defamation or to distribute pornography. The guarantees of freedom of religion and nonestablishment of religion have not been held to exclude reverence or silent meditation from the schools, despite some sweeping assertions by careless commentators. The privilege against self-incrimination has not been held to exclude all confessions made without advice of counsel.

The Court has been moving far and fast toward helping to assure responsible and responsive government. This is altogether fitting, for such a government is the necessary presupposition of the respect—the presumption of constitutionality—that should be accorded to ordinary legislation. Whether the Court will take the path of absolutism or will recognize and resolve genuine dilemmas of right against right is a basic question that largely remains for the future to answer.

[19] Blackmur, *A Burden for Critics,* in LECTURES IN CRITICISM 187, 190 (Coleman ed., 1949; paperback 1961).

3 Civil Rights and the Limits of Law

An ancient Chinese curse carried a terrible doom. "May you live," it ran, "in a time of transition." Painful as the experience may be, it is apt to be fruitful for the development of principles of social action. There is nothing like an economic depression to advance the science of economic thought as well as to enlarge the awareness of moral claims and sharpen the sensitivity to social injustices. Thus, when in the dark days of 1933 a lady asked Mr. Justice Brandeis tremblingly if he thought the worst was over, he replied cheerfully, "Oh certainly, the worst took place before 1929." A similar response is appropriate in a time of legal crisis, when widespread challenges to law and its enforcement compel us to examine the foundations of the duty of law observance and to question the limits of law as a means of social ordering.

The civil rights movement presents such a crisis and offers such a stimulus. The effort to deal with discrimination through law raises questions of the appropriateness of law to cope with prejudice. Moreover, the pressures for preferential treatment of Negroes in respect to education and employment, for example, stir questions of equal protection of the law as a neutral principle. And finally the use of tactics of disobedience to law as a form of protest raises questions of the rule of law as a necessary framework of social expression. In more homely terms, all of these issues can be put as three queries: First,

The James McCormick Mitchell Lecture, delivered November 9, 1964, at the School of Law, State University of New York at Buffalo; reprinted from 14 BUFFALO L. REV. 199 (1964), copyright the Buffalo Law Review.

can you change human nature by law? Second, must not the law be color blind? Third, is not disobedience of law equally reprehensible from whichever side it comes?

First, Can you change human nature by law? No, to be sure, the answer must be, but hopefully, one adds, human nature can change us with the help of law. The hope is that the sanctions of law will not be forever required to curb discrimination; that in due course after civil rights will come civility. This hope rests on a view of human nature as a congeries of discordant elements — a disorderly assembly, if you will — of impulses and controls, a congress, whether of Vienna or otherwise, with reason presiding uneasily in the speaker's seat, where behavior can affect attitudes no less than attitudes can affect behavior. Surely, to come closer to our present concern, segregation laws themselves have influenced attitudes of Negroes and whites to each other as has been demonstrated when, in the armed forces, men of both races were transported from an environment of enforced segregation to one of integration and changed their attitudes as a result. A vivid example of a change taking place, as it were, before the public occurred on a radio program in Little Rock at the time of the school crisis there, when two white and two colored school children participated in an extemporaneous radio discussion of segregation. Let me quote in extenso from the colloquy as it was reported in the New York *Times* of the day.[1]

Mrs. Ricketts (Moderator): Have you really made an effort to find out what they're like?

Kay (White Child): Not until today.

Sammy (White Child): Not until today.

Mrs. Ricketts: And what do you think about it after today?

Kay: Well, you know that my parents and a lot of the other students and their parents think that the Negroes are unequal to us, but I don't know. It seems like they are to me.

Sammy: These people are, we'll have to admit that.

Ernest: I think like we're doing today, discussing our different views,

[1] New York Times, October 20, 1957.

if the people of Little Rock would get together, I believe they would find out a different story, and try to discuss the thing instead of getting out into the streets and kicking people and calling names.

Kay: I think that if our friends had been getting in this discussion today, I think that maybe some of them, not all of them, in time they would change their minds. But probably some of them would change their mind today.

Sammy: I know that it isn't as bad as I thought it was after we got together and discussed it . . .

Mrs. Ricketts: Is there anything finally we want to say that we have to say now?

Kay: Sammy and I both came down here today with our minds set on it that we weren't going to change our minds, that we were fully against integration. But I know now that we're going to change our minds.

Mrs. Ricketts: What do your parents say to that?

Kay: I think I'm going to have a long talk with my parents.

In more scientific terms than I have been using, if one insists on that elaborate demonstration of the obvious by methods that are obscure which is the hallmark of so much current social science, the phenomenon I am discussing is known as cognitive dissonance, a strain between behavior and attitude, a tendency to ameliorate this tension by bringing the two into conformity, which may be done by rationalizing an enforced behavior of nondiscrimination. In this resolution law is an important element, for there is a strong tendency to obey and emulate authoritative models and to accept a fait accompli.

A number of investigations have tended to bear out this judgment. There were some interesting experiments, for example, in connection with department store employment policies. In certain departments of a store, Negro clerks were hired for the first time and customers who had been waited on by the Negro clerks were interviewed thereafter outside the store by interrogators who were part of the project but who did not indicate that they had seen the episode inside. The questions related generally to how the individual on the street would regard service by Negroes in a department store. The interesting thing was that there was a tendency for those who had been served by a Negro in, for example, the clothing department, to say, "Well, I would accept it in a clothing department but I'm not so sure about the food department," and for people who had been served by a Negro in the food department to answer, "Well, I would accept it in a food department but I'm not so sure about the clothing department"; and each would think of the other unexperienced incident as being too intimate a relation to be accepted. But that which had been experienced came to be acquiesced in. The practice of the department store is, in effect, the law of the community of the store.

Two of the great civilizing human traits, it seems to me, are hypocrisy and greed. Hypocrisy is a bridge thrown up between attitude and behavior. Greed is a response to the equalizing power of money. I recall attending a convention in Atlanta a few years ago at which the welcome was given by the then mayor, who had served for more than twenty years and who had a wide basis of community support. Nowhere in the speech were the terms civil rights or Negro rights or equal rights even hinted at. But the theme of the speech was "Atlanta is too busy to hate." Atlanta was seen as a great rising metropolis athwart an intercontinental airway with one of the ten largest airports in the world, and Atlanta was too busy to hate.

One may ask at this juncture, is the role of law then simply an amoral manipulation of behavior? Certainly not, because the moral quality of law is itself a force toward compliance and the change of attitudes. A feeling of guilt upon violation of law becomes a feeling of shame if the law is felt to be morally right, and shame reflects one's innermost nature. But what, you will ask, of the precedent of prohibition. Just as in anthropology the skeptic always says, but what of the Fiji Islanders, or what of Samoa, so in these matters of legal instrumentality toward moral change the question is always, What of prohibition. It is often cited to prove the thesis that you cannot change human nature by law. Actually it seems to me the lesson from prohibition is rather different, namely, that a law which is not an acceptable moral guide will not inspire a change in attitude. The experiment of prohibition was best summed up in the cynical jocularity of Ring Lardner's phrase: "After all," he said, "prohibition is better than no liquor at all." And I think most people came to feel, viewing the lack of observance in the highest and most respected circles of the community, that the prohibitionists' attitude toward strong drink was very much like the old Puritans' toward bear bating: they opposed it not because it gave pain to the bear but because it gave pleasure to the spectator. When Gunnar Myrdal spoke of the American dilemma, he was voicing an optimistic note, for the very existence of a moral contradiction between authoritative ideals and personal conduct is a hopeful basis for altering conduct, and in turn attitudes, to resolve the tension.

Consider now other fields of law to see whether there is any reason to believe that law can alter and has altered attitudes. Is morality a product of law as well as its source and ground? That morality is indeed a source of law is hardly debatable though we may not go to the length of the early chancellor in the Yearbook whom Dean Pound was fond of quoting. When counsel argued to the chancellor in a celebrated passage that some things are for the law, for some there is a subpoena in chancery, and some things are between a man and his confessor, the archbishop who presided over the tribunal answered that the law of his court was in no wise different from the law of God. The pronouncement of the chancellor went like this:

Sir, I know that every law is or ought to be according to the law of God and the law of God is that an executor who is evilly disposed shall not waste all the goods etc. And I know well if he do so and make not amends if he have the power, il sera damne in hell.

And Dean Pound added: "As the most feasible substitute for the condemnation prescribed by the law of God, the chancellor sent the defaulting executor to an English jail."

But morality and law are in reciprocal relation. Moral attitudes and standards may themselves be a product of law.

Consider, for example, conflict of interests laws, laws dealing with fiduciary duties in business. Consider the commonplace now paying half of one's income as taxes through voluntary returns. Consider the exclusion of hearsay evidence; think of the morally tonic effect on members of a jury of sitting through an austerely conducted jury trial, and I think you will agree that standards of right and wrong, of moral judgment are, and have been, affected by requirements of the law that are nicer than those that would occur to what the English call the man in the Clapham omnibus, to us simply the man on the street. There are to be sure limits to the effectiveness or the appropriateness of legal action, as we are reminded by the celebrated remark of Thomas Arnold, the master of Rugby: "Boys, if you're not pure in heart, I'll flog you."

Law may be too crude and its cost too great, as in most family relations or in all but the most insistent calls on the good samaritan. But these are not really relevant to the civil rights issue, where, after all, we are dealing with conduct in business relations, whether employment or the sale of property, or public accomodations. Let me then say a few words about the public accommodations approach in the civil rights law. It seems to me entirely fitting that it should rest on the commerce clause. I am quite unmoved by the notion that the commerce clause does not deal with moral issues. Surely this is the way that Congress has open to it for dealing with any exigent problem, whether it be one of morality or safety or one of economic advancement, when it is aggravated by the uses of the channels of interstate commerce — or, to use a more up-to-date term, when it is aggravated by the use of our great national common market. I am a little sorry that the statutory approach under the commerce clause seems to have been entirely modeled on what might be called the antitrust or labor relations technique, namely through the avenue of effect on commerce. This tends to be rather attenuated in certain eating establishments, and it seems to me it does not bring out as sharply as possible the moral thrust of the commerce power in this context. An alternative approach which could have been added is what might be called the security act or pure food and drug technique, where the law is not conditioned by effects on commerce but by the movement of goods themselves in commerce to facilitate or produce an evil. The regulation of the sale of improperly labeled goods at retail for the sake of protecting the consumer, when those have come directly or indirectly through interstate commerce, and by like token the control of interstate sales of securities in the interest of consumers, are the paradigm cases. This seems to me to be technically easier and also more persuasive to the ordinary man. Surely it is right for Congress to interest itself in a local barbecue stand if the owner of that stand insists on selling meat from Montana and fish from Louisiana and coffee from Colombia and does not limit himself to selling chicken and beans grown on his Alabama farm. If he insists on utilizing all of the great advantages of our national and international common market, which the federal government through Congress and the judiciary has so laboriously worked to maintain and strengthen, if he insists on that, he may be made to utilize the products which he so chooses to receive in a way not to spread and perpetuate what Congress deems to be a moral evil, namely, service limited on the basis purely of color. The legal and the moral themes can be structured to reinforce each other.

I come now to the second of my basic questions, Is not the Constitution color blind? Can a preferential treatment of Negroes be squared with the requirement of equal protection of the laws? Is it not an unconstitutional discrimination in reverse?

A head-on clash of principle can be averted, in most cases wisely in my judgment, by framing programs of aid in terms of reaching the most disadvantaged segment of the community, whether economically, educationally, or politically. And if these happen to be in fact predominantly Negroes, no principle of race-creed classification has been violated. It is worth noting that in the administration of justice something of this sort has already taken place. Decisions excluding coerced confessions, requiring counsel to be provided for indigent defendants, and liberalizing the practice on bail, all redound to the benefit of the most submerged group—in many communities, the Negro. Likewise in the sphere of economic aid. A general program for reducing unemployment will help to absorb the most vulnerable members of the labor force. A burgeoning economy is the best remedy for Negro unemployment as it has been the most effective basis for a more liberal policy of immigration.

But suppose this more general approach is not taken. Then we face something of a liberal dilemma. Drawing on the early Mr. Justice Harlan's dissent in *Plessy v. Ferguson,*[2] the phrase, the Constitution is color blind, many liberals viewed *Brown v. Board of Education*[3] as establishing the color-blind principle for public education. Now, facing de facto segregation and pressures to combat it by treating Negroes more favorably or at any rate by taking color into account, the liberal is puzzled. He too suffers some cognitive dissonance of his own. The first thing to note about Justice Harlan's phrase is that it is not a constitutional text, it is a constitutional metaphor. And then we may take a look at some of Justice Harlan's own efforts to deal with social problems through constitutional abstractions; and we soon find that these are two-edged sword. In *Adair v. United States*[4] he wrote the opinion for the Court holding that the right of an employer to hire and fire at will could not be inerefered with constitutionally by a statute which attempted to protect the employee's right to join the labor union. This statute was a violation, said Justice Harlan, of the liberty of contract of the employer and the employee. In *Connolly v. Union Pipe Company*[5] he wrote for the Court holding than an antitrust law which contained an exemption for agricultural

[2] 163 U.S. 537 (1896).
[3] 347 U.S. 438 (1954).
[4] 208 U.S. 161 (1908).
[5] 184 U.S. 540 (1902).

products violated the guarantee of equal protection of the law. And so before canonizing Mr. Justice Harlan it might be well to listen to an *advocatus diaboli.*

If we look at the Constitution rather than a constitutional metaphor, and at the history of the fourteenth amendment, we find that the most obvious fact about it is that it grew out of the Civil War in an effort to raise Negroes from the level of legal inferiority. Certainly in two situations there can be little doubt of the validity of preferential treatment of Negroes: first, where public facilities are in fact unequal and there is de facto segregation placing the Negro in the unequal facilities; and second, where de facto segregation is a product in part, a a remnant, of the govermental discrimination in the past. There is here, I suggest, an analogy from the law of labor relations. The labor board was upheld very early in its history in deciding that a company-dominated union could be required to disestablish itself, not merely to free itself from employer domination but to disestablish itself at least temporarily in order that the effect of employer domination could be easily dissipated.[6] The disestablishment might, for the time being, deprive the members of the union of the free exercise of the right to choose their own bargaining representatives. But out of abundance of caution and to dispel the lingering effect of past malpractice, complete disestablishment could be required. By analogy it seems to me de facto segregation which is in part a remnant of past governmental discrimination may be corrected as a means of overcoming the effect of what was a violation of the fourteenth amendment.

But suppose these conditions of past discrimination are not present. Still a legislature or a school board ought to be able to take account of the facts of segregation in the interest of promoting long-run de facto desegregation, which is surely a legitimate aim. This is the position taken by both the New York Court of Appeals and the New Jersey Supreme Court,

[6] NLRB v. Pennsylvania Greyhound Lines, 303 U.S. 261 (1938); NLRB v. Bradford Dyeing Assn., 310 U.S. 318 (1940).

there being no issue in the cases of requiring integration but only of permitting the race factor to be taken into account by a school board disposed to do so, without violating the abstract principle of color blindness.[7] This is a question of educational and social policy, a choice of means to a legitimate end, the encouragement of desegregation, as segregation itself would be an illegitimate end.

There is finally the moral, and it may be the legal, difference between a preference in favor of a minority and one against it. Compare a trust fund donated to a university, the income to be used for the education of the descendants of John Hancock, and an unrelated fund for the education of anyone except those descendants. It would not be surprising if the governing board of the university felt differently about the two preferences, and judges might be animated by the same sense of justice in applying the constitutional guarantee of equal protection of the laws.

Let me turn to my third and final question, Is the civil rights movement running a collision course with the law through civil disobedience? When I speak of civil disobedience I use it in a limited and strict sense to mean practices that are nonviolent, measured responses which are highly selective because of their moral quality, and whose practitioners are prepared to pay the penalty of the law by acting openly in an effort to sear the conscience of the community. Now the easy answer to this question is that there may be a moral justification but that this is not a legal defense. This is the answer which is readily given, I would say, by most lawyers and certainly by most bar association groups: a curse on both your houses—on the Faubuses and Barnettes as well as the Martin Luther Kings—so far at least as the legality of their conduct is concerned.

But there are questions for the law in the process of becoming. There are some lessons to be drawn from the history of

[7] Morean v. Board of Education of Montclair, 42 N.J. 237, 200 A.2d 97 (1964); Balaban v. Rubin, 14 N.Y.2d 193, 250 N.Y.S.2d 281, 199 N.E.2d 375 (1964), *cert. denied,* 379 U.S. 881 (1964).

organized labor and the law. At first concerted strikes were regarded as a criminal conspiracy. Then they were viewed by some common law judges and some legislatures as a means to achieve more nearly equal status with ownership in the community of the plant or the industry and therefore were privileged. Then there came with the Wagner Act a legal guarantee of the right, which was in turn followed by limitations on labor organizations in the Taft-Hartley law, when they acted outside the scope of the means spelled out in the law. Now the Negro movement, insofar as it includes demonstrations, boycotts, rent and school strikes, is similarly seeking equal status and recognition in the political and economic communities. The community of the factory provides certain lessons regarding the capacity of the law to adjust to such claims. Also there is some lesson to be drawn from the community of nations. Our long delay in recognizing the Soviet Union and our dispatch of troops there in 1918 poisoned our relations with that nation for a generation.

At the same time, excessive resistance by the victims of the exclusion tends to be self-defeating. It was the Montgomery bus boycott and the Washington march that were the highwater marks of moral self-discipline and effectiveness. But the shutting off of deliveries to hospitals because they engaged in discriminating practices would be morally revolting and self-defeating. The legal order means the domestication of power, that power is to be brought within the community's control. In a free society this means a sharing of rights and duties within the community. It means, to use an old-fashioned but still I think philosophically useful term, a social compact, the principle of the covenant, the idea of reciprocity of rights and duties. In terms of the civil rights movement, this means, I suggest, full participation politically in the right to vote, the right to serve in public office, the right to serve on the police force, to be appointed to the probation service and to those various public agencies and missions which are in their nature policing activities.

Short of cases of exclusion from the political community,

legal history furnishes some further light. The recent rent strikes are a reflection of the fact that our law in this field is a survival from an ancient legal order when land holding rather than contract was the basis of obligations. Instead of enjoying interdependent covenants to pay rent on the one hand and to have repairs made on the other, the tenants were obliged to pay so long as they occupied the premises; the remedy of leaving the premises in case of so-called constructive eviction is all too often unrealistic today in the setting of an overcrowded urban community. Now more modern law is coming to provide for a mutually interdependent covenant, for mutually interdependent conditions, perhaps with provision for payment of rent in escrow.

Even before the law makes adjustments of this kind, before there are changes in the substantive law as there were in the law of stikes, as there are doubtless coming to be in the law of rent, the moral frame in the civil rights movement need not go unrecognized. I refer to the elements of discretion in our legal system which were devised for such contingencies, for a clash between the moral sense of the case and the strict legal obligations: the discretion of the prosecutor in deciding whether or not to bring a case following a one-day school strike, the discretion of a jury whether to convict or acquit, the discretion of a judge in sentencing, the descretion of a governor in pardoning.

To sum up, the civil rights movement is a challenge to law in many ways, to the moral influence of the law, to its impartiality, and to its acceptance and observance. But it is a challenge also to the creativity of law. The civil rights movement has already brought reform in the general fabric of the law. The recent *New York Times* libel case was an outgrowth of the reporting of civil rights protests in Alabama.[8] We now have new law on the subject of the privilege of the press to report on the conduct of public officials. This is not limited, obviously, to

---

[8] New York Times v. Sullivan, 376 U.S. 254 (1964).

the civil rights movement, but it was occasioned by the pressures of that movement. Similarly, we have new law from the Supreme Court regarding the provision of counsel through lay intermediaries, a very sore issue with the organized bar, a decision first produced by the efforts of the NAACP to channel cases to particular counsel or lists of counsel.[9] That decision has already been extended to apply to the railroad brotherhoods in non–civil rights cases.[10] The general body of the law is being altered under the pressures engendered by the civil rights movement in ways that may seem collateral but are nonetheless significant for general legal reform. The creative impulse has surely not been exhausted. Out of the sometimes terrible struggles that threaten to rend the fabric of society, some constructive efforts may still come as they have come in the past with the scourge of wars, depressions, and labor troubles. Out of danger we may pluck security, out of injustice we may hope to discover a wider justice.

[9] NAACP v. Button, 371 U.S. 415 (1963).
[10] Brotherhood of Railroad Trainment v. Virginia, 377 U.S. 1 (1964).

4 The Supreme Court under Attack

The Council of State Governments has proposed, and a number of state legislatures have approved, three constitutional amendments for submission to Congress in order that they may be presented to a national convention and submitted to the states for ratification. These proposed amendments would (1) establish a supreme court of the states composed of the chief justice of each of the fifty states, with authority to decide any case involving an alleged infringement of states' rights; (2) remove the issue of state reapportionment from the federal courts and from the equal protection guarantee of the federal Constitution; (3) set up a new procedure for amending the Constitution, bypassing Congress entirely and enabling two-thirds of the state legislatures to propose an amendment and three-fourths to ratify it without any participation at the national level.

These proposals, clearly a reaction against recent decisions of the Supreme Court, reflect a spirit of localism for whose counterpart we would have to look to the sectional struggles before the Civl War or even to the position of the states under the Articles of Confederation.

Efforts to curb the Court are as old as the Union itself. They have been animated sometimes by local resentment, sometimes by sectional resistance, on occasion by political or class interests, and by collision of the Court with the dominant social forces of the times.

A paper delivered at the University of Pittsburgh, April 29, 1963; reprinted from 25 U. Pitt. L. Rev. 1 (1963).

When the Court held, in 1793, that the state of Georgia could be sued on a contract in the federal courts, the outraged assembly of that state passed a bill declaring that any federal marshal who should try to collect the judgment would be guilty of a felony and would suffer death, without benefit of clergy, by being hanged. When the Court decided that state criminal convictions could be reviewed in the Supreme Court. Chief Justice Roane of Virginia exploded, calling it a "most monstrous and unexampled decision. It can only be accounted for by that love of power which history informs us infects and corrupts all who possess it, and from which even the eminent and upright judges are not exempt." But the South had no monopoly on resistance. During the era of the fugitive slave law it was the Northern states that bridled. Massachusetts legislated for the disbarment of any lawyer appearing in court for a slaveowner. Wisconsin engaged in a tug of war with the Supreme Court over the return of fugitive slaves. From 1821 to 1882 at least ten bills were introduced in Congress to deprive the Supreme Court of its appellate jurisdiction in whole or in part.

Sectionalism was later supplanted by economic class interest as the source of resistance. The decisions of the Court at the turn of the century in the field of labor, the income tax, and corporate regulation, alienated the wage earning and agricultural groups to the point of agitating for the popular recall of judges and of judicial decisions. And under the New Deal the attacks on the Court were mounted by a supremely popular national administration as well as by responsible elements of the bar and the academic legal profession.

In the face of these assults, how has the Court managed to survive? Near the close of his life Chief Justice Marshall sadly concluded: "The Union has been preserved thus far by miracles. I do not think they can continue." Actually the survival of the Union and the Court can be explained in less supernatural terms. As in most secular crises, salvation has come partly from without and partly from within. Constitutional amendments blunted the attacks on the Court over the suability of states and the income tax. From within, the Court has managed to cure itself of self-inflicted wounds through the process of adaptation and overruling, yielding, in the phrase of Justice Brandeis, to the lessons of experience and the force of better reasoning. But the most fundamental explanation of the Court's survival and prestige must rest on public understanding of the role and mission of the Court.

Fifty years ago Justice Holmes, addressing a law school audience, described attacks on the Court then current, and offered a philosophical response:

...We are very quiet there, but it is the quiet of a storm centre, as we all know. Science has taught the world scepticism and has made it legitimate to put everything to the test of proof. Many beautiful and noble reverences are impaired, but in these days no one can complain if any institution, system, or belief is called on to justify its continuance in life. Of course we are not excepted and have not escaped. Doubts are expressed that go to our very being. Not only are we told that when Marshall pronounced an Act of Congress unconstitutional he usurped a power that the Constitution did not give, but we are told that we are the representatives of a class—a tool of the money power. I get letters, not always anonymous, intimating that we are corrupt. Well, gentlemen, I admit that it makes my heart ache. It is very painful, when one spends all the energies of one's soul in trying to do good work, with no thought but that of solving a problem according to the rules by which one is bound, to know that many see sinister motives and would be glad of evidence that one was consciously bad. But we must take such things philosophically and try to see what we can learn from hatred and distrust and whether behind them there may not be some germ of inarticulate truth.

The attacks upon the Court are merely an expression of the unrest that seems to wonder vaguely whether law and order pay. When the ignorant are taught to doubt they do not know what they safely may believe. And it seems to me that at this time we need education in the obvious more than investigation of the obscure.

Today the need for public understanding is greater than ever before, because the attacks on the Court come from a coalition of groups, and the countervailing interests are not nearly so distinct and organized. There is the sectional opposition arising from the desegregation case; the opposition of the officialdom of many states, deriving from decisions in the field of criminal law enforcement; opposition from rural interests growing out of the reapportionment decision; and from important church groups, as a result of the school prayer cases.

Just because the interests served by the Court are relatively less vocal and cohesive, the responsibility devolves on dispassionate agencies like the bar and the universities, not indeed to shield the Court from all criticism but to make sure that judgments of approval or disapproval are raised to the level of genuine understanding.

On this higher level, complaint is made that the Court is reshaping the Constitution, is innovationg, is injecting uncertainty in place of stability. Before taking a closer view, it may be useful to put these complaints into the perspective of constitutional development. Like a work of artistic creation, the Constitution endures because it is capable of responding to the concerns, the needs, the aspirations of successive generations. To Marshall's generation it meant the armament of union, to another age the safeguard of burgeoning wealth, to another the shield of the unorthodox. None of these is wrong; all are encompassed; some become more central as the nagging problems of American life change character. For a long time it was received doctrine that a state could exclude from its borders fugitives from justice, bearers of contagious disease, and paupers. By 1941 the conjunction of these disabilities no longer seemed defensible; the Court, in an opinion by Justice Byrnes, held that pauperism could not be equated constitutionally with criminality and disease for purposes of freedom of movement.

In his little classic, *Microcosmographia Academica,* Professor Cornford of Cambridge addressed himself to the two basic arguments for standing pat, the principle of the opening wedge and the principle of the dangerous precedent:

The *Principle of the Wedge* is that you should not act justly now for fear of raising expectations that you may act still more justly in the future—expectations which you are afraid you will not have the courage to satisfy...

The *Principle of the Dangerous Precedent* is that you should not now do an admittedly right action for fear you, or your equally timid successors, should not have the courage to do right in some future case, which *ex hypothesi,* is essentially different, but superficially resembles the present one. Every public action which is not customary, either is wrong, or, if it is right, is a dangerous precedent. It follows that nothing should ever be done for the first time.

The evolution of constitutional law has been, in fact, a moving consensus. New positions have been taken and then secured, with fresh controversy revolving in turn about progression from the new consensus. Whether the due-process guarantee extended to matters of substance as well as procedure, and whether the safeguards of speech, press, and assembly became applicable against the states by virtue of the fourteenth amendment, were in their day mooted questions; nowadays these are seen as battles long ago, but the scope of these guarantees is a lively issue that brings new disagreement and uncertainty.

Dissents are, in Chief Justice Hughes' phrase, an appeal to the brooding spirit of the law. They are also, to change the figure, the second blade of the shears, against which the cutting edge must work, serving to make a finer and truer line. The practice of dissents is a tribute to the force of reason over fiat, and as such it cannot be tolerated where debate would weaken authority. The German constitutional court avoids the publication of dissenting opinions, though it is rumored that some have been written and filed in the archives, against the day when division will not necessarily connote weakness. Movement does, to be sure, bring uncertainty. And yet, to quote Hughes once more, when in the higher reaches of other disciplines—philosophy, theology, science—the experts disagree, why should we expect in the law to emerge into an icy stratosphere of certainty.

The current development in constitutional law should be viewed in the light of the basic functions of the Court in the decision of cases. Three of these functions will help to explain many of the recent controversial trends.

First of all, the Court has a responsibility to maintain the constitutional order, the distribution of public power, and the limitations on that power. The essential powers of government have been recognized and validated by the Court as never before in our history. Congress enjoys constititional authority over commerce, defense, and the revenues at least as broad as it is likely to wish to exercise. The states are permitted to tax and regulate in ways that were foreclosed or dubious a generation or two ago. Taxation of interstate enterprise, of federal salaries, regulation not only for health, safety, and morals but for aesthetic purposes as well, jurisdiction over out-of-state business, are extensions of public power that liberate the law-making process in the states as well as in the nation.

It is in the realm of procedure that the Court has now been more insistent. And it is appropriate that this should be so. The judges are not experts by virtue of their training or their commissions in the field of economics or public policy. They are, however, the special guardians of legal procedures, of the standards of decency and fair play that should be the counterpoise to the extensive affirmative powers of government. In criminal proscecutions juries are to be fairly selected, evidence is to be legally obtained, and defendants charged with serious offenses are to have the benefit of counsel. Legislative investigations, more frequent and wide-ranging than ever before, are to be conducted with due regard for the right of the witness to know the pertinency of the questions and to be free of public inquisition that is not related to a legislative purpose. We do well to remember the admiration with which the Anglo-American system of procedure is regarded throughout the world. Peoples that have thrown off the colonial political yoke, whether in India or Israel or Nigeria, have been zealous to retain the procedural guarantees which they learned to prize before their independence. In England a few years ago I found myself on a plane seated next to a man who introduced himself as a native of Latvia who had settled in the United Kingdom. When he learned that I was an American lawyer, he told me, in broken English, of an incident just reported in the press. A judge, before sentencing, asked the defendant if he had anything to say, whereupon the convicted man loosed a torrent of abuse against the judge. Sentence was then deferred for twenty-four hours because, the judge said, he did not trust himself to impose sentence in that atmosphere. "Where else," the immigrant asked with pride and awe, "could you find that kind of justice?"

A second great mission of the Court is to maintain a common market of continental extent against state barriers or state trade preferences. To balance the need for local revenue against the claims of freedom of trade has been another of the tasks and achievements of the Court that now serves as a model for emerging federations on other continents. Western European lawyers are astonished at the wealth of experience and analysis to be found in the U.S. Reports on the problems of a working federation.

In the third place, there falls to the Court a vital role in the preservation of an open society, whose government is to remain both responsive and responsible. This too is a corollary of expanding public power. Responsive government requires freedom of expression; responsible government demands fairness of representation. In this context it is not hard to appreciate the central importance of decisions on freedom of press and assembly, on voting rights, and on reapportionment.

The real question is not whether the Court is right in giving central importance to issues of this kind. It is rather whether the Court has been too doctrinaire in resolving specific issues of this kind. No lawyer or judge, on the Court or off, will agree with every decision in these areas. As a teacher of constitutional law I spend much of my time encouraging students to subject Supreme Court opinions, new as well as old, to critical scrutiny, in terms of principle and craftsmanship and viability. Sometimes the estimates are far from approving. But it is well to cultivate perspective, to recognize that although there has been highly significant movement in constitutional doctrine that has to be assimilated rapidly, it has not come as suddenly or as drastically as the more vehement critics assert. The right to counsel for indigent defendants has now been established after twenty years of experiment with a rule that made the requirement turn on the facts of each case and thus converted any trial without counsel into the uncertainties of a potential Supreme Court controversy. In those twenty years the states were afforded time in which to bring their procedures into conformity with the best practice. The same is true of the rule that now excludes illegally obtained evidence from criminal trials in the states, after experiment with a rule that made admissibility turn on the degree of outrageousness of the illegal search and seizure. Legislative investigating committees have not been denied the authority to inquire into the associations of a witness; they must, however, first establish the pertinence of those associations and show probable cause that they have involved illegal or subversive activities. The public schools have, to be sure, been forbidden to install prayers even of a diluted sort; but the alternative would have been to put the Court in the business of picking and choosing among prayers and thus compounding the intrusion of the secular into the religious sphere. Moreover, the Regents Prayer decision does not prevent the public schools from engaging in moral education. They are prevented only from doing it in a way that puts psychological constraint on religious minorities in the coercive atmosphere of the school room.

It is sometimes said that attacks on the Court are to be expected because nobody loves an umpire. It is true that the Court is like an umpire in that the judges must understand the actions and passions of the contestants without becoming embroiled in them. And the Court is like an umpire in that the judges cannot, they must not, measure their success by popular acclaim. But unlike an umpire the Court exposes the reasons for its decisions and even the disagreements entering into them. This practice of candor, which is far from characteristic of courts around the world, presupposes a mature people who in the end will judge their judges rationally. Unless this maturity exists, the whole system is in danger of breaking down.

The future is not likely to bring a lessening of governmental intervention in our personal concerns. And as science advances into outer and inner space — the far reaches of the galaxy and the deep recesses of the mind, — as physical controls become possible over our genetic and our psychic constitutions, we may have reason to be thankful that some limits are set by our legal constitution. We may have reason to be grateful that we are being equipped with legal controls, with decent procedures, with access to the centers of decision-making, and participation in our secular destiny, for our day and for the days we shall not see.

II THE PURSUIT OF JUSTICE

5 Rationality in Judicial Decisions

When James the First royally maintained that he was perfectly competent to decide questions of law by the exercise of reason, Sir Edward Coke respectfully protested, if we can accept his account, that such decisions must be reached by the "artificial reason" of the law, which the King was scarcely qualified to pursue. There have been some who doubted the force of Coke's rejoinder in the context of the common law. Max Weber, for example, regarded Anglo-American law as distinctly inferior in rationality to the systems derived from the Roman law.[1] The common law, he argued, is too akin to the layman's ideal of the practical, the expedient, the expectable, and rests too heavily on the charisma of the judges, while the continental systems are more truly rational in their relentless application of formulated rules to the facts of particular controversies. This is not the place to consider the verisimilitude of Weber's picture of the two legal worlds; but one or two points can be made that will perhaps illuminate in a preliminary way the dimensions of the problem of rationality in judicial decisions.

Weber, as might be expected, denigrated the jury as an irrational intrusion. But it may well be that the rationality of a system as a whole is maintained by the deliberate employment of a less rigorous element at a chosen stage: for example, the assignment by lot of a particular judge to hear a case, or the

Reprinted from Rational Decision (Nomos VII) 109 (C. J. Friedrich ed. 1964), © 1964 the Atherton Press.
[1] Max Weber on Law in Economy and Society 307-08, 316-18 (Rheinstein ed. 1954).

intervention of an executive pardon or the informed hunch of a probation board. Weber, too, selected for illustrative praise the decision of a German court holding that under a code provision punishing the larceny of a chattel the stealing of electric power is not an offense; it was a case of an omitted class of acts that must be rectified by new legislation. One might agree with the conclusion but for more expedient reasons: though the term chattel could be applied sensibly to electric power in some contexts (for example, in a comprehensive constitutional grant of authority to the Government to sell publicly owned chattels or real property), in the context of a criminal law a more restrictive meaning may be called for, in the interest of a general policy that crimes shall be strictly defined.

What I have tried to suggest in this preliminary way is that rationality has some important relation to the context of a system and of a particular class of problems. I find it less helpful to essay a definition than to examine a process in operation. Nevertheless one should, I suppose, indicate broadly the nature of the concept under examination. Rationality is a term of commendation, though not of ultimate praise: a decision may be rational and yet not command approval as a necessary truth or even as right. It is set off against nonrational modes like will, or power, or caprice, or emotion, against irrational modes like recklessness of means or ends or their relation, against rapacity or opacity. It is a warrant not so much of the soundness of a decision as of the course pursued—that the course of inquiry has been kept open and operating in appropriate ways and within appropriate termini. A principal aim of this paper on judicial decisions is to stimulate comparisons with the ways and the termini of the rational process in political and scientific thinking.

A convenient framework is at hand in Benjamin N. Cardozo's analysis of the judicial process.[2] There are, he suggested, four

[2] CARDOZO, THE NATURE OF THE JUDICIAL PROCESS (1921).

elements in judicial reasoning: logic, precedent, history, and social utility. It may be useful to consider these (taking the first two together) from the standpoint of rationality and limitations on it.

First, then, is logic, which embraces the notions of generality, consistency, deduction, and induction.

Generality. In ethical reasoning (of which legal reasoning is essentially an instance, for judicial decisions are aimed at the norm of justice) it is often said that propositions should be general, or should not contain proper names, or should be capable of universalization. In the law, at least, a maxim of this sort is little more than a restatement of problems. Consider the following series of statements beginning with the words "A judge always ought to":

 a. decide by whim
 b. decide for the plaintiff in a negligence case
 c. stretch a statue (Maitland's self-professed rule as a member of the Senate of Cambridge University)
 d. give preference to an injured child in a negligence case
 e. give predominant weight to the welfare of a child in a custody case
 f. uphold an agreement as a valid contract
 g. uphold an agreement as a valid contract if it would be such by the law of any state having relation to the transaction
 h. impose stricter procedural safeguards in capital than in non-capital cases.

The form of these statements is general throughout. Does not their rationality depend on the relevance of the proclaimed standards to the classes described? And does not this depend in the first place on an understanding of the sectors of the law with which the statements are concerned? And does not an understanding involve a good deal of feel for the traditions, assumptions, and practices of the discipline?

Consistency or transitivity. A rational decision, it may be suggested, will respect the principle that if A is preferred to B and B to C, then A must be preferred to C. But this also tends to obscure the real problem, which is whether to view the choices as part of a single field or in pairs that may alter the relevant fields. Anatol Rapoport has put the case of a man faced with the choice of living with one of three women. He prefers A to B and B to C. Is it then irrational to prefer C to A? Not if C is insanely jealous of A, so that to live with A rather than C would provoke an overhanging threat of murder. The law can furnish less fanciful illustrations. A federal statute provides that a lien for federal taxes shall be subordinate only to a pre-existing lien of a mortgage. Thus if there are three claims, that of a prior mortgagee (M), of a tax due to the United States (U) and a tax lien of a state (S), the priorities would seem to be M,U,S. But suppose the state has a statute, enacted within its acknowledged powers, giving priority to state tax claims over the claims of a mortgagee. To follow the state rule would produce the series S, M, U. There is circuity here which somehow has to be resolved. One way of doing so might be to interpret the federal rule as not applying where the claim of a mortgagee and of the state coexist. Another solution might be to preserve the place of the federal claim by giving first priority to the amount and only the amount of the mortgage, but subjecting that amount to the tax lien of the state.[3] In any event the analysis must go deeper than a principle of transitivity and must take account of policies made acutely relevant by what is on the surface a logical dilemma.

Deduction. One need not dwell on familiar logical troubles: what the tortoise said to Achilles in Lewis Carroll's fable, or how deduction from a rule involves the problem of sameness in classifying phenomena under a major premise. In the legal process the difficulties are compounded by virtue of the fact that premises tend to be not so much "rules" as principles or standards, and by the correlative fact that there are commonly two or more such premises available arguably as starting

---

[3] *Cf.* United States v. City of New Britain, 347 U.S. 81 (1954), and the discussion in 95 U. PA. L. REV. 739 (1947).

points for reasoning. In this respect judicial decision tends to resemble efforts at decision by maxims: when we remember that the early bird catches the worm (a rule, to begin with, for the birds), we are at once reminded that haste makes waste. I hope to illustrate what it means to "apply a rule" by the analysis of a case at the end of the paper.

Induction. One need not dwell here on induction as the "scandal of philosophy", nor on the general observation that inductive reasoning is not self-starting or self-limiting; that, as Charner Perry put it some years ago, in beings who act and know there is an irreducible element of chance or will, of intellectual violence in the process of decision.[4] In the legal process induction proceeds from precedents and from facts of life. The use of precedents raises again the problem of sameness and also the problem of the range within which precedents should be reexamined. There is here a parallel with the method of science, since every experiment involves in principle a testing no only of the immediate hypothesis but also of the whole series of postulates of the system within which the experiment is performed. In science and law alike, reasons of economy of effort normally dictate that the experimenter or the judge will not engage in an extensive regressive questioning unless and until his results demand it because they are too awkward, too irreconcilable, or too difficult to work with under the conventional postulates of the system. At that point the postulates may be broken down, or built up, or otherwise reformulated to accommodate the new phenomena in a more satisfying and fruitful way.

In the law the problem is complicated by the assignment of roles: a trial judge has much less freedom than an appellate judge to reexamine precedents; and there is a difference in role between judges and legislatures. The problem is complicated further by the relative importance of stability and justice (of

[4] *Knowledge as a Basis for Social Reform,* 1935 INTERNATIONAL J. OF ETHICS, 267, 276.

which stability is to be sure an element) for different classes of legal transactions and events. A planned transaction, like a mortgage or a marriage, calls for more stability in the use of precedents than, say, a highway collision (though the making of settlements argues for some stability even here).

When one turns from precedents to facts of life as elements of induction, one must recognize that the facts are not given in a raw sense but are themselves part of a social system which makes them intelligible and which must itself be understood. Facts, to be sure, are rarely as raw as we carelessly assume. As recent studies by Jerome Bruner, George Miller, and others have shown, personal values or the norms of syntax and semantics affect the threshold of perception, and "concernedness" helps to define perception's span.[5] Social phenomena serving as the facts of law call for special sensitivity and sophistication. Whether baptism and pagan initiation rites are viewed as parallel phenomena will depend on the orientation of the observer.[6] Judicial review of state taxation in Australia and the United States will be best understood in the context of the whole federal system of each country. On a more elemental level, the claims with which the ongoing law deals are not raw demands but demands that have been shaped by a legal system itself, not the raw appetites for goods or association, but the claims of legal personalities, of debtors and creditors, buyers and sellers, husbands and wives. In this respect the legal process resembles the social sciences and is marked with similar entanglements in building on empiric evidence.

Of *history* it may be said briefly that its usefulness varies inversely with the weight of the demands made upon it. The judge can learn relevant things from a narrative (how habeas corpus began and the functions it served), and, with luck and discretion in interpreting social facts, may learn some things

---

[5] Thirty years ago Whitehead is reported as saying "'Concernedness' is of the essence of perception." 29 J. OF PHILOSOPHY 97 (1932).

[6] See P. WINCH, THE IDEA OF A SOCIAL SCIENCE 108 (1958).

from the history of institutions about the strengths and weaknesses of certain forms of order (arbitration, judicial review of legislation). When he looks to history for a scaling of values, he is confronted, besides all this, with the problem of differentiating history from the historians: in Yeats' phrase, how to know the dancers from the dance; in Santayana's, looking over a crowd to find one's friends. Judges, said Holmes, are apt to be naive, simple-minded men; they need a touch of Mephistopheles. In any search for objectivity through history, they need a touch – perhaps it is the same thing – of philosophy.

Social utility, the fourth of Cardozo's elements, is in a broad sense, as he acknowledged, an inclusive criterion, and it is of this that I want to speak more at length. In the law its limitations are near the surface. Law is a system for imposing a modicum of order on the disorder of human experience without disrespecting or suppressing a measure of spontaneity, diversity, and disarray. How and how much order to impose are questions that cannot always be answered by a utilitarian calculus. Order and freedom are mutually reinforcing to a degree, but at some point become incommensurables. Apparent allegiance to a common ideal of freedom may conceal deep divisions in the valuing of order and disorder: when Benjamin Franklin declared, "Where freedom is, there is my home," Tom Paine answered, "Where freedom is not, there is mine." Similarly with the sanctity of life and the preservation of lives. Is a man justified on utilitarian principles in killing an innocent person in order to save the lives of two others? Of course utilitarian considerations of a long-run kind may enter into a rule; a legal justification in so plainly stated a case might encourage homicides in situations whose exigency is less clear, where a deterrent is wanted. But these long-run considerations can be tenuous at best, and a more intuitive basis for a rule in this case is probably more realistic.

We are concerned, however, with the judicial process rather than with law as a whole, and here the practices of the discipline afford some escape for the judge from the problems of valuation.

First, the judge may take refuge in a "rule" of more or less generality already formulated, either by his predecessors or by the legislature. The starting point or points, in other words, are not at large but are within limits determined. Some rules embody a resolution of values, as in the homicide case. Others are procedural and prophylactic in the sense of forestalling the resolution of wasteful and difficult controversies of fact. The inquiry whether an alleged oral agreement was in fact made or is actually a trumped-up claim may be bypassed by a general provision of the Statute of Frauds requiring a writing for certain kinds of promises. Thus problems of cogency in the establishment of truth are replaced by those of consistency in the application of rules. Such statutes, more often than is generally supposed, leave much to "interpretation" and thus a fathoming of purposes, but at least they circumscribe the scope of inquiry at the outset. In the formulation of such "general rules" by legislatures or courts a good deal of non-rigorous empirical assessment of need and of consequences is indulged in. Social scientists, by and large, have concerned themselves very little with the formation and functioning of rules of substantive law. The reasons for this inattention to a rich quarry of experience are probably various. The problems do not lend themselves readily to experimental study save on a relatively trivial level from which it would be risky to extrapolate. Systematic observation would be costly and often inconclusive because of the number of variables. And, not least, opportunities seem too rare for results that carry a promise of being counter-intuitive.

A second delimiting factor for the judge is the scope of the hearing or trial, as shaped by rules of evidence and procedure. The issues are defined in legal terms, with all that this implies for the exclusion of "remote, collateral, and prejudicial" evidence that might be of interest to an ethicist bent on fixing moral responsibility. As a judge Holmes tried to remember, he said, that he was not God. However unsatisfying judicial judgments may be under the aspect of eternity, if they purported to assess responsibility in a more supernal way they would become intolerable in a community where society and the state are not identical and where first or final causes are not a subject of easy consensus. This may take some of the edge off T. R. Powell's barb: "If you can think of a thing, inextricably attached to something else, without thinking about the thing it is attached to, then you have a legal mind."

The subject of the trial or hearing opens up the familiar issues of the expert witness, cognate to the issue of the social scientist at the rule-making stage. This is surely one of the least satisfactory phases of the judicial process. If the establishment of official, non-partisan experts as an adjunct of the court seems an obvious remedy, it must be remembered that the authority of such officials might in practice be excessive, and that differences among experts on ostensibly technical issues may subtly reflect honest divergences within their profession on more nearly ultimate judgments, whether of the role of punishment, or the desirability of patent privileges, or the virtues of economic competition.

A third delimiting factor for the judge—in addition to the reception of "rules" and the contours of a trial—is the form of his judgment or decree. For reasons which may be bound up with historic procedures, a judge at common law is limited, in general, to categorical sanctions: the defendant is liable to pay the plaintiff's damages or he is not. In admiralty more flexibility is recognized, as in the assessment of damages on the basis of comparative fault. In equity too there is more flexibility, notably in the conditional decree.

Flexibility is a desideratum in the arsenal of sanctions; but a judge does well to respect the limitation of the role of his office, of the record on which he acts, and of his capacity for supervision of a decree. The judge, circumscribed by his station and its duties, will echo Holmes and remind himself that he is not God or even the legislature.

Two special problems deserve attention in a study of rationality: creativity and bias.

To be creative in a discipline is in some sense to remain within it. Creativity involves a tension between vitality and technique; as Jerome Bruner puts it, between passion and decorum, between the frenzy of a mathematical insight and the decorum of an equation.[7] The legal order, and particularly the judicial process, puts a premium on continuity in the midst of change: no Nobel prize is awarded to a judge for the most revolutionary decision of the year. And yet in a deeper sense creativity in judicial thinking may not be radically different from that in science; both depend on seeing new connections, on reexamining postulates, on formulating new statements that promise to be more satisfying (because more inclusive or economical or fruitful) than the old. The amount of innovation in a discipline may be obscured, magnified or minimized, by forms and manners. (A Latin-American visitor once remarked, "In my country we boast of being socialist, but we are not; in your country, you boast that you are not, but you are.") Ancestral voices and communal ghosts may be more powerful in science and in the arts than a new generation may understand or care to acknowledge. "Corpernicus and Kepler," as Michael Polanyi has written, "told Newton where to find discoveries unthinkable to themselves."[8] Of innovation in literature, Harry Levin has observed: "Literary achievements are never quite so personal or original as they may seem, and generally more traditional or conventional. The most powerful writers gain much of their power by being mythmakers, gifted — although they sometimes do not know it — at catching and crystallizing popular fantasies."[9]

In law, and particularly in the judicial process, the voices and the ghosts are not suppressed; they are proudly echoed and paraded, often disguising stranger accents and shapes. Creativity that is too upsetting to legitimate expectations may be

[7] ON KNOWING: ESSAYS FOR THE LEFT HAND 24-25 (1962).

[8] *The Republic of Science*, 1 MINERVA 54, 69 (1962).

[9] *Some Meanings of Myth,* in MYTH AND MYTHMAKING 112 (H.A. Murray ed. 1960).

eschewed by the judges, whose decisions have retrospective effect, and left to the prospective operation of legislation. There are many factors that properly enter into this balance: how firmly grounded, how just, are the vested expectations; how much dislocation would result from an innovating decision; how amenable might the subject be to the rule-making of general legislation; how feasible would it be to enter a judicial declaration applicable only to future transactions.

A vexing problem of rational creativity is the extent to which the new position should be formulated or may properly be left inchoate. In *Hamlet,* that tragic encounter of reason and passion, of intuition and rational proof and spectral evidence, the hero speaks mordantly of "a beast, that wants discourse of reason," and again,

Sure he that made us with such large discourse,
Looking before and after, gave us not
That capability and god-like reason
To fust in us unus'd

"Discourse," articulation, the embodiment of a decision in a reasoned opinion or the amenability of a decision there and then to such an embodiment—how essential is this to rational creativity? Much current criticism of judicial decisions as unprincipled or unarticulated tends to overlook the useful part played in the past by decisions which were fraught with creative ambiguity, which moved in a certain direction but left open the turns that might be taken. One need not subscribe to all of Michael Oakeshott's critique of rational intervention and his enshrining of communal ways to appreciate the force of his observation: "Those who look with suspicion on an achievement because it was not part of the design will, in the end, find themselves having to be suspicious of all the greatest human achievements."[10] Writing of the law of torts in England at the end of the nineteenth century, when the notion of liability

---

[10] *The Universities,* 2 CAMBRIDGE J. 532 (1949).

without fault was making inroads on the unifying concept of blameworthiness, and when the academic jurists were disturbed at the resulting impurity and imprecision of doctrine, Professor Fifoot of Oxford has said: "Faced with the fragments of life, the current law of any place and time can but approximate to a principle or indicate a tendency. Looking back upon the individual torts as they had emerged at the end of the nineteenth century, it requires an act of faith to postulate that principle or to indicate the goal to which they were tending."[11]

Professor Fifoot was referring, among other things, to the well-known case of *Rylands v. Fletcher,* decided by the House of Lords in 1868, which has been the subject of an extensive literature and whose potentialities are even now far from settled. Because the case is not charged with political excitement, and because it has become an influential precedent in a major area of private law, there may be value in examining it as an instance of judicial creativeness whose rationale, to say the least, was not clearly articulated.

The facts were not complicated. The defendant, a mill operator in a mining area, maintained on his land a resevoir for whose construction he had engaged an independent contractor. The contractor negligently failed to discover some abandoned mine shafts which threatened the stability of the reservoir. In time water escaped through the shafts and flooded a neighboring mine owned by the plaintiff. An action was brought against the defendant for damages. Various conventional bases of liability were argued, but none quite fit the case. Though there was culpability on the part of the contractor, the defendant himself was not negligent and was not chargeable by imputation with the fault of an independent contractor who was not strictly an employee. Vicarious liability without fault was therefore inapplicable. Other limited forms of liability without fault were likewise an awkward fit. Trespass on another's land entailed a wilful entry, and here the defendant did not deliber-

---

[11] C. H. S. FIFOOT, JUDGE AND JURIST IN THE REIGN OF QUEEN VICTORIA 56 (1959).

ately discharge the waters. Nuisance entailed a continuing or abiding noxious condition maintained by a defendant, and here the reservoir was not noxious in itself and the flooding was a completed event. To be sure, the escape of cattle would involve liability for their trespass, but to identify escaped water with wandering cattle would compound the animism that led to liability in the latter case. And yet there was something about the Rylands problem that impelled the English court to transcend the limits of the precedents and impose liability. The court spoke of a "non-natural use" of the land for purposes of collecting water in a reservoir, and a consequent liability for the escape of the dangerous substance so collected on the land.[12]

A host of questions perplexed the commentators who tried to fathom the principle underlying the decision. What is a "non-natural" use: suppose the area were devoted more largely to mills than to mines? What if nothing escapes but damage is done, say by the vibrations of a blasting operation? What if the plaintiff too were engaged in an unnatural use of his land? How "absolute" is the liability: suppose the barriers were broken by the action of a stranger or by an act of God? More broadly, could the decision in principle be confined to landowners? Did it entail rather a doctrine of responsibility for the consequences of extra-hazardous undertakings? These questions, implicit from the beginning, have been answered over the succeeding decades, so that the "principle" of the decision is as much its eventual product as its original ground.

After the foregoing paragraphs were written, I rediscovered a passage in the early writings of Holmes which is now itself an ancestral voice that may have become legitimated:[13]

It is the merit of the common law that it decides the case first and

---

[12] The case is reported in (1868) L. R. 3 HL 330. Professor Francis Bohlen sought to explain it through an economic or class-interest interpretation of the judicial process. *The Rule in Rylands v. Fletcher*, 59 U. Pa. L. Rev. 298, 318-20 (1911). This view was vigorously disputed by Dean Roscoe Pound. *The Economic Interpretation and the Law of Torts*, 53 Harv. L. Rev. 365, 383-84 (1940).

[13] *Codes, and the Arrangement of the Law*, 5 Am. L. Rev. 1 (1870), reprinted in 44 Harv. L. Rev. 725 (1931).

determines the principle afterwards. Looking at the forms of logic it might be inferred that when you have a minor premise and a conclusion, there must be a major, which you are also prepared then and there to assert. But in fact lawyers, like other men, frequently see well enough how they ought to decide on a given state of facts without being very clear as to the *ratio decidendi*. In cases of first impression Lord Mansfield's often-quoted advice to the business man who was suddenly appointed judge, that he should state his conclusions and not give his reasons, as his judgment would probably be right and the reasons certainly wrong, is not without its application to more educated courts. It is only after a series of determinations on the same subject-matter, that it becomes necessary to "reconcile the cases," as it is called, that is, by a true induction to state the principle which has until then been obscurely felt. And this statement is often modified more than once by new decisions before the abstracted general rule takes its final shape. A well settled legal doctrine embodies the work of many minds, and has been tested in form as well as substance by trained critics whose practical interest it is to resist it at every step. These are advantages the want of which cannot be supplied by any faculty of generalization, however brilliant...

This is not to exalt blind groping or mystical intuition as marks of a creative judge, but to suggest that insight may outrun foresight, that there may be a time for sowing and a time for winnowing, that the advancement of doctrine need not await an exposition of its full reach, so long as judges are reasonably satisfied that it will not prove to be intractable. These are metaphors which could be annotated extensively from the law of the past.

To turn from creativity to the problem of impartiality or "neutrality" or bias, a judge's root beliefs or presuppositions or, in Holmes' phrase, his "can't helps": what is the role of reason in the congeries of selves that constitutes the personality of the judge? I would suggest four functions that reason might perform to cope with the problem of bias.

1. Distinctions must be drawn between legitimate and illegitimate biases, as the list of statements on page 65 was meant to indicate. It is one thing to indulge a bias in favor of

injured children in an accident case; it is another to be guided by the child's welfare in a custody suit. These distinctions often come down to the received traditions of the discipline, subject, to be sure, to modification like other parts of substantive law. Sometimes two legitimate biases may conflict: in a case of prosecution for bigamy following a marriage after a migratory divorce, working in favor of the validity of such a divorce is the bias against uncertainty in the criminal law, and working toward its invalidity is the bias against competitive depreciation of moral standards through the avenues of a federal system. Neither bias is disreputable, each is relevant, and if all other indicia leave the mind in equilibrium, the one more strongly held may prevail.

2. But reason should not lightly assume that one's biases deserve the strength they have or that they would not be amenable to further scrutiny. Is not this what needs to be said about the non-cognitive character of "values"? To flaunt one's biases as "can't helps" assumes that they are like saying "I dislike asparagus" when they may properly be only of the order "I dislike Picasso."

3. Related to the previous point is the possibility of rationally finding a ground of agreement short of a collision of root beliefs. The judicial process is full of devices for this cushioning: burden of proof, presumptions, delimitation of issues, and so forth—institutional arrangements that have been referred to earlier in connection with social utility and intuition. Moreover, agreement on the facts may forestall a conflict of biases. If I am a vegetarian and you are not, we may agree that a given piece of meat is unfit for consumption without agitating our basic difference, and reason should explore such grounds of consensus to the full (though it is entirely possible that one's assessment of the facts will in turn be somewhat affected by one's general bias).

4. The most troublesome role of reason in coping with bias is an endeavor to offset an illegitimate one by self-awareness and deliberate counter-bias. How delusive or self-defeating may

this effort be? May it indeed produce a counter-distortion rather than neutrality? And may the self-analysis be too superficial, disguising a deeper unconscious desire to arrive at the counter-bias? These psychological questions might be illuminated by that discipline in a way helpful to students and practitioners of the judicial process. The late Judge Jerome Frank suggested psychoanalysis for all judicial appointees. My present question is whether preoccupation with bias, adding oneself to the problem to be decided, may involve a significant risk of distorting oneself, the problem, and the decision.

Some general observations on rationality may tentatively emerge from a study of the judicial process. Rational thinking is to be understood in the context of an activity or set of practices; relevance and bias are meaningful in that context; and this is true also of creativity. Rational thinking involves respect for roles, not only for the place of a given discipline in society but for the allocation of functions within the discipline.

It has been said (in Paul Diesing's study, *Reason in Society*)[14] that the concept of practical reason has taken one or another of three forms among philosophers from Plato onward: creativity (Plato, Hegel, Whitehead); the discovery and application of rules (natural-law theorists); calculation (Hobbes, the utilitarians). The judicial process, at least, suggests that these are interacting and to a degree interfused.

Sinclair Refining Co. v. Atkinson,[15] decided by the Supreme Court of the United States in 1962, is an interesting and not atypical case presenting problems of rationality in decision-making that may illuminate the meaning and relation of creativity, the application of rules, and calculation.

The facts were not in dispute for purposes of the case. The company and a union of its employees entered into a collective bargaining agreement which provided for arbitration of grievances and renounced strikes or slowdowns over any causes

[14] P. 224 (1962).
[15] 370 U.S. 195.

that were arbitrable. In violation of the agreement the union repeatedly engaged in work stoppages on account of arbitrable grievances and did not resort to the arbitration procedure. The company brought suit in a federal court to enjoin such work stoppages. For its defense the union relied on the Norris-LaGuardia Act of 1932, section 7 of which prohibits the federal courts from issuing injunctions against concerted non-violent activity by a union growing out of a labor dispute.

If this were all, it might appear that the course of decision is plain; that the rule of the Norris-LaGuardia Act compels the Court to refuse an injunction. The "rule" is clear; it need not be extracted from decisions, it is actually codified; and it is not of convenient vagueness like standards ("due process" or "prudent investment") or principles ("no one may profit by his own wrong at the expense of another"). And yet this result might well cause disquiet. Does the Act really fetter the courts in enforcing the obligations of a collective agreement? The background of the Act was a history of federal courts' intervention to restrain strikes and picketing in an era before rights of union organization and bargaining were secured; injunctions served to intensify the inferior position of workers and caused widespread hostility and disrespect on the part of labor toward law and courts. So viewed, would not an application of the Act in the circumstances of the present case be perverse? Already the neatness of "applying a rule" is becoming blurred. The calculation of consequences and the investigation of purposes suggest the possibility, at least, that the rule is more complex than it seems. Any reformulation must not do violence to the potentialities of the language used; but the term "labor dispute" may be sufficiently protean to exclude cases where there is a breach of an arbitration agreement and of a no-strike clause. Whether this would involve too much creativity on the part of judges is the resulting question. If this were the whole case, the Justices might well have concluded unanimously that on balance this degree of creativity should be left to Congress.

But that was not the whole case. Other data were at hand

that bore some relevance to the process of decision. In 1934, without amending the Norris-LaGuardia Act, Congress provided in the Railway Labor Act for compulsory arbitration of certain disputes, and the Court thereafter held that despite Norris-LaGuardia an injunction could be issued against a strike called in violation of the later statutory plan. At this point in the analysis, the present Court might rationally have (a) overruled the railway labor decision as an excess of judicial law making; (b) followed it as a precedent where, as here, a plan of arbitration (though here voluntarily adopted) was in force; or (c) distinguished it as apposite only to a legislative scheme of arbitration. The "rule" of the precedent might have been either (b) or (c), depending on the emphasis placed on the factor of legislative intervention.

But there was in fact additional legislative intervention in the background. In 1947, the Taft-Hartley Act conferred authority on the federal courts to entertain suits for the violation of contracts between employers and employees. This provision, the Court had held, authorized mandatory orders compelling a union or an employer to submit a dispute to arbitration. But did it authorize the kind of negative injunction forbidden generally by the Norris-LaGuardia Act? Now, obviously, the decision could not even in form be rested on "application of a rule." There was at least another coordinate rule to be taken into account, that of the 1947 Act.

In the actual decision, the Court divided. The majority opinion was written by Justice Black, who had been a member of the Senate when the Norris-LaGuardia Act was passed in 1932. The dissent, joined in by Justices Douglas and Harlan, was written by Justice Brennan, who had extensive experience in labor law before going on the bench.

The difference in approach of the two groups loses its significance if it is looked at simply as a difference in the application of a rule. Justice Black took the Norris-LaGuardia Act as the primary datum; held the railway cases inapposite; and stressed what would be the legislative character of a repeal of section 7, which Congress had declined to do. The calculation of consequences was for Congress; in any event they were not too serious, since an action for damages and a mandatory order to arbitrate were still available. Justice Brennan took as his primary datum a pattern of legislation, and asked not whether the earlier provision had been repealed but whether it could be "accommodated" with the later legislation. This he did because the consequences of the Norris-LaGuardia Act on the beneficent practices of arbitration agreements he regarded as deeply upsetting. And so he essayed a more creative role, seeking to find connections and reconciliation between otherwise discrete legislative provisions, converting inharmonious rules, if you will, into a more refined and comprehensive principle whose touchstone would be the promotion and safeguarding of collective bargaining. This he attempted to achieve by regarding the Norris-LaGuardia Act as a non-rigid direction, to be followed generally but not in the special circumstances of a case falling within the fostering policy of the later Act.

It is not important here to appraise the two opinions in their outcomes. What is of interest, I believe, is the fusion in actual practice of the types of rationality classically described as rule-application, creativity, and calculation. In that fusion each element, while not losing its distinctiveness, takes on some of the qualities of the others. That this is psychologically true, it may be argued, does not establish that it is logically valid or philosophically useful; perhaps the psychological impurities ought to be burned away in the interest of clear and distinct ideas. It is really, I suggest, a matter of pragmatic emphasis: which aspect, the distinctiveness of the types of rationality or their interaction, is it more useful to stress. I can only say that I believe the interaction to be not merely a valid description but a process the receptive awareness of which can enrich the resourcefulness and fruitfulness of the judicial process.

6   Social Justice and the Law

The meaning of "justice," linguistic philosophers would insist, is to be found in ordinary usage, and ordinary usage is to be found in the *Oxford English Dictionary*. The O.E.D., it seems, is the Q.E.D. I have some misgivings about the uses and usages of dictionaries ever since an illustrious professor of English, taxed with violating a dictionary pronunciation, replied serenly, "That's wrong. I must change that in the next edition." But if ordinary usage is not the be-all and end-all of meaning, perhaps it may be taken, at any rate, as the more modest members of the linguistic school suggest, as the begin-all.

Washington, where so many social concerns are focused, is filled with edifices associated with a variety of human vocations: agriculture (farmers), commerce (business), defense (land, sea, and air forces), labor (wage-earners), justice (lawyers). This survey of ordinary usage is flattering to the legal profession, but it raises a question: is justice then the concern solely of lawyers?

This identification reflects a popular fallacy, or rather a double fallacy: that the pursuit of justice is a responsibility of a professional class, and that it is centered on the process of trial and adjudication. Yet surely the suffragettes who campaigned for the women's right to vote were in as sincere a pursuit of justice as the judges who denied the right to them. The judges, to be sure, were dispensing justice as long as they denied the

Reprinted by permission from SOCIAL JUSTICE 93 (R. Brandt ed. 1962), ©1962 Prentice-Hall, Inc., Englewood Cliffs, New Jersey.

vote to ladies of Republican and Democratic persuasion alike; but the suffragettes were seeking justice in another and broader sense, and in another forum.

From one standpoint, justice is seen in the opposed aspects of individual and social justice. The individual voter may be treated justly if the existing rules are applied to him impartially, but the rules themselves may be inequitable and therefore unjust. This is the familiar dichotomy between internal and external standards, between honor among thieves and the dishonor of thievery. From the standpoint of its relation to law, justice is viewed in one aspect as the canon governing the judge in applying existential rules, and in another aspect, as the canon governing the legislator in altering the rules. The judge addresses himself to standards of consistency, equivalence, predictability, the legislator to fair shares, social utility, and equitable distribution.

If this is the analysis of justice in relation to law that is afforded by self-conscious ordinary usage, it stands in need of critical review. In particular, the distinction between individual and social justice, and between the judicial and the legislative function, must be examined from within the working process of the law.

An inscription on the wall of the Havard Law School library taken from Justinian's *Institutes* reads: "The precepts of the law are these: To live honorably, not to injure another, to render to each his due." (*Honeste vivere, non alienum laedere, suum cuique tribuere.*) Is the last precept the only obligation referable to justice? Are the duties of good faith and due care legitimate concerns of law in society but not exactly of justice? I suggest instead that each of the precepts ought to be comprehended in justice, that each is an aspect of a more general notion.

What then is this more general notion? Professor Vlastos has said that justice implies an allocation according to worth, or need, or merit, or contract. The last criterion is interesting: why contract?

Suppose that I offer a reward of one hundred dollars for the return of a lost ring, of much less intrinsic worth but of great sentimental value to me, and it is returned the next day. Is the finder entitled to the hundred dollars? He is conferring a benefit on me which I have sought and which I have publicly valued at one hundred dollars. But suppose that, completely unaware of the offer, he was moved by innate honesty to trace the ownership of the ring and return it. May I justly refuse to pay the reward? Many courts would say so, and it is hard to disagree. That element is lacking which makes a promise binding: another's legitimate expectation that the promise will be performed, an expectation usually evidenced by reliance on the promise.

Contract, Maitland somewhere remarked, is the greediest of legal categories. The law is addicted to the device of finding "implied" contracts as a way out of novel problems, and of assimilating relations—such as that of public utility and customer—to a contractual mold. The reason, I believe, is that the concept of contract is a paradigm case of justice viewed as the satisfaction of reasonable expectations. The coordinate categories of legal obligation—property and tort—are also analyzable in these terms, but contract has brought their common element close to the surface.

The history of the law of contract bears out this analysis. In early Roman law there was no generalized conception of contract: obligations arose from certain formal acts and from certain special agreements, such as loans, pledges, and partnerships. A more generalized notion produced the so-called innominate contracts, either a delivery of a thing in expectation of counterperformance (*do ut des; do ut facias*), or still more broadly the performance of an act in expectation of counterperformance (*facio ut des; facio ut facias*). Legal action to secure redress for breach of these innominate contracts was grounded on the duty of good faith and, if necessary, resort might be had to an action of *dolus* (roughly, "for deceit"). Thus the elements of an enforceable promise were drawn from both property and tort, from the promisor's having received a benefit and from his causing another to rely on his promise.

English law, while quite independent and markedly different in detail, bears interesting resemblances. Until the fifteenth century the idea of contract was limited to the formal covenant under seal and essentially to an obligation to restore a fixed sum which had been received and was being withheld. The latter obligation was enforced through the action of debt, in which the defendant was entitled to wager of law, trial of the issue by the weight of oath-takers. The more generalized idea of contract grew up from the notion of deceit: the notion that the defendant contrived by his promise to deceive the plaintiff into parting with goods or labor. Indeed, where a debt existed though no promise had in fact been made, the judges ruled early in the sixteenth century that a promise would be conclusively presumed by which the promisee had been put off from pursuing his remedy through an action for debt; and thus the action for breach of contract, with its more rational method of trial, could supersede as well as supplement the older form. Here too contract is seen as a progeny of property and tort: the elements of both *quid pro quo* and reliance entered into its inheritance,[1] and its ancestry may flow back to the unifying idea of the satisfaction of reasonable expectations.

Is not each of Justinian's precepts an instance of the fulfillment of reasonable expectations: that a person may rely on the good faith of another, that he may expect another not to injure him carelessly or wantonly, that he may expect to receive what reasonably may be deemed to be due him? This concept of legal justice may be objected to as either tautologous or uselessly vague. But the content of reasonable expectations, although related to the positive law of the time and place, is not identical

---

[1] For the Roman law see R. Sohm, Institutes of Roman Law 397-99 (2d ed. Leslie transl. 1901); W. W. Buckland, A Textbook of Roman Law 518-23 (1921). For the English development see C. H. S. Fifoot, History and Sources of the Common Law ch. 14 (1949); S. F. C. Milsom, *Not Doing Is No Trespass*, 1954 Camb. L.J. 105-17.

with it. The relation is one of interaction: the law is itself an educative element, as in its distrust of hearsay evidence or its prohibition of conflicts of interest and its imposition of fiduciary duties that are not always self-evident to the man of business; but reasonable expectations are more generally the ground rather than the product of law, as well as a basis for a critique of positive law and thus a ground of law in the process of becoming.

This is, to be sure, a protean concept, but its vagueness has boundaries: it is to be differentiated, on the one hand, from generosity or mercy; on the other, from will or power. Moreover, it connotes rational principles of measure and order. It was both a classical and an Elizabethan view of justice that Shakespeare advanced in *Troilus and Cressida:*

> Observe degree, priority and place,
> Insisture, course, proportion, season, form,
> Office and custom, in all line of order;
> . . . .
>
> O, when degree is shaked,
> Which is the ladder of all high designs,
> The enterprise is sick!
> . . . .
>
> Force should be right; or rather, right and wrong,
> Between whose endless jar justice resides,
> Should lose their names, and so should justice too.

The symbol of the scales reflects the association of justice with the adjudication of adverse claims, and the process of rendering justice may be so depicted. Why not, then, reduce the fulfillment of reasonable expectations to the allocation of benefits or burdens equally according to the measure of need, or merit, or worth? But this analysis seems to drain the process of the vitality and richness that give it and its product meaning in an operational sense. The alternative criteria of equality are themselves in conflict; even when one has been selected, competing claims under it must be subjected to a degree of generalization, so that the principle of the decision may be expressed as an ethical maxim of universal conduct (to use a Kantian concept which is necessarily inconclusive in the realm of practical judgment). The immediate claimants have to be viewed, in other words, as members of classes whose contours are by no means self-evident. Moreover, even when such classes have been tentatively constructed for purposes of assessing the claims of the immediate parties, it may be found that a decision allocating benefits and burdens will produce consequences for, and affect the motivations of, still other groupings, and so the validity and sufficiency of the classes as originally constructed may be opened to question. And finally all of this is bound to be done by one or another form of human arbiter who should be mindful of his station and its duties. This whole congeries of operations cautions against a misleading reduction of the ethical problems involved in reaching judgments of social justice, even when endeavoring to hew as closely as possible to the criterion of equality.

An analysis of a case, which on its surface seems unphilosophic enough, will illustrate my meaning. The Associated Press brought suit against the International News Service to restrain the latter from taking accounts of news events published on AP bulletin boards and distributing these to member papers of the INS. The case ultimately reached the Supreme Court of the United States.[2] A majority of the Court, in what has at least the surface indicia of a progressive opinion, declared that there was a kind of property right in news belonging to him who gathered it; and for another to seize such accounts while still fresh, for his own competitive benefit, was a misappropriation, a legal wrong. There is a reasonable expectation that one will not be victimized by "piracy" or parasitism. The demands of corrective justice, it was felt by the Court's majority, required that reparation be made or at least that an undertaking be given against the repetition of the wrong.

[2] International News Service v. Associated Press, 248 U. S. 215 (1918).

The more interesting and significant analysis was made by Justice Brandeis in a dissenting opinion. He took the position that since news items were confessedly a peculiar kind of property, the Court had latitude in determining whether to protect it. He pointed out the interest of the community in the widest possible dissemination of information. (This counterconsideration is itself a form of equality: equality of access to knowledge and the truth.) He added that quite possibly the Associated Press made it too difficult for nonmembers to become members, through its restrictive bylaws; this in turn was a form of inequality. The Court, Justice Brandeis continued, would achieve more inclusive justice through a conditional decree, granting relief to the Associated Press only on condition that it admit INS member papers to its services on the payment of reasonable fees. In essence this solution would have converted the Associated Press into a public utility, with a duty to serve all comers at reasonable charges. But this solution would in turn give rise to a serious problem: it would promote a monopolistic position of the Associated Press and would require regulation and supervision of its rates and services. In the end Justice Brandeis was constrained to acknowledge that the courts were not equipped for this kind of task and had no directive from Congress to embark on it. His ultimate conclusion was that the Court should leave the parties where it found them, lest in doing justice by halves it not do justice at all.

There are three interrelated elements in the case. First, equality: corrective justice from the standpoint of the Associated Press, and distributive justice from the point of view of the members of the INS. (Who are my peers and what is the measure of our portions?) Second, community: the interest of the reading public in widely diffused and equal access to information. (Who are my neighbors and what are their legitimate concerns in the direction of a wider equality?) Third, authority: the procedural aspect of a just solution. (Who is my judge, and what are the proper dimensions of his title to act?) A closer look at each of these elements, through the medium of legal problems, follows.

Equality: the measure of equivalence or proportionality. The problem is to determine the relevant peer group (to adopt a sociological barbarism), and the criteria of equivalence or proportionality.

Consider what may at first appear to be a pure problem of equality: a requirement that broadcasting networks allot free time to political parties. "Equal time" is the maxim of justice. But what does this signify? As between the Republican and Democratic parties it may be taken to entail absolute equality, the same number of hours and similar times of day. But what of small splinter parties, Socialist or States Rights?

At least three possibilities suggest themselves. There may be formal equality, in which the group unit, not its constituent members, is the relevant measure. Or, there may be proportional equality. Allotment according to size might be deemed an equal allocation according to achievement; but achievement may be itself a function, in part at least, of the power to command the resources of mass communication, the very point at issue. Or, there may be proportional equality inversely to size, giving the smaller parties correspondingly more time. This view might be deemed an allocation proportionate to need—but whose need? Such an allocation would diminish the time available for the major parties, leaving the mass of the electorate who are in all probability going to choose between Republicans and Democrats less informed than they would be under either of the first two solutions. Their need is consequently less satisfied. Moreover, this solution implies a choice in favor of innovation over tradition, the provocative over the familiar—a rational but disputable position. There might very possibly be side effects, such as the stimulation of small parties, with consequences for Presidential and legislative leadership, and for the efficacy of the very procedures instrumental in achieving social justice through governmental action.

All these factors are present in the problem of a just solution of a question phrased initially in terms simply of equality. To rule out side effects as not pertaining to justice but to some other values is like a dentist's claim that he has a cure for pyorrhea which will incidentally paralyze the jaw.

All three solutions are within the spectrum of justice, while some others would be clearly outside; for example, an allocation among bona fide political parties on the basis of the merit of their ideas and platforms. Although merit may be a criterion of just allocation, it is not the business of government to appraise or control the political ideas of the citizenry; it is the business of the citizenry to appraise and control the political programs of the government. It is clear then that an analysis of equality leads to consideration of equality in relation to a wider community and finally to a consideration of the problem of authority.

Consider another example, an actual case in litigation. The Railway Labor Act authorizes union shop contracts, and (let us assume) permits contributions by the union for local political causes. Certain dissident members of the union object to having their dues appropriated to political causes or candidates not of their own personal choice. This controversy bears a curious resemblance to the INS case. The union, like the Associated Press, maintains that it may justly protect itself and its members against pirates or parasites or free riders, and that the interests which the union promotes are common interests, for which all members should pay equal shares. In one respect indeed the union has a stronger case than the AP: it is an open union, to which all employees have access on payment of dues. But in another respect the dissident members have a stronger claim than the INS, for they raise the question of political equality. Who are the peers? As economic men, perhaps, all the members may be treated alike; but as political men they are not to be equated indiscriminately with their fellow workers of the dominant persuasion. The dissident members, in order to restore their political autonomy, are obliged to pay out of a second pocket to offset the invidious contributions channeled through their union dues.

How can this conflict of two kinds of equality be resolved? Is political equality always the more fundamental? This is the philosophy, broadly speaking, of other labor and corporate legislation of Congress in relation to Federal elections. But is it the only just solution? After all, the common economic aims are hard to divorce from their realization through the political process. Moreover, the dissident employees are not forbidden to vote, to campaign, and to spend additionally as they may individually choose. Perhaps justice requires only that the union management show a genuine economic purpose in support of its political expenditures, and maintain open procedures for electing and instructing union management.

Under this analysis, then, the question of equality resolves itself into the appropriate group-categorization of the complainants: as members of a representative guild or as fully autonomous political entities. The problem arises in a lawsuit, and the claim of the plaintiffs rests on the unconstitutionality of an Act of Congress. The ultimate issue may thus become one of authority. If the legislature has taken a reasonable position and the impairment of first amendment freedoms is oblique at best, a court might resolve the issue on the basis of its own limited function in reviewing the validity of legislation.[3]

Community: the interrelation of individual justice and social justice — or rather, the aspect of justice which makes it artificial and unsatisfactory to consider individual justice apart from the interests of larger groups, and the most relevant groupings. At a minimum the individuals immediately involved ought to be treated as members of classes, in recognition of the principle of universality or generality which pervades the ethical concept of justice. But more broadly, there is the question how extensive should be the inquiry into the interests of wider groups and communities. There is always the question, in other words, of the definition of the relevant society whether the immediate problem be that of so-called individual or social justice.

---

[3] The case was decided on grounds of statutory construction, the majority of the Court not reaching the constitutional issue. International Assoc. of Machinists v. Street, 367 U. S. 740 (1961).

Consider a simple case in the law of contract. *A* promises to deliver to *B* one thousand bushels of wheat in six months at one dollar per bushel. The market price rises, at the due date it is one dollar and fifty cents, and no delivery is made. *B* waits, and after another six months, when the market price has reached two dollars, he brings suit. His claim is for one thousand dollars, the difference between what he agreed to pay and what the wheat is now worth or will cost him. The claim seems consonant with the duty of promise-keeping on a principle of *quid pro quo*. Does *B* then recover the one thousand dollars? He does not: he recovers five hundred dollars. Although *B* is wholly the innocent party, he had a duty to minimize the wrongdoer's damages by purchasing promptly from another seller, in the interest of an efficient, non-wasteful system of market exchange, which in turn has been designed to assure equivalence and reciprocity.

For a more dramatic and complex problem of community, suppose that an underdeveloped country expropriates private land holdings and declines to pay the owners the market value of the property taken. Suppose that no distinction is drawn between alien and native land owners, that the local law provides no compensation to either class. Suppose further that the government proposes to use the land for a more equitable allocation of natural resources among its indigent population. The significance of these variations on the theme of equality is brought out in an exchange of messages between the governments of Mexico and the United States in 1938 over the expropriation of Mexican land owned by Americans. The Mexican Minister of Foreign Affairs wrote to the Secretary of State:

I wish to draw your attention very specially to the fact that the agrarian reform is not only one of the aspects of a program of social betterment attempted by a government or a political group for the purpose of trying out new doctrines, but also constitutes the fulfilling of the most important of the demands of the Mexican people, who, in the Revolutionary struggle, for the purpose of obtaining it, sacrificed the very lives of their sons. The political, social, and economic stability and the peace of Mexico depend on the land being placed anew in the hands of the countrypeople who work it; a transformation of the country, that is to say, the future of the nation, could not be halted by the impossibility of paying immediately the value of the properties belonging to a small number of foreigners who seek only a lucrative end . . . as has been stated above, there does not exist in international law any principle universally accepted by countries, nor by the writers of treatises on this subject, that would render obligatory the giving of adequate compensation for expropriation of a general or impersonal character.[4]

The Secretary of State of the United States replied:

There is now announced by your government the astonishing theory that this treasured and cherished principle of equality, designed to protect both human and property rights, is to be invoked, not in the protection of personal rights and liberties, but as a chief ground of depriving and stripping individuals of their conceded rights. It is contended, in a word, that it is wholly justifiable to deprive an individual of his rights if all other persons are equally deprived, and if no victim is allowed to escape.

If the Secretary had been a logician, he might simply have said that equality is a necessary but not a sufficient condition of justice. The real question, however, had shifted from equality to community — to whether the claims were to be measured by the standards and expectations of the local group, or whether there is an international community whose interests and standards are relevant and even decisive.

A related problem is found in the claims of the American Indians for compensation for the taking of their lands. Between 1863 and 1946 these claims were cognizable only through special acts of Congress conferring jurisdiction on the Court of Claims to hear particular grievances. By an act of 1946 Congress established an Indian Claims Commission, with the duty to hear and determine all claims growing out of the uncompensated taking of Indian property or the violation of

[4] 1 G. H. HACKWORTH, DIGEST OF INTERNATIONAL LAW 657-60 (1942).

Indian treaties with the Federal Government. This is a passage of President Truman's statement made in connection with the signing of the bill:[5]

This bill makes perfectly clear what many men and women, here and abroad, have failed to recognize, that in our transactions with the Indian tribes we have at least since the Northwest Ordinance of 1787 set for ourselves the standard of fair and honorable dealings, pledging respect for all Indian property rights. Instead of confiscating Indian lands, we have purchased from the tribes that once owned this continent more than 90% of our public domain, paying them approximately $800,000,000 in the process. It would be a miracle if in the course of these dealings—the largest real estate transaction in history—we had not made some mistakes and occasionally failed to live up to the precise terms of our treaties and agreements with some 200 tribes. But we stand ready to submit all such controversies to the judgment of impartial tribunals. We stand ready to correct any mistakes we have made.

In the voluminous litigation following upon the act, probably the leading case is the claim of the Indians of California, in which liability has been established for 75,000,000 acres, comprising three-fourths of the state, at values measured as of 1851. In similar earlier proceedings, values were taken between forty cents and one dollar and twenty-five cents per acre, owed to some 37,000 Indian claimants. Liability has been established for all of Kansas and forty per cent of Nebraska, and for much of Indiana.[6] Who are to be deemed the beneficiaries of these judgments?

The question is one of community. The victims of the failures of the Government are long since dead. Who are the rightful successors to their claims—their descendants as families or as individuals, or the tribe as a unit, or perhaps the American Indians as a single group? In fact the recoveries have inured to

[5] See F. S. COHEN, THE LEGAL CONSCIENCE 304 (1960). The background of the 1946 Act appears in *Hearings before the House Committee on Indian Affairs*, 79th Cong., 1st Sess. (1945).

[6] New York Times, Aug. 12, 1959, p. 59; *id.*, May 3, 1959, p. 120; *id.*, July 14, 1959, p. 8.

the tribe, whose council may determine their further distribution. In one representative case the Mountain Utes, in Colorado, collected $7,200,000 after sixteen years of litigation in the Court of Claims. The tribal council decided that half of it should go in individual grants of three thousand dollars per capita, the other half to go to the tribe for the expenses of education, health, irrigation, and the buying of new lands.[7] A relevant factor is the effect of such judgments on the likelihood of emancipation from tribal status. So long as these recoveries are possible, members of the tribe may well be inclined to remain within the community to be benefited. This in turn would forestall the development of their individual autonomy and their integration with equal legal status into the larger community. And so what at first seemed a question of equivalence, of corrective justice, involving a determination of the appropriate group to which restitution is due, takes on the problems of community: how does such a grouping affect other aspects of equality in other groupings, actual or potential?

A very different context may also be explored: the free exercise of religion in a secular state. A few states of the Union provide by law that in adoption proceedings the child shall, so far as practicable, be placed with adopting parents of the same religion as that of the child. Is such a law consonant with social justice? In terms of equality, potential adopters of a different faith will argue that they are discriminated against for no valid reason, in relation to adopters who share the child's imputed religion. On the other hand, the church will maintain that its rolls ought not to be depleted by the intervention of the state in the form of adoption proceedings; the relevant classes to be compared, the argument will run, are the church rolls with and without adoption, or perhaps the rolls of two faiths before and after adoption. If the conflict shifts to the question of the child's welfare, similar issues of classification appear. The potential parents will argue that the child should not be

[7] Id., Dec. 2, 1956, p. 109.

disadvantaged in relation to children born into another religious group; the church may counter that the most important element in a child's welfare is spiritual, that the most relevant group is the community of saved souls, from which the state must not remove the child. Thus, the problem entails not merely issues of equality and the subsumption of the contending parties under various possible groups, but also issues of the relevant larger communities, secular or spiritual. There lurks, however, the further and basic issue of authority, the question of the role of the secular agencies in the fortunes of religious groups and the spiritual welfare of individuals.

It is essential therefore to consider the element of authority itself.

Authority: the appropriate person or tribunal to decide, and the appropriate procedures for decision. Lionel Trilling has remarked, in his study of E. M. Forster, that it is not enough to choose the moral result. There is, he adds, a "morality of morality." The course pursued is no less important than the goal achieved; indeed the goal cannot meaningfully be considered apart from the pursuit of it.

It is an historic principle, applied in the celebrated case of Dr. Bonham in Coke's time, that no one shall be a judge in his own cause. Equally well established is the principle that both sides shall be heard. It is a curious point of historical interest that the Fugitive Slave Law of 1850, over which a storm of moral controversy raged, violated both these procedural canons. The law fixed the compensation of the commissioners hearing the cases at ten dollars if the Negro was adjudged a runaway slave of the claimant, and at five dollars if he was not. Moreover, the law prohibited the arrested Negro from testifying in the proceedings. That these statutory vices were largely ignored in contemporary debate but would surely be a primary object of attack today is a measure of the increasing sensitivity of lawyers in America to the procedural aspects of justice. This is not to say that the great substantive issues of justice are less pressing or complex. On the contrary, it is just as those issues grow more difficult and divisive that the procedural injustices about which there can be readier consensus tend to become grounds of decision.

It is in fact in the area of procedure that the widest measure of equality, the least tolerance of classifications, is to be found. Equality before the law is a maxim of legal personality, governing access to courts and treatment before them. Alien and citizen, man and woman, pauper and prince, scoundrel and saint—all have the right to seek justice through the agency of the courts. This has been an evolutionary development, to be sure; the disabilities of married women well into the nineteenth century are a notable reminder of this. The right is, of course, an abstract one unless there is material provision to assert it effectively. This is the current stage of the process, in which the state is assuming an increased responsibility for legal aid to the indigent, some of it under the compulsion of the equal protection guarantee of the Federal Constitution.

Similarly, the right to vote is being increasingly recognized. Here too equality of participation entails a corresponding duty on the state to make it a meaningful reality, through the provision of commensurate educational opportunities. There is a positive feedback principle involved here: the increasing recognition of the right of participation gives rise to an obligation to increase the resources devoted to supporting the right.

Parenthetically, the feedback principle may be useful in approaching other, non-procedural, problems of social justice and the law; for example, the much-discussed question whether there should be a legal duty as well as a moral duty to go to the aid of a stranger in physical peril—whether, that is, good samaritanism ought to be more than a moral duty. In this country the law has hesitated to impose a duty of rescue unless a certain relationship to the victim exists: that the rescuer caused the peril, however innocently, or led the victim to rely on him for protection, or stood in a beneficial relation such as employer to employee or merchant to customer. Perhaps, if the law is to impose a broader social duty of rescue, it should provide correspondingly for public compensation of the rescuer in the event he is injured or suffers financial loss. This is in substance the solution adopted in Austrian law.[8]

To return to the subject of authority. Thus far we have touched on the intrinsic fairness of procedures, and the right of access and participation. Another aspect of authority is concerned with determination of the proper arbiter. In the Associated Press case, according to the dissenting judgment of Justice Brandeis, the Court was neither equipped nor authorized to undertake the kind of supervision and regulation which full justice would have required. In the union shop case, the issue of justice was reduced to the availability of fair procedures within the union organization itself and ultimately to the scope of judicial review in the light of the function allocated to the courts with respect to judging the validity of legislation.

Consider another concrete case, this one a rather familiar illustration of the relation of law and morals. A father dies and his property descends by the statutes of inheritance to his eldest son. Other members of the family allege that in fact the father was murdered by the son for the sake of the inheritance. If this allegation is true, corrective justice would require that title to the property be denied the son and placed in the next heirs of the father. That no one should profit by his own wrong at the expense of another is a convenient moral maxim that covers the case. Suppose, however, that meanwhile the property was sold by the son to an innocent purchaser. If by reason of his crime the title had never been vested in the son it would be held that it could not be transferred to the purchaser. Is the innocent purchaser, who after all paid good money for the property, to be subordinated to the innocent members of the family, who have made no expenditure at all? Furthermore, it must yet be decided whether or not a murder has actually been committed. Shall this be decided by the probate court, without

[8] See J. P. Dawson, *Negotiorum Gestio: The Altruistic Intermeddler,* 74 HARV. L. REV. 1073, 1121 (1961); and generally, G. Hughes, *Criminal Omissions,* 67 YALE L.J. 590 (1958).

the usual safeguards surrounding the defendant in a criminal trial? Perhaps an accommodation of interests could be worked out along these lines: there must be a verdict of guilty in a criminal trial before the title may be attacked in the probate court; the title itself will be unaffected, so that an innocent purchaser will be undisturbed; but the son will be treated as a constructive trustee of the property or its proceeds to the extent that he retains them or holds any assets up to the amount he received.[9]

Such a solution indicates the freedom of judges to "make" law within limits. But what are those limits? Justice Holmes put his view pithily when he said that judges make law interstitially, that they are confined from molar to molecular motion. Justice Frankfurter puts it more colloquially, saying that judges make law at retail, legislators at wholesale.

An analogy to science, suggested in the preceding essay, is relevant here as well, in connection with the authority of the judge. In principle an experiment tests not only the law which is its immediate target of inquiry but the whole system of laws of which this one is a part.[10] Practically, however, the subject of the test will be much more limited, unless and until a more searching reexamination of anterior postulates seems to be required by the puzzling nature of the result or by an intuition that the result may be assimilated in a more satisfying way to the larger body of knowledge.

So also with the judge. Normally, if only by reason of the need for economy of effort, the judge is content to select and "apply" the "rules" of law that appear to be immediately relevant.[11] This process involves an illumination, refinement,

---

[9] Various solutions are considered in 4 A. W. SCOTT, THE LAW OF TRUSTS   492 (2d. ed. 1956).

[10] See M. WHITE, TOWARD REUNION IN PHILOSOPHY 255-58 (1956).

[11] I can only advert to the subtle and important question of what it means to "apply a rule." "The notion of a principle (or maxim) of conduct and the notion of meaningful action are *interwoven*." P. WINCH, THE IDEA OF A SOCIAL SCIENCE 63 (1958).

and development of the rules themselves in changing contexts. Nevertheless occasions arise when this course seems less than satisfactory. The results may no longer appear sufficiently coherent, or predictable, or just, to warrent the judge's stopping at the immediate rules; he is impelled to enter upon a regressive inquiry into the antecedent postulates of the system of rules which he is applying. The theoretical scientist is perhaps more likely than the experimentalist to undertake so searching a reexamination and to frame newer principles. In law the legislator is, for a number of reasons, freer than the judge to engage in this sort of enterprise. By directing itself to the future and making flexible its provisions, legislation can more readily mitigate the unsettling effects of a change; by employing more varied techniques of ascertaining poular and expert opinion, legislation can ground itself more confidently in the necessity for change. The importance of these factors varies greatly with the circumstances, and despite the ready cliché that legislators make the law and judges find it, these considerations are by no means always applicable or decisive.

Much of law is designed to avoid the necessity for the judge to reach Holmes' "can't helps," his ultimate convictions or values. The force of precedent, the close applicability of statute law, the separation of powers, legal presumptions, statutes of limitations, rules of pleading and evidence, and above all the pragmatic assessments of fact that point to one result whichever ultimate values be assumed, all enable the judge in most cases to stop short of a resort to his personal standards. When these prove unavailing, as is more likely in the case of courts of last resort at the frontiers of the law, and most likely in a supreme constitutional court, the judge necessarily resorts to his own scheme of values. It may therefore be said that the most important thing about a judge is his philosophy; and if it be dangerous for him to have one, it is at all events less dangerous than the self-deception of having none.

This discussion of movement in the law leads to a more general consideration of the role of law in relation to drastic social change. Continuity with the past, said Holmes, is not a duty; it is only a necessity. The law faces no greater challenge than when it must reconcile this necessity with sharply rising expectations and pressing demands for radical redistribution made in the name of justice. The role of law here is to mediate, to accommodate, to cushion. Even the thorough recasting of the law after a social upheaval is likely to display such continuity. The French Civil Code of 1803 is a leading example: New and important popular rights were indeed conferred; but the more noteworthy feature of the Code is its continuity with legal doctrine of the past.[12]

Legal institutions have developed a variety of devices for the task of accommodation. The law, for instance, determines where the financial cost of drastic change shall fall. Here the polar positions, in legal terminology, are the "police power" of the state, which may introduce abrupt dislocations for which the community need not pay, and "eminent domain," which involves a "taking" of "property" for which compensation must be made. The essentially pragmatic content of the "police power" was described by Justice Holmes in a celebrated opinion:[13]

When legislatures are held to be authorized to do anything considerably affecting public welfare it is covered by apologetic phrases like the police power, or the statement that the business concerned has been dedicated to a public use. The former expression is convenient, to be sure, to conciliate the mind to something that needs explanation: the fact that the constitutional requirement of compensation when property is taken cannot be pressed to its grammatical extreme; that property rights may be taken for public purposes without pay if you do not take too much; that some play must be allowed to the joints if the machine is to work. But police power is often used in a wider sense to cover, and, as I said, to apologise for the general power of the legislature to make a part of the community uncomfortable by a change.

[12] See C. J. Friedrich, *The Ideological and Philosophical Background,* in THE CODE NAPOLEON AND THE COMMON-LAW WORLD 1, 2-4 (Schwartz ed. 1956); André Tunc, *The Grand Outlines of the Code,* in *id.* at 19, 33-42.

[13] Dissenting in Tyson and Brother v. Banton, 273 U.S. 418, 445-46 (1927).

"Taking," "property," and "public use" are sufficiently protean concepts to permit a diversified allocation of loss consequent on governmental programs of change. If the government requisitions a stock of goods for military or philanthropic purposes it must pay the owner their value; but if it forbids the shipment of goods to their intended purchaser, in order to conserve transportation facilities, there is no taking and hence no liability for loss of profits. Questions arise when the "property" taken is less tangible—for example, the manufacturing capacity of a plant previously serving a particular customer holding a profitable contract. The line between the "taking" and the "frustration" of that contract, or between its "direct" and "indirect" destruction, may be one visible more clearly to the lawyer's eye than to the economist's; such distinctions are a crude way of freeing the community from a collective burden which might retard the rate of social change or the experimental initiative of representative government.

How thorny these questions can be when they emerge on a new state's path to socialism is shown in the recent experience of India. On the basis of—some would say in the teeth of—somewhat ambiguous provisions in the constitution of 1950, the courts ruled that standards of compensation for the great estates nationalized in the land-reform program must not offend the judicial sense of fairness; and that when a local government established a publicly owned utility monopoly there was a "taking" of an existing private business which was displaced. These pronouncements were promptly overriden by constitutional amendments making the legislative standard of compensation for takings non-reviewable and emphasizing the distinction between taking and deprivation.[14]

Compensation from the public at large is not the only technique for dealing with certain losses consequent upon change.

[14] See H. C. L. Merrillat, *Compensation for the Taking of Property: A Historical Footnote to Bela Banerjee's Case,* 1 J. OF THE INDIAN L. INSTITUTE 375 (1959); Merrillat, *C. J. Das: A Decade of Decisions on Right to Property,* 2 J. OF THE INDIAN L. INSTITUTE 183 (1960).

Indeed, when the government is not the immediately responsible cause of the dislocation the problem is generally approached in other ways. The law may, for instance, require minimal standards of pay and compulsory insurance, both of which are forms of social cost accounting that involve changing concepts of community. Whether it be compulsory automobile accident insurance, unemployment insurance, workmen's compensation, or overtime-wage legislation, the response is an amalgam of legal, ethical and economic standards that move away from the identification of responsibility with personal fault and toward a concept of state-wide or industrial responsibility concurrent with the common benefits of the undertaking.

In the community of the corporation, risks are adjusted by law among classes of investors. But the place of the employees in the corporate community has been the slowest to be defined beyond the guarantees of collective bargaining and industrial insurance. The relation of wage earners to bondholders and stockholders in the hierarchy of charges on the company's funds remains to be developed by the law. When rapid technical change is reflected in the displacement of labor, the problem becomes exigent: shall the law impose on the business this cost of a change-over, or is it to be borne by labor with such help as the community is prepared to afford through employment exchanges, retraining centers, work relief, and the like?

Compensation, insurance, priorities of claims are not by any means the only legal resources for accommodating change to continuity. How does the law deal with drastic changes in the price level or shifts in demand which cause deep imbalances in the economy? One way is through the renegotiation of contracts. Another is the institution of the moratorium. In the case of very severe imbalance, the law of bankruptcy may come into play. The classic legal definition of bankruptcy, an excess of liabilities over assests, has in recent times been expanded to include an inability to pay debts as they mature. Thereby the law has widened its ability to make adjustments of debts under conditions of financial stringency. The rule in bankruptcy is one of equality of sacrifice among unsecured creditors, and priorities among secured creditors according to the nature of their liens. As in the case of mergers or the introduction of labor-saving equipment, the relation of labor's claims to those of investors will be one of the pressing problems of the future.

In a more general way law must meet the dilemma of stability and redistribution through its ordinary modes of growth. In a celebrated passage Sir Henry Maine observed that the principal modes of legal development have been fictions, equity, and legislation. It is no accident that each of these is designed for the flexible adaptation of the past to the present. Fictions—the white lies of the law, Jhering called them—are the tribute that change pays to continuity. They make it possible to cope with the new without complete severance from the familiar. But they become dangerous if taken too literally. When the action of debt was usefully circumvented by the fiction of a subsequent deceitful promise to pay, it would have been unfortunate if the judges had gone on to draw the consequence that, as in the case of torts generally, an action could not be maintained after the death of the wrongdoer; luckily the tort aspect of the fiction was not allowed to control. Fictions serve the same function in law and in the life of institutions generally that word-play serves in the life of individuals: we may achieve new intellectual plateaus through the overarching abstractness of concepts.

Equity is the most flexible of legal instruments. In its characteristic sanction—the injunction—it operates prospectively by a command to desist from certain further action on pain of contempt of court, not retrospectively like a judgment at law to pay a certain sum on account of conduct already engaged in.

And the third of Maine's trinity—legislation—is itself characteristically prospective in the operation of its sanctions. Indeed, it is when legislation purports to operate retrospectively that the relations of justice and stability come into clearer focus. Under the Constitution a legislature may not impair the obligation of contracts. But individuals and groups, the courts have repeatedly declared, may not fetter the authority of the legislature over subjects otherwise within the "police power" by making contracts about them. Private interests may not by "prophetic discernment" forestall the reforming and corrective impulse of government. A brewery, for instance, need not be allowed to operate as an oasis in a dry state because it was established by public charter before the legislature introduced prohibition. A sweatshop wage is not immune from a minimum-wage law because it is embodied in a pre-existing contract.

On the other hand, if a legislature grants a perpetual tax exemption in the charter of a private university, it will be preserved against the tax-hungry generations that would mow it down. Why the need for greater revenues should be subordinated to the contract when the need for greater sobriety or affluence is not, cannot be explained in dryly analytical terms. There is involved an implicit judgment that the stability of a sovereign assurance is to be maintained against a general need for public funds though not against a tide of rising moral expectations in the community.

Everyman-his-own-lawyer (who will model himself upon the most pettifogging legal literalist) may seek to resolve these issues by defining "contract" and "impairment." What is a contract as distinct from a mere expectancy or a mere statutory privilege? What is an impairment of the obligation as distinct from a mere incidental or collateral frustration of a contract or diminution in its value or impediment to its enforceability? Questions such as these may veil, but do not conceal, the elements of judgment entailed in valuing the expectations of parties arising from contract or status or relationship and the expectations of the larger community.

An illustrative case is the controversy over the so-called Portal-to-Portal Act. Congress enacted the Fair Labor Standards Act, setting minimum wages, maximum weekly hours, and requirements of overtime pay. On the basis of the precedents, the law was undoubtedly effective to override employment contracts then outstanding. "Congenital infirmity" sufficed for this. The real difficulty arose later. In a series of decisions the Supreme Court construed the Act's provisions to mean that in measuring the compensable work week of miners there must be included the time spent in traveling from portal to portal of the mine, and not merely the time spent at the place of actual mining. These decisions declined to regard as controlling a contrary custom or usage in the industry in connection with wage negotiations. The effect of the decisions was to impose on the companies a very large wage burden which they had not contemplated either before or after the Fair Labor Standards Act. Congress responded by passing the Portal-to-Portal Act, which reinstated the prior understanding that custom would prevail for purposes of computing overtime. Now it was the workers' expectations — of recent origin, perhaps, but nevertheless grounded in the legitimacy of a decision of our highest court — that were blighted. Could Congress thus deprive the workers of these expectations? There was argument in terms of the nature of the expectations: were they contractual, or statutory, or judicially created, or what? Were they "impaired" by a law which purported to restore the original Congressional meaning? Judge Learned Hand, agreeing with his colleagues on the Federal Court of Appeals that the amendatory Act was constitutional, spoke in more ethical terms reminiscent of the psychological basis of Justinian's precepts of law and justice:[15]

With the opposed interests so nearly in balance, it seems to me, not only that Congress was free to make controlling the indirect effects of the new and unexpected reading of the Fair Labor Standards Act, but that it would have been most recreant in its responsibilities if it had not done so. I trust I do not undervalue the importance of not disturbing "vested" rights; but the pith and kernel of our well-founded reluctance to do so is because otherwise the hopes of their possessors will be disappointed and they will be unable *pro tanto* to plan their

[15] Addison v. Huron Stevedoring Corp., 204 F.2d 88, 98-99 (2d Cir. 1953) (concurring).

future. I do not believe that that is so imperious an interest as of itself to justify sacrifices of the general interest, no matter how grave; and, in the case of an assurance so contingent and doubtful as was any that these plaintiffs could have had, it would have been shocking to allow the retention of their bonanzas to bring about the evils described in the declaration. For these reasons I think the Act was constitutional.

There is a certain irony in this episode: the legislature operating retrospectively in order to displace in turn a retrospective displacement by the judiciary; and the judiciary in the end bowing gracefully to the reallocation between stability and change.

Thus law in its groping way seeks to mediate between expectations old and new. When Lincoln proposed that slaveholders be compensated for freeing their slaves he was thinking, as he characteristically did, as a lawyer. Although Franklin Roosevelt's legal training was far less likely to show in his thinking, the New Deal owed so much to the lawyers about him that the measures were at least as remarkable for their grounding in precedent as for their innovations; despite the accelerated pace and the creative novelty of combination, they owed part of their tonic effect to the shock of recognition.

The accommodation between stability and change is representative of the ultimate task of the law — the resolution of the ambiguities and antinomies of human aspiration: personal security and moral responsibility, knowledge and privacy, triumph and fraternity.

7   The Law and the Schools

If you were to look at a book on law and the schools, the chances are that you would find a discussion of the contract rights of teachers, tax exemption of school property, disciplinary powers over pupils, and similar issues on which lawyers might give advice to school administrators. Law, that is, comes in from the outside, and is to be left, a useful but esoteric art, in the hands of the professionals. It is as if science were relevant to the schools only as the basis for the design of buildings, or government only as the source of administrative regulations. The root cause of this comparative neglect of law as an appropriate subject for general education is, I believe, that law is regarded as a system of rules to be mastered by those self-doomed to work with them, and not, like science or government, as an enterprise, an ongoing process, whose study contributes to an enlarged understanding of, and participation in, the world around us.

In the colleges, to be sure, law as a subject of undergraduate study is receiving increasing attention. Surprisingly, perhaps, the most heavily subscribed kind of undergraduate course in law is that in business law. The older and still prevalent form of such a course is one devoted to rules: the requirements of valid contract, the liability of the various signers of a check, and the like—a how-to-keep-the-lawyer-away, or what-to-do-till-the-lawyer-comes sort of exposition. Happily, there is growing dissatisfaction with this conception of legal study, and the younger generation of business-law teachers is

Reprinted from 36 HARV. EDUCATIONAL REV. 470 (1966).

striving to give the subject the intellectual content and stimulus that would warrant its place in a university curriculum.

In liberal arts programs, a variety of approaches is taken, often conditioned by the departmental niche to which the course is allotted and by the general orientation of the department itself. Law in Society is a familiar offering in sociology. It has the virtues and the hazards of any such over-view. It has the virtue of seeing law as more than simply a system of punishments designed to keep order in society. Rather, it shows law to be a system that facilitates organization, association, transactions; that resolves conflicts or deliberately leaves a certain amount of friction; that operates as an educational force; and that can yet be dysfunctional in some of its operations. The hazard of the course is that any attempt at a systematic, functional analysis may compress too much into too few or too general categories and may, as in anthropology, require more refined differentiations. A political-science oriented approach can take a variety of forms. Law may be brought within the fold, domesticated and subdued, as it were, by the pressure-group theorist who assimilates the judicial process to the legislative; or it might be captured by the operations analyst who equates understanding with predictive power and so, programming judicial decisions, gets out of a computer, as from a major premise, all that was put into it, elaborating the obvious by methods that are obscure. These are caricatures, of course, though it is hard to avoid the impression that the work of some of the grimmer practitioners of behavioralism is a caricature of itself. There are partial insights to be gained from all these approaches, and from others; what is intolerable is the claim of any of them to constitute the one true faith, the only road to intellectual salvation. Their tactical legitimacy may well depend on the polemic context in which they are employed: whether to insist that a pitcher is half full or half empty may turn on whether you are combating the illusion that it is completely empty or completely full.

Aside from these rather special approaches, there is a view of law from the inside of the process that seems to me highly fruitful for general education, whether at the university or the school level. What I have in mind is more than a view: it is a vicarious participation in the process of legal thinking through immersion in some of the problems and the literature of the common law.

There is probably no more systematic literature of justification than the reports of decided cases extending back for several hundred years, with conflicting claims and interests laid bare and judgments rendered in the light of reasoned opinions and dissenting opinions, taking account in varying measure of precedent, analogy, logic, history, custom, morality, and social utility. For educational purposes the problem is to extract from this abundant quarry a set of materials that will be intrinsically interesting and comprehensible to particular age groups, that will link themselves to the students' own range of experience and observation. The problem is not as formidable as it may seem, inasmuch as the stuff of law can be related to such normal experiences of schoolchildren as association in clubs, disciplinary proceedings, engaging in simple commercial transactions at the neighborhood shops, and reading facts, opinions, gossip, and untruths in newspapers. The art is to hold the legal materials in a double focus: to see them as significant for their own sake, developments in the rationalizing of certain areas of human experience, and also as exemplifications of the rational process itself, with a wider significance for the developing intellectual style (to use a too pretentious phrase) of the student.

Let me try to be more concrete, setting out in summary form certain modes of thought that are almost inescapably called for in legal reasoning, together with sectors of the law that might appropriately evoke these responses.

1. *Dialectical thinking.* There is a built-in dialectic in law, not merely because of the adversary procedure in litigation but because of the nature of the issues. When Justice Holmes would jauntily enter his study, fling his hat on the

rack, and turn to his law clerk with the challenge, "State any proposition and I'll deny it," he was embodying the spirit of the common law, the rubbing of blade against blade in the scissors of the mind, making a truer and finer line. When Columbia University, a decade ago, celebrated its bicentennial, the theme of the celebration was "The Right to Knowledge and the Free Use Thereof." It is a noble theme, but one that challenges the legal mind to produce countervailing nobilities. Does it matter how the knowledge is acquired, whether by resort to eavesdropping or unauthorized search and seizure of private papers? Does it matter how the knowedge is used, whether by plagiarism or indiscriminate tale-tattling? The legal problems of illegal search and seizure and interference with the right of privacy call for accommodations of a sensitive sort; these are richly documented in the literature and hardly beyond the appreciation of the schoolboy.

In this connection, it seems to me that courses in the Bill of Rights, admirable as they are in intent, lose much of their value unless they are conceived in a dialectical way. Granted that it is important to know about the guarantee of a fair trial under the fifth amendment and the guarantee of a free press under the first. What is more important is to see the two in confrontation, in the context of the problem of press coverage of pre-trial investigations and trial reporting, and to try to resolve the clash by more refined principles than either of them alone. It is important pragmatically if we are to learn to mute the clangor of clashing isms; it is important for learning because we do not really "know" a principle until we know its opposing principles and reshape them all in the process. Better that students be encouraged to feel this implicitly, kinesthetically, than that they be taught from outside, as it were, the theories of scholasticism, Hegelianism, or Morris R. Cohen's principle of polarity.

2. *Contextual thinking.* Questions like "What caused the Civil War?" are a staple of the schools. Would it be thought an impertinence if a student, before responding further, were to

put a question of his own: "What exactly do you mean by 'caused'?" or "Why should we want an answer to that question?" This kind of response, pertinent or impertinent, is endemic in legal analysis. Consider, for example, the problem of legal cause in the law of torts. If a child is drowning offshore while two observers watch passively on the beach, one the child's nursemaid and the other a stranger, has either "caused" the child's death? If an intoxicated man, having been served by a too compliant bartender, playfully slaps the head of a companion who has an abnormally thin skull, who or what caused the resulting injury to the victim? It will surely be evident that to answer the question some decision on the purpose of the inquiry will have to be taken. The question may be asked of a lawyer, a moralist, a sociologist, or a physician, and the answer may vary accordingly. Was the question asked to assess legal liability, to affix moral blame, to promote understanding of human actions, or to aid in taking corrective or preventive measures? In the process, such concepts as concurrent cause, proximate cause, cause versus condition, and purposive identification of cause will have emerged without their formidable labels. Ideally, a discussion of this kind could end with this interchange between teacher and student: "Have you ever heard of Mill's theory of cause in history?" "No sir." "Well, you've just discovered it."

3. *Ethical thinking.* The concept of commutative justice is central to much of our treatment of social issues. It is also central to that great corpus known as the law of contracts, which deals essentially with the making, keeping, and breaking of promises. What kinds of promises should be binding and what not binding? What circumstances should qualify as excuses for non-performance? What remedies should be available in case of breach?—these are the major classes of issues raised in this branch of the law. In considering them, the student will have to consider questions of public policy regarding illegal or odious undertakings, the extent to which supervening unforeseen events ought to release one from an

undertaking, and the rationale of enforcing promises at all, as reflected in the law of damages — whether it be based on the reliance by the promisee upon the expected benefits that performance by the promisor would bring him, or on the promisor's having received a *quid pro quo* for his promise. The meaning of just expectations, on which the social order ultimately rests, can here be explored in considerable depth, without ranging beyond the student's personal field of reference.

4. *Genetic thinking.* The responsiveness of the social organization to changes in modes of production, distribution, and labor is a recurring theme in social studies. The pace, the pains, and the progress in this adaptive process are documented in quite human terms in the law reports. The subject of industrial accidents is a notable example, moving from the plight of the injured worker whose claim would be defeated by the employer's defense — either of the worker's contributory negligence, his assumtion of the risk of the job, or the causative conduct of a fellow-employee — through the abolition of these defenses by legislation, to the provision for workmen's compensation as a cost of the business irrespective of the negligence of employer or employee. A comparable evolution emerges from a study of the manufacturer's liability for defective products in the hands of the consumer, a progression that eventually enabled the consumer to sue the remote manufacturer and that has tended to supplant the criterion of proof of negligent manufacture with an implied absolute warranty on the manufacturer's part. These responses to changing patterns of industrial and commercial life give point to the remark of the late Professor Hocking, the Harvard philosopher, that to teach social studies without law is like teaching vertebrate anatomy without the backbone.

5. *Associative thinking.* Movement occurs not only through organic institutional changes but through the adaptive and assimilative processes of the mind. We live by metaphor; we advance by simile; we rise by concepts. The legal right of privacy is a fairly recent notion, which can be traced, in one

sense, from protection against eavesdropping (itself a metaphor), through offensive shadowing (a metaphor but also "like eavesdropping"), to the gossip sheet and unauthorized use of name or photograph (the general concept of privacy). Related to this process is the human addiction to fictions, to thinking "as if" one thing were another, an addiction particularly strong, no doubt too strong, in the law. Legal fictions (the "white lies of the law") can be looked at in many ways, but for purposes of comparing them with fictions elsewhere two categories suggest themselves: (a) normative fictions, like models or ideal types: the "reasonable man," or "everyone is presumed to know the law"; (b) categorizing fictions, whereby the new is assimilated to the familiar, the tribute that change pays to continuity — for example, the protection of interests of personality, such as privacy, as if they were "property rights," and the treatment of corporations as if they were legal "persons."

The conspicuousness of fictions in the law may serve to point to their prevalence in other more respectable disciplines — political science or economics or the natural sciences — and to suggest their uses and abuses and their relation to hypotheses and myths.

6. *Institutional thinking.* Perhaps the most distinctive feature of a legal system is the central position of a procedural framework, with specialized organs and ways of operation, underscoring the interrelation of ends and means. The amenability of a given problem to resolution by codified rules, or by generalized principles and *ad hoc* decision, or by unstructured nonlegal methods, is an inquiry that serves to sharpen an understanding of the problem itself. Given an apparent agreement in the abstract on an issue, say, of mercy-killing or the right of privacy, the effort to put the agreement into an institutional form with attention to who decides disputes, by what procedures, under what standards, with what sanctions, may uncover some latent differences and some consequent reshaping of the ends themselves. The effort may, at the same time, suggest some ways of resolving or bypassing initial differences

through agreement on procedures. A simple exercise in negotiating and drafting an uncomplicated contract can prove illuminating for an understanding of international disputes and constitution-making.

7. *Self-critical thinking.* Occasions arise when old doctrine has been so radically reinterpreted, when fictions have become so attenuated, that an abandonment of the old in favor of a fresh formulation seems inescapable. The phenomenon of judicial overrulings is familiar enough and is almost always accompanied by a reasoned articulation. The factors that lead judges to reach such conclusions are not very different, *mutatis mutandis,* from those that lead theoretical scientists to opt, at a certain point, for change over continuity. The decision whether to continue the process of assimilation and adjustment or to abandon antecedent positions is in either field a quasi-ethical judgment. The elements that ought to enter into such a choice can be analyzed in notable episodes of the judicial, no less than the scientific, process.

If these seven intellectual traits, or some of them, seem worthy of more deliberate cultivation in the schools, and if the law appears to offer some particularly apt opportunities in this direction, the mechanics of the educational enterprise (the preparation of teachers, the assembling of materials and their sequential use) can be explored by teachers and lawyers together. I should confess, finally, that this essay, like the approaches to which I alluded at the outset, should be taken in a polemic context: that the cardinal sin of our classrooms is one-dimensional thinking, all warp and no woof, making for glibness of mind that knows the answers without really knowing the questions. It is the cardinal sin, I would maintain, because it characterizes some of the most academically successful products of the system. What I have tried to suggest is essentially an antidote to glibness that can be ingested without tears.

III APPRECIATIONS: A GALLERY OF JUDGES

8 Mr. Justice Brandeis

Louis D. Brandeis has become part of our national heritage, like Woodrow Wilson, that other child of 1856. But any inheritance really belongs to the legatees only as they strive to make it part of their own deepest nature. This is simply to paraphrase one of Brandeis' own favorite passages from Goethe: "You must labor to possess that which you have inherited."

This centennial observance serves to acknowledge the special relation in which Brandeis stood to Harvard University. Unlike the present generation of Harvard Law School students, for most of whom Harvard is an alma mater once removed, Brandeis owed no divided academic loyalty. His close and continuing relations with the guiding spirits of the law school and the university – notably with his mentor in constitutional law, J. B. Thayer; with Ezra Thayer, who went into the Brandeis law office; with Dean Ames and President Eliot; his lectureship in the law of evidence from 1882 to 1883; his fathering of the Harvard Law School Association in 1886, for which the university awarded him its master-of-arts degree; his drawing on the school for his law clerks year after year, through the good offices of Professor Frankfurter – these ties surely justify the identification of him with our university without making us guilty of that delightful provincialism which led one of our number (or was it an outlander?) to

An address delivered on November 13, 1956, in Sanders Theatre, Cambridge, at a meeting held under the auspices of the President and Fellows of Harvard College to commemorate the one-hundredth anniversary of the birth of Justice Brandeis; reprinted from 70 HARV. L. REV. 769 (1957).

describe Dr. Eliot's Five-Foot Bookshelf as *"The Odyssey* and other Harvard Classics."

But it is not of these familiar ties that one needs to speak on this occasion. There was in Brandeis a deep sense of attachment to the small community, and particularly in his later years this sentiment—it was more a rationally held obligation than an emotional bond—led him to affirm his Kentucky origins and recognize a duty unfulfilled. Whether the home of his childhood was suddenly presented to view by fond recollection may be doubted; this revival of the domicile of origin, so to speak, was rather the deliberate living out of a philosophy, and so it may repay more than a glance as a clue to the Brandeis mind and method.

What he did for his native community can be described briefly and colorlessly. It consisted in donating, between 1924 and 1929, substantial segments of his library to the University of Louisville, together with a few thousand dollars for the usual costs of binding, cataloguing, shelving, and supplementing the collections. So described, the deed seems worthy enough but hardly of conspicuous note. That, however, was not the real story. The actual event is best recaptured in the contemporary documents which passed between Brandeis and those whom he drafted into the enterprise, the members of his family then living in Kentucky; those living elsewhere were "disqualified for the present by non-residence." Writing to his nephew early in 1925, he expressed his conception of the role of the donor to a university:

> If the University is to become a worthy institution—it must be through its faculty and officers. They are to build up a library. You and I are to help them. And, of course, your part will be an important and continuous one and it is my purpose to keep on helping them to build up the Department.[1]

In November 1924, soon after he had made his first gifts to the university library, he wrote to his nephew:

[1] FLEXNER, MR. JUSTICE BRANDEIS AND THE UNIVERSITY OF LOUISVILLE 5 (1938).

I assumed that the University of Louisville is poor in possessions – including instructors. What I aim to do is to make them rich in ideals and eager in the desire to attain them. I want the authorities to dream of the University as it should be; and I hope to encourage this dreaming by making possible the first steps towards realization.

The only assurance I care to exact is that a desire for high standards is felt, and that an effort will be made to carry out the project as suggested.

Teachers are largely a meek, down-trodden, unappreciated body of men. To know that others believe in them, consider them capable of high thinking and doing, and are willing to help them out – may enable them to accomplish more than even they think possible.[2]

To his brother he described his image of a local university – not, be it noted, a red-brick, ivyless institution to care for the underprivileged, but an enterprise with a distinctive and irreplaceable role in the educational process:

Money alone cannot build a worthy University. Too much money – or too quick money – may mar one; particularly if it is foreign money. To become great, a University must express the people whom it serves, and must express the people and the community at their best. The aim must be high and the vision broad; the goal seemingly attainable but beyond the immediate reach. It was with these requisites in mind that I made the three essays referred to. To indicate, through the Department of Sociology, the purpose to influence the life of the State socially and economically. To indicate, through the Department of Fine Arts and of Music, the purpose to promote that development which is compounded in the term culture. To indicate, through the proposal concerning the World War history, the purpose not only to encourage research and learning, but to influence the political life of the State and the Nation by a deep and far-reaching study of history, and enquiry into the causes and consequences of present ills, and a consideration of the proper aspirations of the United States and of the functions of the State. History teaches, I believe, that the present tendency towards centralization must be arrested, if we are to attain the American ideals, and that for it must be substituted intense development of life through activities in the

[2] *Ibid.*

several States and localities. The problem is a very difficult one, but the local University is the most hopeful instrument for any attempt at solution.[3]

The collections ranged from the World War to fine arts, from English and German literature to Palestine. Each of the collections was to serve as a magnetic core that would attract not merely additional materials but the active participation of an interested group in the community. One subcollection, on the liberation of nationalities, may serve to exemplify the grand design:

The liberation of lesser nationalities is prominent among the hopeful results of the War. And yet their independence was won less by arms than the slow process of education. It was largely the work of far-seeing, patient, persistent devoted men and women, who awakened in the rising generation an interest in the language, the literature, the traditions of their people, and through the acquistion of knowledge, developed the striving for liberty and opportunity and the fuller life ...

These struggles, rich in heroic incident and noble achievement, present material for some of the most promising chapters in the history of mankind. The University should have in its library, not only the books in which the events are summarized, but, so far as possible, also the contemporary publications which were themselves acts of liberation, or which record in detail events of importance. Louisville has among its citizens men and women of many of these liberated nationalities; and among these doubtless some who aided materially in this struggle for independence. That the University purposed making such a collection, the cooperation to that end of these of its citizens would, when announced, be an event of civic significance. It would indicate the breadth of Louisville's hospitality; its appreciation of all contributions to civilization, regardless of nationality of those who made them, and that what is noble and fine in the traditions of all peoples of which its population is composed, is to be cherished as a subject for generous study. Thus would be made clear that the University is the University for all, regardless of race or

[3] *Id.* at 7-8.

creed and however recent their emigration to America, and that all should endeavor to work through it for the city's finest development.[4]

There is a characteristic insight, almost by way of an aside, in a reference to another of the collections:

The American Legion is an outgrowth of the War which is likely to exert considerable influence on our life and government. It seemed to me desirable, therefore, that the University should have a complete set of its publications and, if possible, a full record of its proceedings. From enclosed letter you will see that these are promised.[5]

Each collection was to bear a simple bookmark with a dedication to a Kentuckian most worthy to be remembered in that branch of knowledge: a "romantic German piano teacher" who organized the first chamber and orchestral music in Louisville; a humble bookkeeper who was a founder and informal librarian of a library association with quarters over a drug store, where "many of us made, and often on his introduction, our first acquaintance with modern English writers and with the British periodicals . . . " The law school received extensive collections of materials similarly dedicated to Kentuckians: Vice-Presidents, Speakers of the House, chairmen of the Senate and House Committees on the Judiciary, and also — a typical Brandeisian touch, arduously familiar to his law clerks — to "Kentuckians, not previously mentioned, who, prior to the creation of standing Committees on the Judiciary in the House and Senate, served on select committees and gave consideration to legislation of the character later considered by the Committees on the Judiciary" — followed by ten names with dates of service.

When a man's characteristics, which are writ large in his work, are thus reduced to miniature they may take on the aspect of caricature. But an image does emerge: a man with a simple idea, a glowing idea capable of kindling many hearts — like Bishop Grundtvig of Denmark and his folk high

---

[4] *Id.* at 32-33.
[5] *Id.* at 32.

schools for adults, whose story was translated from the German by Mrs. Brandeis under the title "Democracy in Denmark." A self-reliant leader whose lieutenants must be educated in the grand design and then strategically deployed—the little band of his uncles and his cousins and his aunts—no strangers and no outsiders. "Have you talked this over fully with the members of the History Department?," he reminded his nephew. "And have you shown them my original letter to you, so that they may know what is expected of them and of you?" A commander who insisted on mastering the details of execution: "master of both microscope and telescope," Chief Justice Hughes was later to describe him.[6] Letters to his cousin explained how the materials were to be surveyed, in what order bound, catalogued, and shelved, and how monthly progress reports should be sent: "This division of the task before us into sections, will insure accuracy." Each letter was internally organized into divisions—first, second, third, etc., with numbered subdivisions. If, as someone has said, Lord Eldon's love letters read like the charging part of a bill in equity, Brandeis' personal communications read like the text of a Brandeis brief.

There was, finally, the inevitable problem of obstacles and the discouragement felt by some of the little company of troops. But Brandeis himself felt no discouragement. He had no romantic illusions about human nature. How could he, who had all his life fought against inertia, obtuseness, self-interest, and worse; who was branded by some of his respectable contemporaries as an enemy of society; who had accepted hostility as a test of his own purposes and capacity to persuade; who was puritan enough to have subscribed entirely to John Milton's view of the human condition in the *Areopagitica:* "Assuredly we bring not innocence into the world, we bring impurity much rather; that which purifies us is trial, and trial is by what is contrary." "I want to say today," he wrote to his brother,

that I am not in the least discouraged by any of the events or attitudes

[6] Hughes, *Mr. Justice Brandeis,* in MR. JUSTICE BRANDEIS 3 (Frankfurter ed. 1932).

to which you refer. The difficulties are inherent in the situation ... There is no obstacle, so far as I see, that cannot be overcome with the requisite thinking, tact, and persistence. Some opposition is rather to be desired, as an incentive to our and others' thinking, and as a means of stirring up interest. But of course, we must be sure that we set the right course and maintain it ...

The need of money [for the University] is great and urgent. The value of money as a means of achieving things is familiar to them [the Trustees]. To devote themselves to the obvious need and to pursue familiar ways is natural. It does not require thinking or vision. I do not criticize it. I accept it as a fact. While I recognize it as an obstacle, I am convinced that it is not an insuperable one; and in some respects is only temporary in its intensity. It is in other respects permanent, and inevitable probably in any Board of Trustees charged with the duties of administrative supervision.[7]

I cannot refrain from adding the following passage in the letter. The necessary thinking, he remarked, must come to a great extent "from the customarily downtrodden members of the faculty who should be encouraged and taught to overcome their meekness."

Pointing doubtless to the model with which he was happily familiar in Cambridge, he proffered some advice for the board:

Your Trustees should learn that if they want to reach sound judgment and a real understanding of University affairs, they will have to do, as Trustees elsewhere have done: —

Give the mornings and afternoons to concentration on serious University problems and not the evenings after the vitality and energies are spent and their judgment naturally impaired.[8]

This last point was one on which he felt strongly as a guide to the management of affairs. The breakdown of the NRA between 1933 and 1935 he attributed to the superhuman task it had assumed, and especially to the fatal errors made by harried civil servants who were working almost around the clock and who had to make important decisions by the midnight lamp. I came across, just the other day, a most comfort-

[7] FLEXNER, op. cit. supra note 1, at 81-82.
[8] Id. at 82-83.

able and utterly subversive passage in an essay of Bertrand Russell that bears on this theme. "Bagehot speaks somewhere," he says, "of men he knew in the City who went bankrupt because they worked eight hours a day, but would have been rich if they had confined themselves to four hours. I think many learned men could profit by this analogy."[9] Brandeis would not have taken this suggestion quite literally. Multiply Bagehot's figures by three and you would come closer to Brandeis' regimen.

If I may pursue a moment further this digression from his idea of a university, let me say that I came to know him and observe his mode of life when he was in his seventy-sixth year. At that time it was his firm rule not to engage in judicial labors after nightfall. It was a rule, I should add, that he did not enforce on his law clerks. But neither did he enforce on them the positive side of his daily schedule, which called for a good day's work to be accomplished in the early hours before breakfast. Of this the law clerks were made cognizant only by circumstantial evidence—the drafts of opinions revised, the volumes consulted and strewn on the floor of the study adjoining the law clerk's room, the brief note left on the law clerk's desk with its embarrassing message: "Please see me when you come in. L. D. B." The note would have seemed more of a reprimand than it was, or was meant to be, had not the law clerk himself virtually synchronized his hours to the Justice's in the nighttime. Indeed, there is a treasured story of perfect synchronization on one occasion when the bleary-eyed law clerk, slipping a memorandum of nocturnal research under the Justice's apartment door sometime before dawn, felt it being retrieved on the other side. How could an errant twenty-five resist the moral compulsion of the self-discipline of seventy-six? The relations between law clerk and Justice were those of a working partnership. Two copies of each revision of an opinion were always made by the printer (Brandeis employed no

---

[9] RUSSELL, PORTRAITS FROM MEMORY 200 (1956).

stenographer but used the printer's overnight service in place of a typist): one copy for the Justice, one for the law clerk. Draft opinions went through dozens, sometimes scores, of revisions. Shakespeare, it is said, never blotted a line, while Anatole France liked to have eight proofs and Balzac might require as many as twenty-seven. Holmes and Cardozo belonged to the school of Shakespeare, Brandeis to that of Balzac and Anatole France. "Take infinite pains," said Michelangelo, "to make something that looks effortless." The law clerk was encouraged to embody his research in a form that could be absorbed directly into an opinion, though the Justice was unsparing with those drafts as he was with his own. The illusion was carefully fostered that the Justice was relying, indeed depending, on the criticism and collaboration of his law clerk. How could one fail to miss the moral implications of responsibility?

And that brings me back to the significance of the Louisville experiment, on which I may already have dwelt excessively. If so, it is because I am confident that implicit in the little episode, no less than in any of Brandeis' larger ventures, are to be found the major themes of his thought and the major strands of his character. To understand any one of the fruits of his thinking is like contemplating the flower in the crannied wall: to know it, root and branch and all, is to know the mind of its creator. The library at Louisville might have been savings-bank life insurance in Massachusetts, or the Palestine Economic Corporation, or the sliding scale for gas rates, or the protocol for labor relations in the garment trade, or the co-operative movement, or federalism and judicial review of the legislation of the states. In all his endeavors there was a steady vision of the creative powers of ordinary men and there was the resourcefulness to devise structures and processes to release those powers. The ancient democratic faith of the Stoics — no man is so like unto himself as each is like to all — was more than a dogma for him. It was an empirical fact borne in on him by immersion in affairs, and to disregard it was both a moral offense and a practical peril. At the root of his philosophy, in short, lay the issue of responsibility – the diffusion of responsibility, the assumption of responsibility, and the identification of responsibility. It is of these interwoven themes that I wish particularly to speak.

The diffusion of responsibility is an injunction that casts a wide net. It is a hard doctrine, especially for those who have sat in the seats of the mighty or to whom those eminences appear to be beckoning. When the Hoover administration was disbanding in 1933, one of the officials of the Department of Justice, making a farewell call on Brandeis, asked for advice about his career. Ought he to stay in Washington or perhaps go to New York, where he had some alluring prospects? The Justice's counsel was his familiar one: take your training and talents back to the service of your own community, your hinterland, and lead a full life there. To which the unhappy friend answered plaintively, "But Mr. Justice – Fargo, North Dakota!" It was a hard doctrine, and sometimes beyond comprehension. The Justice was expounding to a certain foreign ambassador the same philosophy that Washington was not America and that young men in particular should not overstay their time in the capital. Nodding sympathetically the ambassador interposed, "Yes, the climate in Washington is so bad!" Perhaps he spoke more wisely than he knew.

It is impossible to speak of diffusion of responsibility without coming to grips with "the curse of bigness," that Brandeisian phrase which is, I venture to think, as much misunderstood by some as the federalist spirit was by the ambassador in Washington. It has been charged against Brandeis that he would bring about the Balkanization, if not indeed the Bermudaization, of America; that he ignored the curse of smallness; that he undervalued the blessings of efficiency.

To this line of argument there are three things to be said. First, he was no scorner of efficiency. How could he be, who urged upon the railroads that they could save a million dollars a day by applying the principles of Frederick W. Taylor's concept of scientific management, and who braved the wrath of

labor unions by insisting that the precepts of scientific management must be accepted by the workers as well? What he denied
was the bland assumption that there is somehow a one-to-one
correlation between size and efficiency. His own experience led
him to conclude that frequently bigness is a prize sought for
reasons unrelated to efficiency, that it may mask inefficiency,
and that in any case it raises the most serious problems of the
development of character for those at the top as well as for
those at the bottom. What he asked of economists was a study
of optimum size in various lines of enterprise. Perhaps we shall
live, as he did not, to witness their report.

In the second place, he was concerned to preserve the values
of size while minimizing its vices. This is a problem which is so
pervasive that it has not gone unnoticed even in the administrative halls of our universities. Brandeis saw that the problem
of size was essentially the same in private and public undertakings because when the convenient labels are scratched the
familiar flesh tones of human beings are laid bare. Of one thing
we may be sure: as bigness poses the problem of power, the
answer did not lie for him in countervailing power, save in that
desperate state of extremity when fire has to be fought with
fire. He refused to accept the concentration of power as either
so inevitable or so irredressable as it has generally come to be
regarded. When asked how small enterprise could hope to
survive against the giants, he would point to the co-operative
movement as one resource not sufficiently explored. In government, too, co-operative federalism seemed to him a device full of
possibilities: interstate compacts, federal regulation of commerce in aid of state or local controls, federal taxation with a
credit for payments to state funds—these were techniques for
avoiding, in the classic phrase of the critics of federalism,
apoplexy at the center and anemia at the extremities. It would
be a mistake to suppose that he distrusted power as such. He
enlisted power, but power that would be self-liquidating. In
that view he regarded the ill-fated NRA as an exemplar of
power at its worst; we learned from it how not to bring human

authority to bear on human beings, and the NRA should for that reason have been set up, he suggested, as an instructional experiment in the Office of Education. By the same token, a statute like the Public Utility Holding Company Act, which brought about the simplification of financial structures and ended geographic scatteration of utility systems, thereby making them at last intelligible to their own managers as well as to the federal and state commissions charged with their continuing regulation, was a healthy use of public power. The criterion was not how drastic the power, but how conducive its exercise to the ultimate diffusion of responsibility.

The third and perhaps the most vital point to be made on this issue of bigness is that—to adopt the form of alternative pleading—even if the correlation of size and efficiency were clearer than it is, the price in many realms would be too great. Men are finite beings with a capacity—a destiny, if you prefer—for the cultivation of excellence. The pursuit of excellence is likely at best to be a heartbreaking adventure; but it is tragic folly when undertaken by man in his pride or in his subjection. "Care is taken," Brandeis would quote from Goethe, "that the trees do not scrape the skies." He would, I think, have found wisdom in this passage from E. M. Forster's novel, *Howards End,* where Uncle Ernst, having moved to England from Germany, is speaking to his German nephew:

It is the vice of a vulgar mind to be thrilled by bigness, to think that a thousand square miles are a thousand times more wonderful than one square mile, and that a million square miles are almost the same as heaven. That is not imagination. No, it kills it. When their poets over here try to celebrate bigness they are dead at once, and naturally. Your poets too are dying, your philosophers, your musicians, to whom Europe has listened for two hundred years. Gone. Gone with the little courts that nurtured them—gone with Esterhaz and Weimar. What? What's that? Your Universities? Oh, yes, you have learned men, who collect more facts than do the learned men of England. They collect facts, and facts, and empires of facts. But which of them will rekindle the light within?[10]

[10] FORSTER, HOWARDS END 36 (1921).

If, as Brandeis believed, responsibility is the great developer of men, then responsibility diffused must also be assumed and discharged. This simple theme too had its manifold variations. How did he put his views on woman suffrage? "We cannot relieve her from the duty of taking part in public affairs." [11] That is no doubt innocuous enough. Do you want a variation more arresting? When he was consulted in 1913 by President Wilson regarding the appointment of an industrial commission, he gave this advice: "[I] t seems to me very important that one of the representatives of organized labor should be an I.W.W. man." [12] And a little later: "If you have any doubt as to the advisability of appointing any I.W.W. man, I hope you will look at [John Graham] Brooks' book on 'American Syndicalism.' "[13] That book was a fervent, almost religious, plea for recognition of what the author called the "used and ignored masses." How quaint and remote it seems, incidentally, when our chief executives could be expected to have time to read books!

The opportunity to serve was also an obligation. On an occasion in the 1930's a friend reported to Brandeis that certain New Yorkers were trying to persuade Al Smith, then in retirement, to run for the Mayor's office in that city, and that Al was resisting because he had to recoup his financial losses, he was no longer young, there was illness in the family, and he had given a fair portion of his life to public service. And those reasons, the friend remarked to Brandeis, are practically conclusive, unless you were to say that a man's duty to his community is never ended. Fixing on the last words, the

[11] Quoted in Strauss Magazine Theatre Program, March 31, 1913 (Brandeis Papers, University of Louisville Library).

[12] Letter to President Wilson, May 19, 1913 (Woodrow Wilson Papers, File VI-158, Library of Congress). Brandeis' view of the IWW as a force to be domesticated on the road to "the sharing of responsibility" and "full-grown industrial democracy" may also be found in BRANDEIS, *How Far Have We Come on the Road to Industrial Democracy?*, in THE CURSE OF BIGNESS 43-47 (Fraenkel ed. 1935).

[13] Letter to President Wilson, May 27, 1913 (Woodrow Wilson Papers, File VI-158, Library of Congress), referring to BROOKS, AMERICAN SYNDICALISM (1913).

Justice said solemnly, "Isn't that the answer?" It was an answer that goes back by direct ascent twenty-five hundred years, to a passage Brandeis was fond of quoting from Pericles' Funeral Oration: "An Athenian spends himself in the service of the city as if his body were not his own, and counts his mind most his own when it is employed upon her business."

The third leg of the tripod of responsibility remains to be examined: its identification. Brandeis was not troubled by philosophic doubts about human responsibility. On that issue he employed, as Cardozo said of the common law, a robust common sense. And that, after all, may be where our contemporary philosophy leaves the matter. If, as has been said of certain European philosophy, it was nonsense on stilts, may it not be said without Philistinism that modern Anglo-American philosophy has simply lifted the stilts and put them under common sense? However that may be, Brandeis was under no metaphysical inhibitions in assessing praise and blame. When he noted that someone in Washington had done a particularly praiseworthy act, whether it was in testifying wisely before a committee, or publishing a sagacious paper, or accepting a call to be a professor, the individual was likely to receive an invitation to the next Sunday tea at the Brandeis apartment. Though the deed of valor may not have been spoken of, perhaps because a judge could not discreetly do so, the significance of the occasion was not lost. Although no citation was read and no medal bestowed, it was a kind of unofficial ceremony for the award of an Order of Merit.

More striking, however, were Brandeis' standards of blameworthiness. He refused to accept as explanations of misfortune vast impersonal dooms visited upon innocent victims by forces of history or secular tides or other animistic anonymities. When he was asked in the dark days of the depression whether he thought the worst was over he replied almost cheerfully, "Oh yes, the worst took place in the prosperous days before 1929." This is from memory; but I have recently seen a letter to Harold Laski which supplies the necessary documentation for biographical scholarship: "The widespread suffering, the economic helplessness and the general dejection are appalling; and most painful the absence of any sense of shame on the part of those primarily responsible for existing conditions. But the process of debunking continues; and if the depression is long continued—which seems likely—America will gain much from her sad experience."[14] There follows in the letter an interesting reference, which is also relevant to the issue of responsibility: "The Unemployment Reserve Act recently adopted in Wisconsin is our first step in grappling with irregularity of employment. Possibly you saw Elizabeth's [his daughter's] recent articles in the Survey Graphic. She and Paul [her husband] have had the largest part both in drafting the bill and in securing its passage." What is significant about this act, apart from its authorship, is that it attacked the problem of unemployment—or irregularity of employment, as Brandeis preferred to put it—as a responsibility of industrial concerns and not as an inevitable impersonal doom. This the act did by requiring individual plant reserves, gearing the employer's annual contributions to his record of maintaining regularity in his own payrolls. The plan was thus not so much a program of relief for the unemployed as an incentive to management to make regularity of employment a basic charge on a company's operations. So conceived, it was by no means popular among professional social workers who were more concerned with providing a broad state-wide fund to cushion the recurring distress of unemployment.

The whole question of the identification of responsibility can in fact be put dramatically in terms of a philosophy of insurance. For Brandeis, the insurance principle had taken over too large a sector of modern life, accentuating the drift, already too strong, toward the anonymity and the obscuring of responsibility that accompanies giant corporate or public enterprise. The

[14] Letter to Harold Laski, Feb. 28, 1932 (made available through the courtesy of Professor Joseph Goldstein of the Yale Law School).

first case on which I worked as a law clerk involved a
fidelity-insurance company. After the opinion was delivered,
the Justice asked whether I had ever heard his lecture on
fidelity insurance. As I had not, he exposed me to it. Fidelity
insurance he pronounced an abomination. To think, he said, of
insuring management against the consequences of its own
failure to know and supervise its trusted employees. It was of a
piece with the practice of states and the United States of taking
a pledge of assets of banks to secure public deposits. Some
disastrous bank failures, he believed, could have been averted
if government had retained an incentive, as an unsecured
depositor, to exercise vigilance in overseeing the bank's affairs.
Unfortunately it was not until much later, when I could no
longer reopen the question with him, that I came upon a very
different philosophical view of the matter, oddly enough in the
writing of Josiah Royce. "Ours is already an age and a civilization
of insurance," Royce observed, and he added this comforting
observation: "[F]idelity insurance, working in more or less
indirect fashion, enables countless young men to begin life in
positions of trust, and thus to find their places as people worthy
of confidence in a world where they might otherwise be doomed
to live only as temporary employes."[15] A Brandeisian end, you
will observe, reached by un-Brandeisian means. I leave it to you
to decide—and not merely as a rhetorical question—whether
the colleague of James and Santayana or the counselor at law
was in this instance the more profound moral philosopher.

On this note let me leave the general theme of responsibility,
so intricately woven in the thought of Brandeis, and turn to his
judicial phase. The transition is by no means abrupt, but it
presents some subtleties of its own.

Of course, many of his opinions were labors of love. That was
particularly true of cases where the legislative policy under
review was congenial to his deep convictions and there was no
tension between those convictions and his role as a judge. In

---

[15] Royce, The Hope of the Great Community 72-73 (1916).

such cases he labored mightily to explicate to his brethren (not always successfully), to the profession, and to the future the rational grounds of the legislation under attack—grounds as often as not more deeply bedded in reason and history than the sponsors of the legislation could have imagined. And so, on the Court as at the bar, he was able to transform the little case before him into an instance of a larger truth; he had the art of seeing, as Holmes would say, the general in the particular. One or two illustrations must suffice.

In 1876 Congress provided that postmasters, appointed by the President with the advice and consent of the Senate, could be removed from office only with the same consent. Not until 1923 was this legislation challenged in the Supreme Court—and then three years were consumed before a decision was reached—in a case from the Court of Claims with the telltale reproachful title *Myers, Administratrix v. United States.*[16] President Wilson had removed a first-class postmaster without obtaining the Senate's approval. Was the act of Congress an unconstitutional interference with the executive power of the President? Chief Justice Taft—more solicitous, it seems, of the prerogatives of the chief magistracy out of office than in—thought that it was, wrote an opinion of seventy pages, and carried a majority of the Court. Mr. Justice Holmes saw the issue differently. Since Congress could vest the appointing power in the head of the department instead of in the President and thereby avoid any question of presidential power, Congress could do the lesser thing of retaining the appointing power in the President subject to the condition it imposed on removals. The case was an exercise in simple logic, and less than a page sufficed for his dissent. To Mr. Justice Brandeis the issue appeared different still. The act of Congress reflected a democratic impulse, an appreciation of the safeguards of shared responsibility, that was wholly compatible with the principle of separation of powers and the nature of the executive

[16] 272 U.S. 52 (1926).

office. This view he developed in an opinion of fifty-five pages, including eighty-seven footnotes stocked with heirlooms drawn from the dusty corners of American history. To quote from Brandeis' opinions is, as Mr. Justice Frankfurter has remarked, to pull threads from a pattern, while to quote from Holmes is to string pearls. And yet even when abstracted from the architecture of the opinion this concluding passage bears unmistakably the master's mark:

The doctrine of the separation of powers was adopted by the Convention of 1787, not to promote efficiency but to preclude the exercise of arbitrary power. The purpose was, not to avoid friction, but, by means of the inevitable friction incident to the distribution of the governmental powers among three departments, to save the people from autocracy ... Nothing in support of the claim of uncontrollable power can be inferred from the silence of the Convention of 1787 on the subject of removal. For the outstanding fact remains that every specific proposal to confer such uncontrollable power upon the President was rejected. In America, as in England, the conviction prevailed then that the people must look to representative assemblies for the protection of their liberties. And protection of the individual, even if he be an official, from the arbitrary or capricious exercise of power was then believed to be an essential of free government. [17]

My second illustration of a judical labor of love is the dissenting opinion in the Florida-chain-store-tax case of 1933.[18] A tax graduated according to the number of counties in which the chain operated was held by the majority to be a denial of equal protection of the laws. Mr. Justice Cardozo, dissenting, focusing on the precise question, endeavored to show that in the South, at least, the county was a distinctive unit of government and business and not an inadmissible basis of classification for purposes of taxation. Brandeis took the opportunity to examine the deeper-lying convictions that produced this legislation; these he articulated with an unclouded vigor that bespeaks a

[17] *Id.* at 293-95 (dissenting opinion).
[18] Louis K. Liggett Co. v. Lee, 288 U.S. 517, 541 (1933).

single-minded man – single-minded because his role as a judge charged with forbearance toward acts of a legislature coincided with his persuasion of the wisdom of the law. The people of Florida might be astonished to learn how profoundly wise they were in their response in 1931 to the challenge of chain stores:

There is a widespread belief... that the true prosperity of our past came not from big business, but through the courage, the energy and the resourcefulness of small men; that only by releasing from corporate control the faculties of the unknown many, only by reopening to them the opportunities for leadership, can confidence in our future be restored and the existing misery be overcome; and that only through participation by the many in the responsibilities and determinations of business, can Americans secure the moral and intellectual development which is essential to the maintenance of liberty. If the citizens of Florida share that belief, I know of nothing in the Federal Constitution which precludes the State from endeavoring to give it effect and prevent domination in intrastate commerce by subjecting corporate chains to discriminatory license fees. To that extent, the citizens of each State are still masters of their destiny. [19]

These cases of removal from office and of the chain-store tax raised no inner tensions for a judge of Brandeis' persuasion. Complexities are introduced when private judgment and the judicial function do not coincide but sharply diverge. Just a year before the chain-store case the Court was called on to review the validity of an Oklahoma statute which required certificates of convenience and necessity as a condition of entering the ice business – this as a means of stabilizing the industry against free competition within it.[20] Such a measure was surely unpalatable to Brandeis. It would mask and protect entrenched inefficiency, or it would require a degree of public supervision of rates and services that was in all likelihood beyond the competence of the public authorities. Yet he insisted, against the Court's majority, that the law was not repugnant to the Constitution, and he lavished on his opinion

[19] *Id.* at 580 (dissenting opinion).
[20] New State Ice Co. v. Liebmann, 285 U.S. 262 (1932).

the same care and labor that he devoted, for example, to the chain-store dissent. Only a note of skepticism, uncommon in his opinions, betrayed his private judgment of the law. For the rest, his opinion is a ringing affirmation of the right of legislative experiment toward the control of economic ills. He wrote, in one of his most coldly passionate opinions:

The objections to the proposal are obvious and grave. The remedy might bring evils worse than the present disease. The obstacles to success seem insuperable. The economic and social sciences are largely uncharted seas. We have been none too successful in the modest essays in economic control already entered upon. The new proposal involves a vast extension of the area of control. Merely to acquire the knowledge essential as a basis for the exercise of this multitude of judgments would be a formidable task; and each of the thousands of these judgments would call for some measure of prophecy. Even more serious are the obstacles to success inherent in the demands which execution of the project would make upon human intelligence and upon the character of men. Man is weak and his judgment is at best fallible.

Yet the advances in the exact sciences and the achievements in invention remind us that the seemingly impossible sometimes happens...

To stay experimentation in things social and economic is a grave responsibility.Denial of the right to experiment may be fraught with serious consequences to the Nation. It is one of the happy incidents of the federal system that a single courageous State may, if its citizens choose, serve as a laboratory; and try novel social and economic experiments without risk to the rest of the country. This Court has the power to prevent an experiment. We may strike down the statute which embodies it on the ground that, in our opinion, the measure is arbitrary, capricious or unreasonable. We have power to do this, because the due process clause has been held by the Court applicable to matters of substantive law as well as to matters of procedure. But in the exercise of this high power, we must be ever on our guard, lest we erect our prejudices into legal principles. If we would guide by the light of reason, we must let our minds be bold. [21]

---

[21] *Id.* at 309-11 (dissenting opinion).

Complexities arose too when the judge's role was at odds with the partisan interests Brandeis might have been expected to support. His role was to create and maintain the structures and processes of a working democratic federalism — to maintain them so that the creative energies of a free people might find expression. The problems of federalism loomed large in that judicial task. State laws might conflict or overlap, and parties' rights might depend on the forum in which a case was brought. Brandeis was alert to find in the Constitution adequate resources to avoid on the one hand the anarchy of multiple state laws and on the other the supplanting of state laws by national legislation with its expanding national bureaucracy. One resource which promised a *via media* was the full faith and credit clause, whereby the Court could impose standards requiring a state to recognize the laws and judgments of sister states. Brandeis was a leader in the attempt to put new life into the full faith and credit clause, just as he was hospitable to the possibilities of the interstate compact clause[22] and the federal tax with a credit geared to state laws.[23] In a series of cases he wrote opinions for the Court applying the full faith and credit clause to limit the choice of law by the state courts and incidentally to reject the claims of a widow,[24] an orphan,[25] and a workingman.[26] Brandeis was a compassionate man; without compassion he could not have driven himself to almost incredible labors for his fellow men. But he was not a sentimentalist. He had never allowed his energies to be drained, or his greater usefulness debilitated, by yielding to pity for the individual case at the cost of a more inclusive

[22] See, *e.g.*, Hinderlider v. La Plata River & Cherry Creek Ditch Co., 304 U.S. 92 (1938).

[23] On the federal tax-credit device his interpellations in the oral argument of the federal-unemployment-insurance-tax cases, Steward Mach. Co. v. Davis, 301 U.S. 548 (1937); Carmichael v. Southern Coal & Coke Co., 301 U.S. 495 (1937), are instructive. See S. Doc. No. 53, 75th Cong., 1st Sess. 15-17, 68-72, 78 (1937) (transcript of argument).

[24] John Hancock Mut. Life Ins. Co. v. Yates, 299 U.S. 178 (1936).

[25] Yarborough v. Yarborough, 290 U.S. 202 (1933).

[26] Bradford Elec. Light Co. v. Clapper, 286 U.S. 145 (1932).

rescue and reform. Least of all on the Court would he compromise his moral authority by succumbing to expediency, though it bore the face of grief. He was, after all, a constitutional judge, not a jury lawyer.

I have spoken of his hospitality to legislative experiment, whether it seemed to him wise or foolish, and his concern for process and structure as the central mission of the Court. These attitudes were a reflection, on the bench, of his general philosophy of responsibility. It should not have caused surprise that he laid great store by the observance of technical jurisdictional and procedural requirements. So far from being, as some observers have argued, in contradiction to his spacious view of the powers of government, his concern for these limitations on the powers of the Court was in harmony with his deepest convictions about the allocation of responsibility, the fallibility of judgment, and the wisdom of self-restraint. Once more he would turn to Goethe for the telling phrase: "Self-limitation is the first mark of the master." The most important thing we decide, he used to say, is what not to decide. And so it was a fighting issue for him when the Court interpreted the act regulating the Court's appellate jurisdiction to favor obligatory rather than discretionary review of an important class of state-court decisions.[27] His dissenting opinion,[28] insisting that certiorari and not appeal was the proper route to review, is as deeply felt as if he had been writing on an illegal search and seizure.

There is a certain irony in this obsession with self-limitation on the part of one who undertook and carried through almost superhuman exertions as a matter of course. But concentration of energy is energy squared. The canons of judicial self-restraint, which he elaborated most powerfully in the *TVA* case,[29] were not simply a device to head off the Court from a decision distasteful to him on the merits. If that is not plain enough from the *TVA* case itself, where a majority was mar-

[27] Dahnke-Walker Milling Co. v. Bondurant, 257 U.S. 282 (1921).
[28] *Id.* at 293.
[29] Ashwander v. TVA, 297 U.S. 288, 341 (1936) (concurring opinion).

shaled in support of constitutionality, it becomes even plainer on an examination of his working papers in the child-labor-tax cases;[30] for there it appears that his resistance to a decision on the merits, for lack of equity jurisdiction, caused a long delay during which the membership of the Court changed and what had apparently been a majority for sustaining the law was lost when the case was finally decided.

So intense was his feeling for self-limitation that he opposed the plan for the Supreme Court building on the ground that to be enshrined in a marble palace would make it harder for the Justices to maintain their humility (such as it may have been). The action of the Court in recommending the construction of the building was, it is rumored, one of those five-to-four decisions. When the building was erected it confirmed his worst fears. It was not he, to be sure, but Mr. Justice Cardozo, who said that the Justices ought now to ride to work on the backs of white elephants. But it was Brandeis who declined to use the offices provided for him or even to set foot inside them. They were used as an exhibition suite and he resolutely continued to work in his study at home.

In two notable cases he departed from his canons of self-restraint by venturing an opinion of unconstitutionality when such a pronouncement was unnecessary. I refer to the *Willing* case,[31] rejecting federal declaratory judgments, and *Erie R.R. v. Tompkins*,[32] rejecting a general federal common law. But it is worth observing that in each case if he was guilty of violating his own principles he did so in the interest of enforcing a larger self-restraint on federal courts in the name of the Constitution. Such are the crosscurrents through which judges navigate.

In one realm the currents were strikingly at odds: the realm

[30] Atherton Mills v. Johnston, 259 U.S. 13 (1922); Bailey v. George, 259 U.S. 16 (1922); Child Labor Tax Case, 259 U.S. 20 (1922); see BICKEL, THE UN-PUBLISHED OPINIONS OF MR. JUSTICE BRANDEIS: THE SUPREME COURT AT WORK ch. 1 (1957).

[31] Willing v. Chicago Auditorium Ass'n, 277 U.S. 274 (1928).

[32] 304 U.S. 64 (1938).

of governmental curbs on freedom of speech and assembly. The usual tolerance of legislative experiment runs head-on into the task of maintaining free and clear from governmental obstruction the processes of political criticism, political change, and political self-correction. There is a point at which tolerance of legislative experiment ends and the naysaying mission of the Court begins. Where that point lies is one of the most anguishing problems a judge can face. Brandeis and Holmes, for all their judicial kinship, did not always agree in marking the point. When Nebraska forbade the teaching of modern foreign languages in the primary grades, Holmes would have let the experiment alone; Brandeis joined in an opinion of the Court holding that this obstruction to knowledge could not stand.[33] What is perhaps Brandeis' most eloquent expression of fundamental rights is to be found in his concurring opinion in the criminal-syndicalism case involving Anita Whitney,[34] which has made its way into the anthologies of freedom. Despite its familiarity, I quote it now because I wish to make the point that it was not simply written for the anthologies.

Those who won our independence believed that the final end of the State was to make men free to develop their faculties; and that in its government the deliberative forces should prevail over the arbitrary. They valued liberty both as an end and as a means. They believed liberty to be the secret of happiness and courage to be the secret of liberty. They believed that freedom to think as you will and to speak as you think are means indispensable to the discovery and spread of political truth; that without free speech and assembly discussion would be futile; that with them, discussion affords ordinarily adequate protection against the dissemination of noxious doctrine; that the greatest menace to freedom is an inert people; that public discussion is a political duty; and that this should be a fundamental principle of the American government.[35]

It is hardly necessary to recall that the noble phrase "They believed liberty to be the secret of happiness and courage to be

---

[33] Meyer v. Nebraska, 262 U.S. 390 (1923).
[34] Whitney v. California, 274 U.S. 357 (1927).
[35] *Id.* at 375 (concurring opinion).

the secret of liberty" is taken straight out of Pericles' Funeral Oration. (*The Greek Commonwealth,* by Sir Alfred Zimmern, was the book most likely to be recommended by Brandeis to friends in his late years.) But observe the circumspection and caution of Brandeis even in this stirring passage: the circumspection that led him to speak not of the discovery of truth but only of "political" truth, thus averting the shafts that have been leveled by the natural-law philosophers at Holmes; the caution that led him to insert "ordinarily" in relying on discussion as an adequate protection against noxious doctrine. He recognized, in short, that there was a genuine problem here for judges and that not even the eloquence of Pericles could of itself furnish the final answer. Remember, too, that Brandeis' was a concurring opinion, joining in the affirmance of Miss Whitney's conviction, but on the ground that she had not properly raised the issue of clear and present danger in the trial court and so could not call upon the Supreme Court to pass upon the question. And so Brandeis, who would have given priority in this case to the mandate for maintaining structure and process over tolerance for legislative experiment, in the end gave primacy to the canon of self-limitation. That was still the first mark of the master.

We have been led, you will have noted, into a discussion of judicial ethics—natural enough in considering any Supreme Court Justice, but inevitable in the case of one for whom the nice problems of moral responsibility were at the heart of the conduct of office, as of life. Our academic friends outside the law school sometimes chide us for not teaching ethics. They have looked into the official catalogue and they do not find the word. Yet if the day-by-day study of the law is not an exercise in ethical judgment of the most demanding kind I do not know what it is. Not long ago I came across an analysis of ethical judgment by Professor C. I. Lewis which I found highly suggestive for the law. Right conduct, he suggested, must meet three tests: the socially just character of the end, and the "technical" and the "prudential" rightness of the conduct; is it an appropriate means and one which will bring satisfaction over the long run as well as the short?[36] I am oversimplifying and probably distorting, but if you will apply this analysis to the judicial work of Justice Brandeis you will see, I believe, why it is proper to speak in a refined and not a gross sense of his morality of mind.

Your final impression may be of a man who placed on the life of reason an insupportable burden, who did not reckon sufficiently with those irrational forces in human nature whose exposure was the life work of another child of 1856, Sigmund Freud. And yet Brandeis had no illusions about human strength and reason; on the contrary, it was just the weakness and fallibility of man that gave point and direction to his philosophy. And not even the Freudians—they least of all—would deny the value of measured responsibility in maintaining mental health; nor would they forsake reason in combating unreason. Substitute for the soft nineteenth-century phrases "sentiment" and "custom" our harsher "subconscious drives" and "entrenched ideologies," and it should still be possible to agree with that incorrigible Victorian, John Morley:

> Ambrose's famous saying, that "it hath not pleased the Lord to give his people salvation in dialectic," has a profound meaning far beyond its applications to theology. It is deeply true that our ruling convictions are less the product of ratiocination than of sympathy, imagination, usage, tradition. But from this it does not follow that the reasoning faculties are to be further discouraged. On the contrary, just because the other elements are so strong that they can be trusted to take care of themselves, it is expedient to give special countenance to the intellectual habits, which alone can check and rectify the constantly aberrating tendencies of sentiment on the one side, and custom on the other.[37]

The world's ills are hardly to be ascribed to an oversupply of rationality. When a certain university was casting about to fill

---

[36] LEWIS, THE GROUND AND NATURE OF THE RIGHT 79-82 (1955).
[37] MORLEY, ON COMPROMISE 135-36 (1893).

a senior place in its department of philosophy, Isaiah Berlin was heard to remark ruefully, "There seems to be a world-wide slump in sages."

The distinctive quality of Brandeis is that with immense resourcefulness he found ways to build the ancient ideals we profess into the structure of twentieth-century America. His power derived from a fusion of three traditions: the Biblical tradition, with the moral law of responsibility at the core; the classical tradition, with its stress on the inner check, the law of restraint, proportion, and order, achieved by working against a resisting medium; and not least, the common-law tradition teaching that the life of the law is response to human needs, that through knowledge and understanding and immersion in the realities of life law can be made, in Mansfield's phrase, to work itself pure. This harmonious fusion of traditions accounts for the essential simplicity beneath the manifold expressions of his gifts. It explains, too, why his real significance goes beyond this or that specific measure identified with his name. Like all great teaching, as has been said of history itself, his meaning is not to make us clever for another time, but wise for always.

9   Mr. Justice Frankfurter

To commemorate in the *University of Chicago Law Review* the twentieth anniversary of the appointment of Mr. Justice Frankfurter to the Supreme Court is a singularly, or should I say trebly, appropriate act of dedication. In the first place, the Justice is by temperament and conviction preeminently a teacher. He himself enjoys telling of an incident not long after he went on the Court when in the course of an animated discussion at conference one of the brethren referred, not in entire forgetfulness, to the views just expressed by "Professor Frankfurter"—to which the Justice interposed that he could not imagine a more honorable or flattering title.

The dedication is appropriate in the second place for the very reason that Mr. Justice Frankfurter has no provincial links to this locality or to this University. The dedication connotes the Justice's position in the great community of legal scholarship unbounded by place or school. Twenty-five years ago Oxford University recognized this position by conferring on Professor Frankfurter its degree of Doctor of Laws. Indeed, the University orator in composing the citation was able, through a Vergilian pun, to suggest that the event had been anciently foreshadowed: *"Felix qui potuit reorum cognoscere causas."* However that may be, whether the ascription of happiness to one who understands lawsuits is a Roman or only an Oxonian philosophy, surely no Supreme Court Justice has been more

An address delivered at the University of Chicago Law School on March 2, 1959, in observance of the twentieth anniversary of Mr. Justice Frankfurter on the Supreme Court; reprinted from 26 U. CHI. L. REV. 205 (1959).

solicitous of the place of our law in the current of Anglo-American legal history or more watchful of contemporary developments in the law of England and the Commonwealth.

And in the third place it is appropriate and heartening that this School chooses to honor a judge at the height of his powers. The custom that such distinction should await extinction is surely honored in the breach. In England until recently it was a tradition that living authors were not to be cited as authority in judicial opinions. On one occasion the Lord Chief Justice, despite the tradition, could not refrain from citing Professor Holdsworth's *History of English Law,* but when he did so he was careful to refer to Professor Holdsworth as one "who is happily not an authority." The reporter of the decisions, in puzzling over this passage, concluded that it must have been a slip of the pen, and so when it was published it read "Professor Holdsworth who is unhappily not an authority."

What picture of Felix Frankfurter as a teacher can be conveyed to those who did not have the fortune to know him in the classroom? To describe the special qualities of a great teacher almost eludes the power of words; in this, testimonial evidence is much less effective than real evidence. Perhaps the most touching description of a great teacher that I have seen is the picture given of Willard Gibbs, the Yale mathematician, by his biographer, Muriel Rukeyser. She tells of Gibbs, standing in front of a class, beside a blackboard on which an abstruse equation had been worked out, tears streaming down his face and the students gazing at the board with the look of those who had just seen angels. The sight of angels is an image that is denied to most students of the law, even I daresay at Chicago, and certainly at Harvard. But what we did see was the illumination created by an incandescent mind, sometimes by the darting gleam of fireworks.

Professor Frankfurter taught a course in Public Utilities known affectionately as the "Case of the Month Club." For him a case was not the illustration of some principle or point of law; to approach it thus would for him have been a sacrilege. A case was explored as a process, through the record, the briefs, the counsel, the judges, the statute, its legislative background, indeed the geography of the area involved, preferably to be reported on by a student who came from that locality. The law of public utilities was learned almost by osmosis as you breathed it in while absorbing the insights of lawyership.

Then there were the seminars in Administrative Law and Federal Jurisdiction, where the intensity of a smaller group narrowed the gap over which the sparks traveled, and where the most recondite research became as exciting as the most recent Supreme Court advance sheets because it was felt that the voices of the past, if only they were unlocked, would have something vital to say to us about our urgent problems. Paging the reports, paging the statute books, even paging the statute books of the American colonies, was for many a student an enthralling adventure.

History was always a primary interest of Professor Frankfurter, but not history as inert knowledge. He viewed the study of history much as Holmes did, as a way of emancipating ourselves from fetters forged of our own misunderstanding.[1] Two of his most notable law review articles were of this character. One, the study of jury trial for petty federal crimes, showed that the Constitution viewed historically allowed a classification of crimes that would tolerate trials without jury in a substantial group of cases.[2] This at a time when the enforcement of the Volstead Act posed serious problems of judicial administration for the federal courts on their criminal side. The other paper, curiously cognate to this, was an historical study of criminal contempt to determine whether jury trial

---

[1] Holmes employed a different metaphor: "When you get the dragon out of his cave on to the plain and in the daylight, you can count his teeth and claws, and see just what is his strength. But to get him out is only the first step. The next is either to kill him, or to tame him and make him a useful animal." *The Path of the Law,* in COLLECTED LEGAL PAPERS 167, 187 (1920).

[2] Frankfurter & Corcoran, *Petty Offenses and The Constitutional Guaranty of Trial by Jury,* 39 HARV. L. REV. 917 (1926).

might constitutionally be provided, and this at a time when the validity of the jury provision of the Clayton Act was actively in litigation.[3] It is interesting that in each instance the study demonstrated that constitutional history left scope to Congress to settle the issue without coercion by the supposed compulsion of the Constitution. In the article on petty offenses Professor Frankfurter concluded with words which, though written in 1926, could be matched in his opinions today. He said this:

One can say with assurance, then, that so far as history is a guide, those multitudinous infractions of the detailed rules of modern society which we significantly group as police regulations need not be enforced with all the paraphernalia of jury trials. The profound reasons for a popular share in the administration of criminal justice did not cover this extensive range of petty offenses. Such is the verdict of the history that went into the Constitution. But it does not consider the influences which modify the sway of the common law in the application even of constitutional clauses rooted in its history. Still less are we here concerned with the wisdom of doing what the Constitution allows. American social policy suffers all too much from the dictation of abstract questions of constitutional powers. The historic availability of summary judgment is by no means proof of its desirability in the enforcement of a particular law. That is a problem for statecraft, whatever may be the opportunities which the Constitution affords. But Congress should know the alternatives which constitutionally are open to it . . . If [this paper] be lacking in the definiteness of a yardstick, we can only conclude by saying that history presents a body of experience expressive of the judgment of its time, but does not save Congress nor the Supreme Court from the necessity for judgment in giving past history present application.[4]

As one reviews Professor Frankfurter's scholarly works one is impressed with their dominant concern for procedure in the large sense: that pioneering volume, *The Business of the*

---

[3] Frankfurter & Landis, *Power of Congress over Procedure in Criminal Contempts in "Inferior" Federal Courts — A Study in Separation of Powers,* 37 HARV. L. REV. 1010 (1924). See Michaelson v. United States, 266 U.S. 42 (1924), decided four months after the publication of the article.

[4] Frankfurter & Corcoran, *op. cit. supra* note 2, at 981.

Supreme Court, the casebooks on federal jurisdiction and administrative law, the fruitful study of the labor injunction, and the courageous book which reflected the most painful experience of his life, *The Sacco-Vanzetti Case.* These were all studies of procedure in the context of very concrete issues which transcended procedure but which are made more tractable through the lawyer's contribution of a right structure for their solution.

Significant as his scholarly writings have been, it would be hard to place them higher in importance than his evocative powers with his students. What he said of Judge Cardozo, as Chief Judge of New York, will best convey what I mean. "One is told," he said, "that the same men were somehow or other better when he was chief judge than they were the next day, after he had ceased to be chief judge. That's a common experience in life. One man is able to bring things out of you that are there if they're evoked, if they're sufficiently stimulated, sufficiently directed."[5] It is fair to ask whether Frankfurter was not thinking of the formative influences on himself when he spoke of a common experience in life. Of these influences, beyond the intimacies of family life, one would have to include the teachers in the public schools of New York (his feeling for the public schools can be seen in the flag-salute cases and in the released time for religious education cases) and the Harvard Law School faculty, in particular Dean Ames, who conveyed a deep sense of legal history and ethics under the rubric of Torts or Trusts, and the shade of James Bradley Thayer, the teacher of Brandeis and the colleague of Holmes, whose spacious view of constitutional powers and whose correspondingly guarded conception of judicial review has been high in the consciousness of Judge Learned Hand and of Mr. Justice Frankfurter. Then there was Henry L. Stimson, Frankfurter's chief as United States Attorney in New York and as Secretary of War in Washington, whose standards of austerity and integrity in the enforcement

[5] *Chief Justices I have Known,* 39 VA. L. REV. 883, 902 (1953), reprinted in OF LAW AND MEN, 111, 134 (1956).

of the law are strongly reflected in the Justice's own outlook. And above all there was the long and intimate friendship with Holmes and Brandeis, of which the Justice's own unstinting tributes make it superfluous to speak.

And yet a man is more than the sum of influences playing upon him. These do not so much instill as they evoke. The relation is not merely influence, but affinity. And so in the end we are brought back to the mysterious alchemy of the self. None of us can know another in the way we know ourselves. We cannot transcend the limitations of our own consciousness and project ourselves into the consciousness of another any more than we can jump out of our own skins, though to try to know another who is an altogether richer being than oneself is a healthy exercise in stretching one's mental and spiritual integument.

This digression on the nature of the self is perhaps as good an introduction as any to the judicial philosophy of Mr. Justice Frankfurter. The cardinal themes in that philosophy can be viewed under the aspect of those objects to which Justice ought to owe the profoundest respect. Of these there are three, I would suggest, that are basic in the thought of Mr. Justice Frankfurter: first, respect for the integrity of the individual; second, respect for the structure of government with its distribution of what the military call roles and missions; and third, self-respect. Let me touch on each of these in turn.

First, the integrity of the individual. The philosophers put it that a man is a subject not an object. The British speak of the liberty of the subject. Bills of rights, with their due-process clauses, are yet another mode of formulation. Mr. Justice Frankfurter has never been fearful that adherence to those guarantees would weaken society's defenses. Twenty-five years ago while he was at Harvard, in his introduction to the Gluecks' early study of juvenile delinquency he wrote this:

In the main our whole process of criminal justice is crude and amateurish, economically costly and morally cheap. But the center of gravity of our problems of crime lies outside the courtroom. The crucial difficulties are unrelated to defects in trial procedure, and we are doomed to deep disappointment if we look for substantial diminution of crime to departure from those essential safeguards of liberty that have been enshrined in our bill of rights.[6]

The integrity of the person is the principle which underlies his *McNabb*[7] opinion on the fruits of questioning an accused during a period of unlawful detention. The same principle can be discerned in the very different context of *Sibbach v. Wilson*,[8] where in a dissenting opinion he questioned the federal rule of civil procedure authorizing a compulsory physical examination for a party in a personal injury case. Such a requirement, he believed, touched so sensitively the interests of personality that it ought to await a clear authorization by the legislature and not be imposed by mere rule of court. He has found himself dissenting also from judgments upholding federal searches and seizures without a warrant: violation of the integrity of one's papers and effects, an extension of one's personality, is justified only under the strict safeguards of a specific warrant. In the *Harris* case, in a dissenting opinion, he said:

If I begin with some general observations, it is not because I am unmindful of Mr. Justice Holmes' caution that "General propositions do not decide concrete cases . . ." Whether they do or not often depends on the strength of the conviction with which such "general propositions" are held. A principle may be accepted "in principle," but the impact of an immediate situation may lead to deviation from the principle. Or, while accepted "in principle," a competing principle may seem more important. Both these considerations have doubtless influenced the application of the search and seizure provisions of the Bill of Rights. Thus, one's views regarding circumstances like those here presented ultimately depend upon one's understanding of the history and the function of the Fourth Amendment. A decision may

[6] Introduction to S. & E. GLUECK, ONE THOUSAND JUVENILE DELINQUENTS viii (1934).
[7] McNabb v. United States, 318 U.S. 332 (1943).
[8] Sibbach v. Wilson and Co., 312 U.S. 1, 16 (1941) (dissent).

turn on whether one gives that amendment a place second to none in the Bill of Rights, or considers it on the whole a kind of a nuisance, a serious impediment in the war against crime.[9]

And from the same case:

> For me the background is respect for that provision of the Bill of Rights which is central to the enjoyment of the other guarantees of the Bill of Rights. How can there be freedom of thought or freedom of speech or freedom of religion, if the police can, without warrant, search your house and mine from garrett to cellar merely because they are executing a warrant of arrest? How can men feel free if all their papers can be searched, as an incident to the arrest of someone in the house, on the chance that something may turn up, or rather, be turned up? Yesterday the justifying document was an illicit ration book, tomorrow it may be some suspect piece of literature.[10]

Even when the issue involved the procedure of a state rather than that of the federal court, with the corresponding latitude a state enjoyed to admit or exclude illegally obtained evidence, to employ or not to employ its rules of evidence to keep out relevant and trustworthy evidence because of its origin, even here he balked when the illegal source was grossly offensive to standards of decent official behavior. In the stomach pump case he said:

> Due process of law, "itself a historical product"... is not to be turned into a destructive dogma against the States in the administration of their systems of criminal justice. However, this Court too has its responsibilities. Regard for the requirements of the Due Process Clause "inescapably imposes upon this Court an exercise of judgment upon the whole course of the proceedings in order to ascertain whether they offend those canons of decency and fairness which express the notions of justice of English-speaking peoples even toward those charged with the most heinous offenses..." These standards of justice are not authoritatively formulated anywhere as though they were specifics.

[9] Harris v. United States, 331 U.S. 145, 155, 157 (1947) (dissent).
[10] *Id.* at 163.

Due process of law is a summarized constitutional guarantee of respect for those personal immunities which, as Mr. Justice Cardozo twice wrote for the Court, are "so rooted in the traditions and conscience of our people as to be ranked as fundamental" . . . or are "implicit in the concept of ordered liberty" . . . The Court's function in the observance of this settled conception of the Due Process Clause does not leave us without adequate guides in subjecting State criminal procedures to constitutional judgment. In dealing not with the machinery of government but with human rights, the absence of formal exactitude, or want of fixity of meaning, is not an unusual or even regrettable attribute of constitutional provisions. Words being symbols do not speak without a gloss. On the one hand the gloss may be the deposit of history, whereby a term gains technical content . . . When the gloss has thus not been fixed but is a function of the process of judgment, the judgment is bound to fall differently at different times and differently at the same time through different judges. Even more specific provisions, such as the guarantee of freedom of speech and the detailed protection against unreasonable searches and seizures, have inevitably evoked as sharp divisions in this Court as the least specific and most comprehensive protection of liberties, the Due Process Clause.[11]

This stomach pump case, you will recall, produced a great debate within the Court. Two concurring Justices took the position that the evidence dredged up by the stomach pump must be excluded under the specific guarantee of the privilege against self-incrimination. They bridled at what they regarded as the natural-law and subjective analysis of due process by Mr. Justice Frankfurter. But once the privilege against self-incrimination is applied beyond the sphere of oral testimony, there is no literal guide to its stopping place. The concurring Justices acknowledged that to compel an accused to stand up in court, to turn this way and that, or to put on an article of clothing before the jury would not violate the privilege against self-incrimination. But they would rule out the results of a scientific blood test if carried out without the consent of the defendant. What, then, of the cutting of a strand

[11] Rochin v. California, 342 U.S. 165, 168-70 (1952).

of hair? They would draw the line somewhere on the basis of physical integrity, and though they might draw it more restrictively, it is hard to see how this invocation of the privilege against self-incrimination furnishes that objective and unmistakable criterion that is lacking in the due-process clause.

The same fundamental respect for human integrity comes through the Justice's opinions on the question of the right to a hearing, as when a claim of insanity is made on behalf of a prisoner condemned to death.[12] Here again he found himself in a minority. Of a piece with this concern is the Justice's position on capital punishment. Again he sees the issue in terms of procedure. He said in testimony before the British Royal Commission on Capital Punishment a few years ago:

I am strongly against capital punishment for reasons that are not related to concern for the murderer or the risk of convicting the innocent, and for reasons and considerations that might not be applicable to your country at all. When life is at hazard in a trial, it sensationalizes the whole thing almost unwittingly; the effect on juries, the Bar, the public, the judiciary, I regard, as very bad. I think scientifically the claim of deterrence is not worth much. Whatever proof there may be in my judgment does not outweigh the social loss due to the inherent sensationalism of a trial for life.[13]

This is a rather different view of the issue of capital punishment than you will find expressed in the conventional discussions.

The same emphasis on fair procedure as the Court's fundamental concern is to be found in his opinions on administrative law. An alien against whom a deportation order has been issued ought, he felt, to be able to invoke the declaratory judgment procedure and not be confined to habeas corpus; the alien ought, that is, to be able to challenge the order even though not in custody, provided that the governing statutes are

[12] Caritativo v. California, 357 U.S. 549, 550 (1958) (dissent); Solesbee v. Balkcom, 339 U.S. 9, 14 (1950) (dissent).
[13] OF LAW AND MEN 77, 81 (1956).

susceptible of a reading either way.[14] Once more he was in dissent.

The whole subject of standing to challenge administrative action received full-scale treatment in one of his most massive and deeply felt opinions, that in the *Joint Anti-Fascist Committee* case:

> Man being what he is cannot safely be trusted with complete immunity from outward responsibility in depriving others of their rights. At least such is the conviction underlying our Bill of Rights. That a conclusion satisfies one's private conscience does not attest its reliability. The validity and moral authority of a conclusion largely depend on the mode by which it was reached. Secrecy is not congenial to truth-seeking and self-righteousness gives too slender an assurance of rightness. No better instrument has been devised for arriving at truth than to give a person in jeopardy of serious loss notice of the case against him and opportunity to meet it. Nor has a better way been found for generating the feeling, so important to a popular government, that justice has been done.[15]

A procedural guarantee which is at the core of the rule of law, of Dicey's Rule of Law if you please, is the suability of public offficials for illegal actions which they have taken or threatened. How to reconcile this essential of the rule of law with the traditional doctrine of sovereign immunity from suit has been the subject of some of the Justice's most important and revealing opinions. When issues of fundamental human liberty are discussed, the problem of immunity of the sovereign or suability is frequently overlooked, but to me, and I surmise to the Justice, it is at the very core of the guarantee of liberty. It is fitting therefore that one of the two opinions the Justice delivered on his first opinion day twenty years ago was on this theme, and another of his massive dissents, in the *Larson* case,[16] was in protest against an extension of sovereign immunity.

[14] Heikkila v. Barber, 345 U.S. 229, 237 (1953) (dissent).

[15] Joint Anti-Fascist Refuge Committee v. McGrath, 341 U.S. 123, 149, 171-72 (1951) (concurring).

[16] Keifer & Keifer v. RFC, 306 U.S. 381 (1939); Larson v. Domestic and Foreign Commerce Corp., 337 U.S. 682, 705 (1949) (dissent).

I have said nothing thus far of the liberty of speech which many would regard as the cornerstone of respect for integrity of the individual. Surely no one can read Mr. Justice Frankfurter's opinion in the Michigan obscenity case[17] striking down a law which made the test of legality for all distribution the effect of the printed matter on the susceptibilities of youth, or his concurring opinion in the *Sweezy* case[18] setting up the freedom of the academic lecture room against an attenuated claim of the internal security of the state, no one can read these opinions without recognizing his sensitivity to freedom of expression. But he has not been prepared to regard this freedom in as absolute terms as some of his brethren, as, for example, in the case of contempt of court by newspapers in the Los Angeles Times—Harry Bridges affair.[19] This is not the occasion to deal in detail with the issue of freedom of speech and the press. I can do no better for present purposes than to quote from a recent piece by Philip Toynbee, the English literary critic, which appeared in a recent issue of the London *Observer* and which could some day find its way into an opinion of Mr. Justice Frankfurter. I quote this with the thought that it will be sufficient to illuminate the issue of freedom of expression as seen by an observer with the disinterestedness of distance and with another professional background. What Philip Toynbee wrote with specific reference to obscenity and the law could be taken *mutatis mutandis* as a more general commentary on our problem.

The smut-hounds are guilty of elevating personal prejudice above both art and freedom. The art-heretics are guilty of elevating art above life, the part above the whole, the by-product above the living process of creation. It is the old argument which divided some of us at the time of Monte Cassino, when a few held that the monastery should be spared even at the cost of soldiers' lives while the same majority considered this to be the most odious of blasphemies. Suppose that after an air raid a man had lain buried under St. Paul's in such a way

---

[17] Butler v. Michigan, 352 U.S. 380 (1957).
[18] Sweezy v. New Hampshire, 354 U.S. 234, 255 (1957) (concurring).
[19] Bridges v. California, 314 U.S. 252, 279 (1941) (dissent).

that he could be rescued only by the demolition of the whole cathedral. Who but a monster would have hardened his heart against the victim's cries rather than against the man-made monument above him? And just as there is a lunatic fringe of art lovers, so there is a lunatic fringe of libertarians who hold that the freedom to talk or print is, in all circumstances, sacrosanct. They would protest against any action being taken to prevent the publication of anti-Semitic pamphlets in modern Germany or of incitements to race-violence in Notting Hill. It is another heresy which prefers the part to the whole and attempts to deal with the complexity of life by a single supreme simplicity.[20]

A "single supreme simplicity" is exactly what Mr. Justice Frankfurter is wary of.

This is a convenient point at which to turn to the second kind of respect in the Justice's philosophy: respect for the structure of government and the assignment of roles and missions. If a judge could think only of respect for integrity or personality, all would be peace and quiet in the dovecote. As soon as you introduce such considerations as the federal system, the relation of courts to legislatures, the limits of effective judicial action, and the congeries of cautions known as political questions, you have indeed set the cat among the chickens. The *Francis*[21] case from Louisiana is an illustration. That was the case of the unfortunate criminal defendant who, upon being placed in the electric chair pursuant to a death sentence, found that the current failed and that the electrocution was therefore frustrated, and who maintained that to be subjected to a second ordeal would violate the guarantee against double jeopardy and cruel and unusual punishment as well as the standard of due process of law. Mr. Justice Frankfurter, with his avowed and deeply felt repugnance toward capital punishment, must surely have felt sympathy for the defendant's claim, and yet he was unable to find in the clauses of the Constitution a ground for

[20] Toynbee, *Two Kinds of Extremism*, The Observer, Feb. 8, 1959, p. 20, cols. 5-6.

[21] Francis v. Resweber, 329 U.S. 459, 466 (1947) (concurring).

preventing a second attempt on the part of the state. He more than implied in his opinion that the case ought to commend itself as one for executive commutation.

The most vexing problem of judicial review in terms of the structure of government is the question of a double standard or a preferred position for certain constitutional guarantees. Mr. Justice Frankfurter has resisted the claim for any such priorities, though he has described approvingly a scale of values which he discerned in the opinions of Mr. Justice Holmes. He said this in writing of Holmes:

Social development is an effective process of trial and error only if there is the fullest possible opportunity for the free play of the mind. He therefore attributed very different legal significance to those liberties which history has attested as the indispensable conditions of a free society from that which he attached to liberties which derived merely from shifting economic arrangement. [22]

This is not the occasion to examine the myriad judgments arrived at by Mr. Justice Frankfurter in this troubled area. Doubtless no two thinkers would stand in complete agreement, given the complexity of the issues. But it may be important to notice the frank and ever-present concern of the Justice that the issues be seen in the full on their several levels, and his cognate concern lest a purely private judgment of preference be taken as a constitutional command. To avoid this he relies heavily, may it not be too heavily, on the teachings of history. Now history can show us a number of things. First, it can show us specific events: what was done, for example, about habeas corpus in the Act of 1679. In the second place, history can give us a narrative; it can tell us what was the practice regarding jury trial for contempt in the centuries preceding our Constitution. But when history is called on to furnish a guide to the priority of values, I wonder whether it is being given a burden

[22] Article on Holmes in 21 DICTIONARY OF AMERICAN BIOGRAPHY 417, 424 (1944), reprinted in OF LAW AND MEN 158, 175 (1956). See also FRANKFURTER, MR. JUSTICE HOLMES AND THE CONSTITUTION 51 (1938).

heavier than it can bear alone. Here, as it seems to me, history becomes the creative art of the historian. Santayana has spoken of an "estimate of evolution" as "a sort of retrospective politics," engaged in as one "might look over a crowd to find his friends." [23] From Lord Acton has come a similar warning against confounding the historian with the history:

> Whatever a man's notions of these later centuries are, such, in the main, the man himself will be. Under the name of History, they cover the articles of his philosophic, his religious and his political creed. They give his measure, they denote his character: and, as praise is the shipwreck of historians, his preferences betray him more than his aversions. Modern history touches us so nearly, it is so deep a question of life and death, that we are bound to find our way through it, and to owe our insight to ourselves. [24]

I wonder whether history does not have to yield here to philosophy. History or historians may suggest, to be sure, some lessons about the effectiveness of institutional arrangements. But would it really matter, for constitutional law, if a historian argued persuasively that English literature had its greatest flowering during a period of the licensing of books and plays?

A philosophy, of course, need not be merely personal. In large terms our professed philosophy is that of representative self-government, a secular state, a division of authority, and the protection of minority rights. While important variances within these very broad conceptions are inevitable, we are not without safeguards against excessively personal judicial judgments. One safeguard is the practice of deciding no more than is necessary to the case — in constitutional law to decide, if possible, on a non-constitutional rather than a constitutional ground. The whole tenor of the Supreme Court's decisions in the last few years in the field of internal security reflects this caution, by giving to the legislature or to the executive an opportunity for sober second thought. And this practice, it must

[23] Santayana, *Reason in Science,* in The Life of Reason 401-2 (rev. ed. 1955).
[24] Acton, A Lecture on the Study of History 73 (1905).

be clear to any reader of the opinions of the Court, is particularly congenial to, and characteristic of, Mr. Justice Frankfurter. Another safeguard is craftsmanship — the careful articulation of the grounds of decision and a reexamination from time to time of the assumptions on which rules and doctrines rest. If the unexamined life is not worth living, the unexamined premise is not worth its implications.

This is the meaning of the third and final form of respect of which I have spoken, namely self-respect, and I shall let Mr. Justice Frankfurter describe it in his own words from the *Larson* case on sovereign immunity.

Case-by-case adjudication gives to the judicial process the impact of actuality and thereby saves it from the hazards of generalization insufficiently nourished by experience. There is, however, an attendant weakness to a system that purports to pass merely on what are deemed to be the particular circumstances of a case. Consciously or unconsciously the pronouncements in an opinion too often exceed the justification of the circumstances on which they are based, or contrariwise, judicial preoccupation with the claims of the immediate leads to a succession of *ad hoc* determinations making for eventual confusion and conflict. There comes a time when the general considerations underlying each specific situation must be exposed in order to bring the too unruly instances into more fruitful harmony. The case before us presents one of those problems for the rational solution of which it becomes necessary, as a matter of judicial self-respect, to take soundings in order to know where we are and whither we are going.[25]

One is reminded of the moving and profound story told of Gertrude Stein on her death bed. She was heard to murmur, "What is the answer?" and after an awkward and prolonged silence, "In that case, what is the question?"

Some of Mr. Justice Frankfurter's greatest opinions have inquired into and reformulated "the questions" — his opinions, for example, on standing to challenge administrative action, on review of negative orders in administrative law, on sovereign

[25] Larson v. Domestic and Foreign Commerce Corp., 337 U.S. 682, 705-6 (1949) (dissent).

immunity, on inter-governmental relations. The value of these opinions makes one all the more regretful that the volume of the Court's business requires that these explorations be undertaken only now and then, and against undue pressure of time. The full potentialities of the Court for the clarification and advancement of fundamental law may well entail a more selective granting of review and more systematic procedures within the Court for consultation, interchange, and collaborative endeavor leading toward persuasive and scholarly exposition. Mr. Justice Frankfurter, at all events, places his ultimate faith in articulated reason, though he has no illusions about the fragile instrument that reason is. As he has more than once put it, "How slender a reed is reason, how recent its emergence in man." He must have relished the citation read by President Lowell of Harvard in awarding an honorary degree to William Morton Wheeler, the eminent entomologist: "Profound student of the social life of insects, who has shown that they also can maintain complex communities without the use of reason."

For an infusion of a modicum of reason into its relationships the human hive, in its less recalcitrant moments, looks to its teachers and its judges. Mr. Justice Frankfurter has shown, for many more than his twenty years of judicial service, how this highest of human enterprises can be carried on at once without illusion and with buoyancy, courage, and faith.

10 Individual and Commonwealth in the Thought of Mr. Justice Jackson

Few would disagree with the remark of a German jurist that "to recognize the true boundaries between the individual and the community is the highest problem that thoughtful consideration of human society has to solve."[1] The problem is one that faces both the philosopher and the judge, at all events a judge who is a member of the Supreme Court of the United States. The two vocations may seem at first blush to be incommensurable. To the lawyer the philosopher may appear to be entirely at large in his constructions, while the philosopher may regard the judge as utterly confined by philosophic postulates laid down by the framers of the Constitution, and hence incapable of interesting or important systematic thought about the individual and the commonwealth.

Both views, it must be said, rest on misconceptions. The philosopher is constrained not only by the universe of discourse inherited from his predecessors but by the concerns, the assumptions, the needs, and the intellectual mood of his own society. "What we have to look out for," an English historian of ideas has observed, "in reading the philosophers of Western Europe, is the emotional or social determinant which makes their work what it is, and this is usually implicit rather than explicit... [What] will seem 'true' or 'explanatory' to any age or

Reprinted from 8 STAN. L. REV. 9 (1955).
[1] JELLINEK, THE DECLARATION OF THE RIGHTS OF MAN AND OF CITIZENS 98 (1901).

individual is what satisfies current demands and interests."[2] If this is true of metaphysics, how much more apt is it of social philosophy. And if the philosopher is implicitly constrained by the demands and interests of his time, the constitutional judge is in considerable measure emancipated by them. Perhaps it is enough, in order to make the point, to mention the school segregation cases.

The judge's emancipation, so far as it is proper, reflects the fact that the crucial terms of the Constitution are-open-ended, as, for example, due process and equal protection of the laws, or ambiguous, like the first amendment guarantees against laws respecting an establishment of religion or prohibiting the free exercise thereof. When a state provides for religious instruction on a voluntary basis in the public schools or contributes to the support of parochial schools, does it violate the establishment clause or does it, on the contrary, carry out the guarantee of free exercise of religion for those sectarians who believe that education and religion are inevitably interfused? Ambiguities become open-ended, or at any rate double-ended; they make possible the creation and functioning of constitutions. Jacques Maritain relates that at a meeting of a United Nations commission on human rights someone expressed astonishment that certain champions of violently opposed ideologies had agreed on a list of those rights. "Yes," they said, "we agree about the rights but on condition that no one asks us why."[3] Differences over the "why" portend controversy over the "what". Yet if there is at the same time agreement on the process of resolving such controversies, the ambiguities may prove to be not only life-giving but life-saving in the history of a constitution. This is a lesson which is now being learned in the effort to formulate universal covenants of human rights. "The promulgation of a world declaration of rights depends," Richard McKeon has said, "as bills of rights seem always to have de-

---

[2] WILLEY, THE SEVENTEENTH CENTURY BACKGROUND 99 (Anchor ed. 1953).
[3] Maritain, *Introduction,* in HUMAN RIGHTS I (UNESCO, 1948).

pended, on the existence of a broad region of interpretation within which court decisions and administrative and legislative action have worked progressively to a practical definition and within which divergent philosophies have worked to less ambiguous or conflicting theoretic bases."[4]

The position of judges as constitutional mediators implies that the most important thing about them is their philosophy. Political allegiance, wealth, previous clients are important only if and so far they serve to fix a man's outlook. It is of course dangerous that judges should be philosophers — almost as dangerous as if they were not. It is dangerous too if judges fail to include in their philosophy the special question of the role of judges in relation to other organs of government, which are charged in the first instance with constitutional interpretation. As philosophers, Supreme Court Justices are not so much kings as elder cousins once removed.

On and off the bench Mr. Justice Jackson has stated with uncommon directness his outlook and insights on the individual and the community and on the judge's responsibility toward that relationship. In his Godkin lectures published in 1955 he chose to stress the latter issue, particularly in the address entitled "The Supreme Court as a Political Institution."[5] In a mood of *désistement* reminiscent of Judge Learned Hand's position that judicial review of legislation is not needed by a healthy society and will not restore an ailing one, Mr. Justice Jackson reproached the "cult of libertarian judicial activists."[6] Recalling with a wry thrust the libertarian attack on the judicial activists of the 1930's, he argued the consistency of his own attitude and its identification with democratic principles.

[4] McKeon, *The Philosophic Bases and Material Circumstances of the Rights of Man,* in *id.* at 33-34.

[5] JACKSON, THE SUPREME COURT IN THE AMERICAN SYSTEM OF GOVERNMENT 53-83 (1955).

[6] *Id.* at 57. See also HAND, *The Contribution of an Independent Judiciary to Civilization,* in THE SPIRIT OF LIBERTY 172, 181 (Dilliard ed. 1952).

I may be biased against this [activist] attitude because it is so contrary to the doctrines of the critics of the Court, of whom I was one, at the time of the Roosevelt proposal to reorganize the judiciary. But it seems to me a doctrine wholly incompatible with faith in democracy, and in so far as it encourages a belief that the judges may be left to correct the result of public indifference to issues of liberty in choosing Presidents, Senators, and Representatives, it is a vicious teaching.[7]

In the same spirit he had written in the *Dennis* case[8] of the legislation under which the Communist leaders were convicted: "While I think there was power in Congress to enact this statute and that, as applied in this case, it cannot be held unconstitutional, I add that I have little faith in the long-range effectiveness of this conviction to stop the rise of the Communist movement."[9]

There is much that is persuasive in this nay-saying counsel. Judges are at best fallible in their understanding; they necessarily come to an interpretation of broad constitutional guarantees conditioned by fragmentary experience, accidents of association and inadequacies of prior study as well as of opportunities for further study. All of these may affect their appraisal of those basic affirmations of our society that are the essence of due process of law—affirmations which are chosen and cherished with the help of traditions filtered through a study of the past. Unsatisfactory judicial vetoes, moreover, are difficult to overcome. Judicial review may weaken the responsibility of lawmakers to enforce constitutional limitations in the legislative stage. And judicial review has a habit of coming late, after irremediable harm has been done. Finally, constitutional guarantees by and large are directed against official action alone; private acts of overbearing or discrimination must be left for the most part to the processes of ordinary legislation, not to the self-executing standards of the Constitution.

[7] JACKSON, *op. cit. supra* note 5, at 58.
[8] Dennis v. United States, 341 U.S. 494 (1951).
[9] *Id.* at 577-78 (concurring opinion). See also Harisiades v. Shaughnessy, 342 U.S. 580 (1952). "We, in our own private opinions, need not concur in Congress' policies to hold its enactments constitutional. Judicially we must tolerate what personally we may regard as a legislative mistake." *Id.* at 590.

But when all these concessions have been made the nay-saying counsel must yield substantial ground. The fact is that the judges do have a responsibility to apply constitutional guarantees, not excluding those stated in the open-ended or ambiguous terms of the first, fifth, and fourteenth amendments, and every Justice has on occasion joined in exercising those responsibilities. The moral and educational effect of a number of those decisions has been great, indeed comparable to the sobering effect of questions in the House of Commons or even to the English literary classics of the liberal spirit — the essays of the trinity of Johns: Milton, Locke, and Mill.

Comparison with the lamented and ill-fated judicial vetoes of a prior generation is not wholly apt. Those vetoes of economic measures such as price control and minimum wage laws proceeded on doctrinaire grounds excluding those subjects from legislative control, whereas the judicial negatives in current controversy relate to defects in legislative standards or severity — problems, for example, of controlling inflammatory street speakers or regulating sound trucks or door-to-door solicitation, where the subject is not declared immune from public control but rather subject to it in certain forms but not in others. The parallel is not so much to the butcher-knife treatment of economic measures under the due process clause in the 1920's as to the scalpel operations today on state laws affecting interstate commerce.[10]

Mr. Justice Jackson was far from taking his negativism as a rule of judicial quietism. It was only a caution, not a dogma, and a caution which did not keep him from breaking the sound barrier explosively and repeatedly. Liberty of conscience and the right to procedural decencies were the causes that most emphatically drew from Mr. Justice Jackson his full powers of indignation and rebuke on behalf of man against the State.

---

[10] In the preceding two paragraphs I have drawn on an earlier paper of mine, *The Supreme Court and Civil Liberties,* 4 VAND. L. REV. 533, 551-54 (1951). A somewhat similar theme has been richly developed in an address by Judge Wyzanski. See Wyzanski, *Process and Pattern: The Search for Standards in the Law,* 30 IND. L.J. 133 (1955).

In placing liberty of conscience at the head of human freedoms Mr. Justice Jackson showed himself a true son of Pennsylvania, whose constitution as early as 1701 recognized that
"no People can be truly happy, though under the greatest
Enjoyment of Civil Liberties, if abridged of the Freedom of
their Consciences, as to their Religious Profession and Worship." Any discussion of the Justice's dedication to liberty of
conscience must start with his opinion for the Court in the
Barnette flag-salute case.[11] The child of Jehovah's Witnesses
who believed that to salute the flag was to bow down before a
graven image faced expulsion from the public schools for his
nonconformity. An obvious analysis of the problem would have
been in terms of religious liberty and its limits, or more
precisely whether an idiosyncratic religious belief, characterized by most as a secular concern, may exempt the believer
from a certain organized observance. Had the belief taken the
form of a doctrine that to pay taxes is sinful, the answer would
not have been doubtful. Or had the ritual taken the form of
bending the knee and crossing oneself, there would again have
scarcely been a doubt. On the sliding scale of measurement
which is the constitutional judge's professional instrument,
how vital was the secular observance without exemption as
compared with the offensiveness of it to a religious dissenter?[12]
This analysis was avoided by Mr. Justice Jackson. He elected
to minimize the religious factor and to treat the problem under
the aspect of freedom of the mind, or integrity of belief whether
or not religious in nature. This enlarged view of the case rested
on an interpretation of the child's conduct as a refusal to

[11] West Virginia State Bd. of Educ. v. Barnette, 319 U.S. 624, 147 A.L.R. 674
(1943).

[12] At this point I put to one side the question of the weight to be accorded the
legislative judgment in the calculus; nor am I dealing with areas where a mere
rational basis may be enough to sustain legislation. An illustration of what is
meant by the sliding scale is Lovell v. City of Griffin, 303 U.S. 444 (1938),
invalidating an ordinance prohibiting distribution of handbills without a
license. The ordinance was a rational means of preventing littering of the
streets; but the means was excessively oppressive of freedom of communication
in relation to the end served.

proclaim by gesture what he did not believe—that the flag is entitled to a show of allegiance. In this view the penalty of expulsion for a repugnant belief approached the English schoolmaster's admonition: "Boys, if you're not pure in heart I'll flog you." Mr. Justice Jackson's opinion rested, then, on the principle of integrity of belief and communication, and its moral tone had something of the high ethical spirit of one who believes that to tell a lie is to sin against language. "To sustain the compulsory flag salute we are required to say that a Bill of Rights which guards the individual's right to speak his own mind, left it open to public authorities to compel him to utter what is not in his mind." [13]

Belief rarely comes into collision with the law except as the motive power of conduct which touches and concerns the community. What are the limits to the sacrosanct character of belief in contest with organized society? Mr. Justice Jackson essayed an answer in another Jehovah's Witness case, this one involving violation of child-labor laws by families selling literature of the sect on the streets at night.[14] Joining in an affirmance of conviction, the Justice stated his position compendiously. "I think the limits begin to operate whenever activities begin to affect or collide with liberties of others or of the public. Religious activities which concern only members of the faith are and ought to be free—as nearly absolutely free as

[13] West Virginia State Bd. of Educ. v. Barnette, 319 U.S. 624, 634, 147 A.L.R. 674, 679 (1943). For purposes of comparison on the problem of distinguishing secular from religious symbolism, see BURY, HISTORY OF FREEDOM OF THOUGHT 43-44 (1913). "The objection of the Christians—they and the Jews were the only objectors—to the worship of the Emperors was, in the eyes of the Romans, one of the most sinister signs that their religion was dangerous. The purpose of this worship was to symbolize the unity and solidarity of an Empire which embraced so many peoples of different beliefs and different gods; its intention was political, to promote union and loyalty; and it is not surprising that those who denounced it should be suspected of a disloyal spirit. But it must be noted that there was no necessity for any citizen to take part in this worship. No conformity was required from any inhabitants of the Empire who were not serving the State as soldiers or civil functionaries."

[14] Prince v. Massachusetts, 321 U.S. 158, 176 (1944) (concurring opinion).

anything can be." [15] Of course it is not difficult to show that the problem has thereby really been transferred to the ambiguities of "concern," and that even abstention by dissenters may lose the claim to immunity — as in the case of the English lord who, on receiving notice of income taxes at increased rates, is said to have replied tactfully, "I do not think I shall join the Inland Revenue this year." The Justice's formulation does not dispense with the necessity of judgment, of measurement if you will on the sliding scale. But for present purposes its significance is clear as a philosophic premise which served to give a steady direction to the Justice's thinking.

To what extraordinary lengths he carried his devotion to the sanctity of belief may be seen in two cases, one involving a purely secular creed, the other involving a claim to spiritual revelation. The first case, *American Communications Ass'n, CIO v. Douds,*[16] required the Court to pass on the loyalty oath provisions of the Taft-Hartley Act. Mr. Justice Jackson concurred wholeheartedly in sustaining the compulsory pledge of nonmembership in the Communist Party, but he rejected with emphasis the obligatory oath of nonbelief in violent overthrow of the Government. "I think that under our system, it is time enough for the law to lay hold of the citizen when he acts illegally, or in some rare circumstances when his thoughts are given illegal utterance. I think we must let his mind alone." [17] And in a passage reminiscent of the spirit of Holmes and Brandeis, but encased in his own burnished wit, he described the civic value of dissent:

Progress generally begins in skepticism about accepted truths ... The danger that citizens will think wrongly is serious, but less dangerous than atrophy from not thinking at all ... Thought control is a copyright of totalitarianism, and we have no claim to it. It is not the function of our Government to keep the citizen from falling

[15] *Id.* at 177.
[16] 339 U.S. 382 (1950).
[17] *Id.* at 444 (concurring and dissenting opinion).

into error; it is the function of the citizen to keep the Government from falling into error.[18]

The second case, *United States v. Ballard*,[19] is complementary in that it called for appreciation not of the civic but of the spiritual virtue of nonconformist belief, and in a most improbable setting. The leaders of a commercially prosperous California sect were convicted of using the mails to defraud. Despite the fact that bad faith was found by the jury, as it had to be for conviction, and that the record contained such items as the defendants' selection of the name Ray-O-Light for their celestial messenger after reading an advertisement for Ray-O-Vac flashlights, Mr. Justice Jackson would have uprooted the whole prosecution, believing as he did that an inquiry into the good faith of the accused could not in practice be kept distinct from an inquiry into the truth or falsity of their doctrine.[20] Here, to be sure, there was no doubt about the public, outreaching character of the defendants' conduct, to follow the line of distinction laid down in the Justice's Jehovah's Witness opinions. But here there was the special, and to him fatal, element of scrutiny of doctrine itself. "I would dismiss the indictment," he wrote, "and have done with this business of judicially examining other people's faiths." [21] The spiritual temple of the mind, dubious though it might be in this case, remained a sanctuary into which no search warrant could give a right of entry.

When we turn to outright proselytizing, unembarrassed by any inquiry into the validity of beliefs, much greater latitude is allowed the State by way of regulation, in the thought of Mr. Justice Jackson; but even here there are limits on the State, lest the right of expression of belief become illusory. In *Thomas*

[18] *Id.* at 442-43.
[19] 322 U.S. 78 (1944).
[20] *Id.* at 92 (dissenting opinion).
[21] *Id.* at 95.

v. Collins[22] the Justice concurred in invalidating a requirement that labor organizers register and carry identification cards, when applied as a condition to making a public speech espousing unionism.

It is not often in this country that we now meet with direct and candid efforts to stop speaking or publication as such. Modern inroads on these rights come from associating the speaking with some other factor which the state may regulate so as to bring the whole within official control. Here, speech admittedly otherwise beyond the reach of the states is attempted to be brought within its licensing system by associating it with "solicitation." Speech of employers otherwise beyond reach of the Federal Government is brought within the Labor Board's power to suppress by associating it with "coercion" or "domination." Speech of political malcontents is sought to be reached by associating it with some variety of "sedition." Whether in a particular case the association or characterization is a proven and valid one often is difficult to resolve. If this Court may not or does not in proper cases inquire whether speech or publication is properly condemned by association, its claim to guardianship of free speech and press is but a hollow one.[23]

When dealing with inflammatory speech, street meetings, and door-to-door visitations, the Justice was readier than some of his colleagues to sustain the countervailing claim of the public order. A series of these issues reached the Court after his return from Nuremberg, and his acquaintance with European experience colored his opinions, if it was not actually decisive in his judgments. Even a system of licensing, with indifferent standards, seemed to him justifiable in the regulation of street speakers having a background of incitation[24] or in the control of sound trucks seeking the use of parks or highways.[25] With a kind of deliberate perversity, the Justice argued that to require permission in advance is more consonant with the protection of liberty of speech than to put the speakers to

[22] 323 U.S. 516 (1945)

[23] *Id.* at 547 (concurring opinion).

[24] See Kunz v. New York, 340 U.S. 290, 295 (1951) (dissenting opinion).

[25] See Kovacs v. Cooper, 336 U.S. 77, 97, 10 A.L.R.2d 608, 622 (1949) (concurring opinion), discussing Saia v. New York, 334 U.S. 558 (1948).

the hazard of surveillance and arrest for inciting to violence or for producing loud and raucous noises. As for the lack of standards governing the issuance of licenses, the Justice answered, in a not uncharacteristic vein, by needling his brethren of the majority.

Of course, standards for administrative action are always desirable, and the more exact the better. But I do not see how this Court can condemn municipal ordinances for not setting forth comprehensive First Amendment standards. This Court never has announced what those standards must be, it does not now say what they are, and it is not clear that any majority could agree on them.[26]

One is tempted to find a similar streak of perversity in Mr. Justice Jackson's dissent in the doorbell-ringing case, where he would have upheld an ordinance forbidding such approaches by solicitors, when applied to itinerant Jehovah's Witnesses.[27] Describing the problem in his Godkin lectures, the Justice concluded: "If the Court holds that the right of free speech includes the right to enter upon private property and summon the owner to the door, it necessarily holds that a majority of a community are without the right to protect their hours of rest against such religiously inspired aggression.[28] Actually the issue was hardly of such heroic dimensions. It was simply whether, in accommodating the interests of public order on the one hand and of willing speakers and hearers in the peaceable communication of ideas on the other, the majority may forbid access to all homes (unless, perhaps, the individual householder extends an invitation) or must allow access unless the individual householder posts a prohibitory warning. In the

[26] Kunz v. New York, 340 U.S. 290, 308 (1951) (dissenting opinion). Other examples of the attack *ad hominem* are to be found in Zorach v. Clauson, 343 U.S. 306, 323 (1952) (dissenting opinion), and Magnolia Petroleum Co. v. Hunt, 320 U.S. 430, 446, 150 A.L.R. 413, 423 (1943) (concurring opinion). In delivering the former opinion the Justice began by saying, "I had better read what my office staff has deleted down to the residue."

[27] Douglas v. City of Jeannette, 319 U.S. 157, 166 (1943) (concurring and dissenting opinion).

[28] JACKSON, THE SUPREME COURT IN THE AMERICAN SYSTEM OF GOVERNMENT 77 (1955).

latter event the majority protects itself by putting the force of the state behind the law of private trepass.

But it is less important to debate the merits of particular decisions than to indicate—what is in any event much clearer—the direction of Mr. Justice Jackson's thinking. Intrusive, aggressive, disorder-inciting conduct secured no immunity, in his view, by reason of the fact that it was verbal in character. In the *Terminiello* case[29] he voiced his concern over the extent of protection accorded to such conduct.

> This Court has gone far toward accepting the doctrine that civil liberty means the removal of all restraints from these crowds and that all local attempts to maintain order are impairments of the liberty of the citizen. The choice is not between order and liberty. It is between liberty with order and anarchy without either. There is danger that, if the Court does not temper its doctrinaire logic with a little practical wisdom, it will convert the constitutional Bill of Rights into a suicide pact.[30]

The relation of the first amendment to conspiracies was a major theme in Mr. Justice Jackson's concurring opinion in the *Dennis* case.[31] Acknowledging, as he had earlier insisted, that on the procedural side prosecutions for conspiracy could be a "dragnet device," [32] he laid hold of the concept of conspiracy as an escape from the problems of the first amendment, in particular the test of clear and present danger. The Nuremberg experience had borne in on him the distinctive character of the idea of criminal conspiracy in Anglo-American law and he pressed it into service. But the opinion finally falls away from reliance on that concept, as the Justice is forced to narrow it in the context of advocacy of ideas to conspiracies to advocate a crime, and then to differentiate more trivial conspiracies of that sort, so that ultimately the opinion rests on the special enormities of the Communist Party. "Unless," he concluded,

29 Terminiello v. Chicago, 337 U.S. 1 (1949).

30 *Id.* at 37 (dissenting opinion).

31 Dennis v. United States, 341 U.S. 494, 572 (1951).

32 *Id.* at 572, referring to his concurring opinion in Krulewitch v. United States, 336 U.S. 440, 445 (1949).

"we are to hold our Government captive in a judge-made verbal trap, we must approach the problem of a well-organized, nation-wide conspiracy, such as I have described, as realistically as our predecessors faced the trivialities that were being prosecuted until they were checked with a rule of reason." [33] Escape from the trap would have been possible, of course, through a prosecution for conspiracy to overthrow the Government, or for conspiracy to commit sabotage or espionage or to train members in those practices. Whether the first amendment permits Congress to speculate on the dangers in the indefinite future stemming from minds prepared by present organized propaganda would appear to be an unavoidable question. The Justice deftly turned it around, posing it as a task in prophecy pressed upon the Court, which the Court need not and should not assume: "No doctrine can be sound whose application requires us to make a prophecy of that sort in the guise of a legal decision. The judicial process simply is not adequate to a trial of such far-flung issues." [34] And so in the end he rested on his philosophy of *désistement*, never very far in the background when issues of great political import had been resolved by other departments of government. It was a philosophy revealed most strikingly in his refusal to pass judgment on the validity of the wartime Japanese evacuation orders.[35]

Perhaps the most balanced and matured statement of the Justice's first amendment views is found in the group libel case, *Beauharnais v. Illinois*.[36] Dissenting from a judgment

[33] Dennis v. United States, *supra* note 31, at 568-690.
[34] *Id.* at 570.
[35] Korematsu v. United States, 323 U.S. 214, 257 (1944) (dissenting opinion).
[36] 343 U.S. 250, 287 (1952) (dissenting opinion). In this opinion the Justice distinguished between the first and fourteenth amendments, regarding the latter as allowing greater latitude to the states than the former does to Congress. The distinction is a little surprising in view of his strict application of the establishment of religion clause to the states. See Everson v. Board of Educ., 330 U.S. 1, 18, 168 A.L.R. 1392, 1406 (1947) (dissenting opinion). The assimilation of that clause to the fourteenth amendment seems more difficult, textually and historically, than the assimilation of the first amendment's other guarantees, including that of the free exercise of religion. See Snee, *Religious Disestablishment and the Fourteenth Amendment,* 1954 WASH. U.L.Q. 371.

affirming a conviction, he was prepared to sustain a carefully drawn statute penalizing group libel; but he deemed the Illinois statute and the procedure in the trial court deficient in necessary safeguards for the accused, in particular the right to present evidence of truth as a defense and the burden which should rest on the prosecution to establish a clear and present danger of violence. The weighing of public order against public expression, the avoidance of the notion that if one does not give three cheers he gives none at all, the emphasis on privileges and procedural safeguards, the willingness to utilize the clear and present danger test as a practical check in circumstances different form *Dennis,* the drawing of lessons from legal history—these are the marks of a mind which accepts the responsibility of the judicial task while conscious of the risks of overreaching.

Group libel statutes represent a commendable desire to reduce sinister abuses of our freedoms of expression—abuses which I have had occasion to learn can tear apart a society, brutalize its dominant elements, and persecute, even to extermination, its minorities. While laws or prosecutions might not alleviate racial or sectarian hatreds and may even invest scoundrels with a specious martyrdom, I should be loath to foreclose the States from a considerable latitude of experimentation in this field. Such efforts, if properly applied, do not justify frenetic forebodings of crushed liberty. But these acts present most difficult policy and technical problems, as thoughtful writers who have canvassed the problem more comprehensively than is appropriate in a judicial opinion have well pointed out.

No group interest in any particular prosecution should forget that the shoe may be on the other foot in some prosecution tomorrow. In these, as in other matters, our guiding spirit should be that each freedom is balanced with a responsibility, and every power of the State must be checked with safeguards. Such is the spirit of our Americal law of criminal libel, which concedes the power to the State, but only as a power restricted by recognition of individual rights.[37]

---

[37] Beauharnais v. Illinois, 343 U.S. 250, 304-5 (1952) (dissenting opinion).

The stress on procedural rights will serve as a transition from the substantive issues of the nonconforming conscience and nonconforming expression to another great theme in the philosophy of Mr. Justice Jackson – the individual's right to a full and fair hearing before the force of the state is brought to bear on him. The Court's responsibility in this area of human freedom was for the Justice paramount, for the arbitrary administration of justice is both an indignity to the claims of humanity and a damaging reproach to the legal order itself. Some of the most biting animadversions to be found in the writing of one whose bite was uncommonly deep are contained in his opinions on the denial of a fair hearing. They are the more striking as they occur in cases dealing with exclusion or deportation of aliens, a subject on which, in its substantive aspect, the Justice went very far in deferring to the will of Congress. The strange and ignoble *Mezei* case,[38] where an alien was left to languish on Ellis Island, not permitted to enter and not eligible for repatriation, aroused to the full his gift of ironic verbal swordplay; the buttons were off the foils when he wrote:

This man, who seems to have led a life of unrelieved insignificance, must have been astonished to find himself suddenly putting the Government of the United States in such fear that it was afraid to tell him why it was afraid of him ...

... Government counsel ingeniously argued that Ellis Island is his "refuge" when he is free to take leave in any direction except west. This might mean freedom, if only he were an amphibian![39]

There follows a remarkably candid treatment of due process in its procedural and substantive aspects.

Procedural fairness, if not all that originally was meant by due process of law, is at least what it most uncompromisingly requires. Procedural due process is more elemental and less flexible than substantive due process. It yields less to the times, varies less with

---

[38] Shaughnessy v. United States *ex rel.* Mezei, 345 U.S. 206 (1953).
[39] *Id.* at 219-20 (dissenting opinion).

conditions, and defers much less to legislative judgment. Insofar as it is technical law, it must be a specialized responsibility within the competence of the judiciary on which they do not bend before political branches of the Government, as they should on matters of policy which comprise substantive law.

. . . Let it not be overlooked that due process of law is not for the sole benefit of an accused. It is the best insurance for the Government itself against those blunders which leave lasting stains on a system of justice but which are bound to occur on *ex parte* consideration. *Cf. Knauff v. Shaughnessy,* 338 U.S. 537, which was a near miss, saved by further administrative and congressional hearings from perpetrating an injustice.[40]

The celebrated war-bride case, referred to in the foregoing passage, had drawn from the Justice a resounding dissent which should recall to sanity those who have suffered aberrations in the cause of security.

Now this American citizen is told he cannot bring his wife to the United States, but he will not be told why. He must abandon his bride to live in his own country or forsake his country to live with his bride.

So he went to court and sought a writ of *habeas corpus,* which we never tire of citing to Europe as the unanswerable evidence that our free country permits no arbitrary official detention. And the Government tells the Court that not even a court can find out why the girl is excluded. But it says we must find that Congress authorized this treatment of war brides and, even if we cannot get any reason for it, we must say it is legal; security requires it.

Security is like liberty in that many are the crimes committed in its name. The menace to the security of this country, be it great as it may, from this girl's admission is as nothing compared to the menace to free institutions inherent in procedures of this pattern. In the name of security the police state justifies its arbitrary oppressions on evidence that is secret, because security might be prejudiced if it were brought to light in hearings. The plea that evidence of guilt must be secret is abhorrent to free men, because it provides a cloak for the malevolent,

[40] *Id.* at 224-25.

the misinformed, the meddlesome, and the corrupt to play the role of informer undetected and uncorrected.[41]

It would be an overstatement to say that the Justice was concerned with procedure in all its aspects. In criminal cases he tended to focus on the reliability of the evidence and not on the procedures by which it was obtained. This was true at least in cases coming from the state courts.[42] The irregularities or illegalities which may have attended the securing of the evidence seemed to him to be collateral issues unless these abuses vitiated the trustworthiness of the evidence itself. This attitude rested partly on a concern for the immediacies of criminal trials, partly on skepticism that exclusionary rules of evidence would promote reform in police administration. In the *Irvine* case,[43] involving particularly odious acts of state law enforcement officers in uncovering evidence, the Justice, while joining in the decision upholding the use of the evidence, took the unusual course of suggesting that a copy of the record be sent to the Attorney General of the United States for possible action under the civil rights laws – a course the more surprising in view of his strong apprehensions about the possible oppression resulting from a national police force exercising surveillance over local law enforcement.[44] He drew a bright line

[41] United States *ex rel.* Knauff v. Shaughnessy, 338 U.S. 537, 550-51 (1950) (dissenting opinion). The Justice's concern for procedural fairness is hard to reconcile with his concurring opinion in Dennis v. United States, 339 U.S. 162, 173 (1950), holding that in a prosecution of a Communist Party officer for contempt of the House Un-American Activities Committee, jurors were not challengeable for bias on the ground that they were Government employees. Having earlier urged unsuccessfully that such employees should be disqualified generally in federal prosecutions, the Justice felt that the Court should either accept his position or refrain from making what he regarded as an arbitrary "exception."

[42] *Compare* Irvine v. California, 347 U.S. 128 (1954); Stein v. New York, 346 U.S. 156 (1953), *with* Brinegar v. United States, 338 U.S. 160, 180 (1949) (dissenting opinion); McDonald v. United States, 335 U.S. 451, 457 (1948) (concurring opinion).

[43] Irvine v. California, *supra* note 42.

[44] JACKSON, THE SUPREME COURT IN THE AMERICAN SYSTEM OF GOVERNMENT 70 (1955).

between use of the fourteenth amendment as a shield in criminal cases against extrinsic abuses and its use as a sword to attack those abuses directly. The brightness of the line is reminiscent of the distinction taken between the internal creed of a religious sect and its external impingements, in the case of Jehovah's Witnesses, or between an oath of nonbelief and an oath of nonmembership, in the case of Communists.

As a complement to the basic themes of liberty of conscience and fair hearing, one final note in the Justice's thinking ought to be marked—the priority deserved by the guarantee of equal protection of the laws. His position was stated with his customary candor.

My philosophy as to the relative readiness with which we should resort to these two clauses [due process and equal protection] is almost diametrically opposed to the philosophy which prevails on this Court...

The burden should rest heavily upon one who would persuade us to use the due process clause to strike down a substantive law or ordinance... Invalidation of a statute or an ordinance on due process grounds leaves ungoverned and ungovernable conduct which many people find objectionable.

Invocation of the equal protection clause, on the other hand, does not disable any governmental body from dealing with the subject at hand... The framers of the Constitution knew, and we should not forget today, that there is no more effective practical guaranty against arbitrary and unreasonable government than to require that the principles of law which officials would impose upon a minority must be imposed generally. Conversely, nothing opens the door to arbitrary action so effectively as to allow those officials to pick and choose only a few to whom they will apply legislation and thus to escape the political retribution that might be visited upon them if larger numbers were affected.[45]

The pattern of Mr. Justice Jackson's view of individual and commonwealth has now emerged, largely in his own words.

[45] Railway Express Agency, Inc. v. New York, 336 U.S. 106, 111-13 (1949) (concurring opinion).

What must be cherished and secured above all — what the Constitution means to be secured — is human personality. Its cultivation is both a civic necessity and a spiritual duty.[46] The right to be oneself, to differ in thought and word, to express one's nonconformity in peaceable persuasion, to be treated by one's fellows wielding public power as a rational subject and not a mere object, to be treated evenhandedly — these claims as ancient as religious sensibilities, formulated with modest British insularity as the immemorial rights of Englishmen, and retransformed in eighteenth-century America into rights of man, remain the central concern of a civilization torn between the angel and the dynamo.

In this recognition, Mr. Justice Jackson's understanding coalesced with his temperament. Convivial he was, and joyful in companionship, but he did not wear his heart upon his sleeve or expose the deepest recesses of the spirit to the outside gaze. Fresh and unconventional ideas were welcome to him as they can only be to a lover of irony and paradox. But his mind recoiled from organized pressures, as it did from the seduction of opportunism.[47]

If this portrait leaves some features blurred, it is not disturbing. What is disturbing is the risk of the opposite distortion, an excessive tidiness in the portrayal of a complex and altogether unmechanical individual. The intellecutal portrait of a judge resembles a treatise on a legal subject. Anyone who has lived

---

[46] The interrelation of these ends has been described by Reinhold Niebuhr in THE CHILDREN OF LIGHT AND THE CHILDREN OF DARKNESS (1946). "A society which exempts ultimate principles from criticisms will find difficulty in dealing with the historical forces which have appropriated these truths as their special possession. Another and contrasting justification for a free society must be added. Sometimes new truth rides into history upon the back of an error. An authoritarian society would have prevented the new truth with the error..." *Id.* at 75-76. "Though the individual is organically related to the community there is a point in human freedom where the individual transcends both his own community and the total historical process..." *Id.* at 79.

[47] Consider, for example, his scornful reference to a brief amicus curiae filed by a newspaper association, whose only contribution, he asserted, was the fact that its membership embraced over 700 publishers interested in the outcome. Craig v. Harney, 331 U.S. 367, 397 (1947) (dissenting opinion).

through a complicated and lively case is appalled to find it embedded in a treatise as a citation for an abstract proposition of law. It is all a good deal like trimming a great oak to make it neat as a hedge, or devising categories for Latin ablatives when the language is no longer living. The risk is especially great in the case of Mr. Justice Jackson, for one of the most tragic aspects of his death is that he had never ceased to rethink and refine his premises. His philosophy was, in the figure applied to the common law, working itself pure. In that process, incomplete though it was, he struck off what Emerson called "blazing ubiquities," which will kindle many a heart in the ceaseless struggle for the life of the spirit.

11 Chief Justice Stone and the Conflict of Laws

A few years ago Chief Justice Stone remarked that if he were devising a law-school curriculum he would regard Conflict of Laws as a study serving in place of a course in Jurisprudence. His point was not, of course, that legal studies should be divorced from philosophy, but that the philosophic content of Conflict of Laws should be made more patent.[1] This essay is in the nature of an annotation to the observation of Chief Justice Stone, with special reference to his own conflict-of-laws opinions, and will not undertake a catalogue of those opinions.

The conflict of laws adds a new dimension to the realm of legal thinking. As in relativity the standpoint of the observer is of central importance, so in the conflict of laws the position of the forum apart from some of the elements of an event gives perforce a larger perspective. It is not possible, as it is in some problems of purely internal law, to ignore the availibility of more than one legal premise from which to work toward a solution. By hypothesis there are at least two possibly applicable rules or systems of law in a multistate problem. Choice is inescapable and must be explicit. In making that choice, two

Reprinted from 59 HARV. L. REV. 1210 (1946).
[1] We have the testimony of Mr. Justice Frankfurter, which others will confirm, that at least one course in Conflict of Laws fulfilled Chief Justice Stone's conception: "But every really good course in law is a course in Jurisprudence. For us this was peculiarly true of Professor Beale's course on the Conflict of Laws." Frankfurter, *Joseph Henry Beale* 56 HARV. L. REV. 701, 703, (1943).

problems of legal philosophy are relevant: the nature of law, and the ends of law. The first of these has received considerable — one may venture to say disproportionate — attention in discussions of conflict of laws. How to explain the use by the forum of the law of another state is indeed a fascinating juristic inquiry. Does the forum "enforce" the law of another sovereign; does it "incorporate" the foreign law into its domestic law, *pro hac vice;* does it enforce rights which have been "created" by foreign law, or by that truncated portion of foreign law that would control if the multistate elements were absent; does it fashion its own law in the image, partial or complete, of the foreign law? These formulations have been the subject of much controversial discussion, in which judges have been avouched as exponents of one or another of the theories: Holmes and Cardozo as standard-bearers for the vested-rights approach, Judge Learned Hand for the "local law" or "law of the forum."[2] While the conflicting versions of the nature of law in conflict-of-laws cases do suggest differences in the rigidity or latitude with which a forum should resolve conflict-of-laws issues, it may be doubted whether the controversy furrows deeply enough into the soil of our legal thinking to mark the direction a judge will travel in arriving at his ultimate judgment.[3] Chief Justice Stone has not been identified with one or another of these polemic schools. The suggestiveness of his work in

[2] *Cf.* Holmes, J., in Slater v. Mexican Nat. R.R., 194 U.S. 120 (1904); Cardozo, J., in Loucks v. Standard Oil Co. of New York, 224 N.Y. 99, 120 N.E. 198 (1918); L. Hand, J., in Guinness v. Miller, 291 Fed. 768 (S.D.N.Y. 1923); see Cheatham, *American Theories of Conflict of Laws: Their Role and Utility* 58 HARV. L. REV. 361 (1945); Dodd, *The Power of the Supreme Court to Review State Decisions in the Field of Conflict of Laws* 39 HARV. L. REV. 533, 535-37 (1926).

[3] In Siegmann v. Meyer, 100 F.2d. 367 (2d Cir. 1938), Judge Learned Hand, declaring fidelity to the theory of "local law" or "law of the forum," examined the foreign law from the standpoint of its territorial jurisdiction, for "no state can create personal obligations against those who are neither physically present within its boundaries, nor resident there, nor bound to it by allegiance" — citing the *Restatement of Conflict of Laws.* Exponents of the vested-rights theory would be quite satisfied with this, and might insist that Judge Hand's is a dual, or at least a divided, allegiance.

Conflict of Laws lies rather in the other major field of legal philosophy, which is perhaps less cultivated but more fertile – the ends or objectives of Conflict of Laws.

It is frequently asserted, or assumed, that the dominant objective, indeed the very *raison d'être,* of Conflict of laws is uniformity. It is true that this body of law is occasioned by the diversity of domestic laws, and the necessity of resolving their applicability in some tolerably certain way, so that the identity of the forum will be minimized. But to state this proposition is to announce at best a destination, not to provide directions for reaching it. Uniformity can be achieved most naturally by the adoption of uniform rules of conflict of laws. Failing this, given conflicting rules of conflict of laws, uniformity can be attained conceivably either by the mandate of Congress or the Constitution, compelling a particular choice, or by a system, such as the renvoi, for resolving the conflict of conflicts rules; of each of these, more hereafter. At the lowest level in the dialectic of the subject, the level of simple and unfettered choice of law, uniformity is a by-product. It will be attained according to the measure of universality with which conflicts rules commend themselves by their good sense to the judgment of courts and legislatures.

If this is so, what objectives other than uniformity can be suggested for the choice of law? The question brings to a close a prologue and introduces one of Chief Justice Stone's earliest and most suggestive opinions in this field.

Seeman v. Philadelphia Warehouse Co.,[4] decided in 1927, arose in a federal court for the Southern District of New York in that spacious era before the *Erie* case, when federal judges in diversity cases were more than echoes of half-heard whispers of the state tribunals. The warehouse company brought suit in the federal court to recover a quantity of canned salmon which had been pledged to it as security for a loan. The defendants

---

[4] 274 U.S. 403 (1927).

were innocent purchasers of the salmon from the pledgors, who had fraudulently regained possession. The defense to the warehouse company's claim rested on the contention that the original transaction of pledge was usurious and void under New York law, which the defendants insisted was applicable. The warehouse company was a Philadelphia enterprise whose business had been held by the Pennsylvania courts not to offend against the usury laws of that state. The business consisted of the lending of funds or of credit—the distinction was regarded by counsel as critical under New York law—by issuing to the borrower a note of the warehouse company, payable to its order, and discounted by a note broker who was recommended by the company to the borrower, and to whom in practice the company itself took the note for discount and receipt of the net proceeds. The borrower was obligated to pay the company a commission of three per cent, in addition to repaying the proceeds of the note plus the discount. The aggregate of the commission charged by the company and the discount charged by the broker exceeded the lawful rate of six per cent for loans of money under New York law. The contacts with Pennsylvania and New York were fairly evenly divided. The negotiations took place in New York, where the borrower's place of business was situated, and the proceeds of the note were sent to the borrower there; the discounting, however, occurred in Pennsylvania, and the borrower's obligation to repay called for performance there.

In the district court, Judge Mack charged the jury that the contract was made in New York, and he left open only the question whether the transaction was a sale of credit or a disguised loan of money.[5] The jury, evidently taking the latter view, returned a verdict for the defendants. The record preserves the colloquy of court and counsel on the issue of the applicable law; the argument was made to turn on whether the contract was bilateral or unilateral, and where, on each hy-

[5] Transcript of Record, pp. 264-74, Seeman v. Philadelphia Warehouse Co., 274 U.S. 403 (1927).

pothesis, the last act occurred which gave rise to a binding obligation. Judge Mack was of opinion that, at least if the jury should find that the transaction was in substance a loan of money, the contract was formed by an offer of the borrower, accepted by the act of the lender in turning over the proceeds of the note in New York; "there was an option," said the court, "on the part of the plaintiff [lender] to convert this into a binding obligation, by its unilateral act."[6] It must be remembered that the case was decided at a time when the rule of place-of-making had apparently been erected into a constitutional principle by the Supreme Court, if its decisions in the insurance field could be regarded as generally controlling.[7]

In the circuit court of appeals, the judgment was reversed.[8] The opinion, by Judge Manton, took the position that there was no evidence that the transaction was other than it purported to be, a sale of credit; that the contract was made in Pennsylvania, having been formed when the warehouse company issued its note and discounted it for the borrower's convenience; and that, in any event, performance, that is, repayment, was to be made in Pennsylvania, and "the law of the place of performance controls . . ."[9] So plenitudinous an opinion would seem to have left no room for originality on review by the Supreme Court. Nonetheless that Court, speaking through Mr. Justice Stone, put aside the embarrassment of riches that had been served up to it, and, without drawing on anything offered by counsel or lower courts, affirmed the judgment of the circuit court of appeals because the contract was valid if the amount payable as interest was allowable under the law of either Pennsylvania or New York. As the Pennsylvania law concededly supported the transaction, it was sustained.

The decision is noteworthy for renouncing a geographical test in favor of a teleological one in the choice of law. Not place

[6] *Id.* at 261.
[7] *Cf.* Aetna Life Ins. Co. v. Dunken, 266 U.S. 389 (1924); Mutual Life Ins. Co. v. Liebing, 259 U.S. 209 (1922).
[8] 7 F.2d 999 (2d Cir. 1925).
[9] *Id.* at 1002.

but purpose was decisive. *Ut res magis valeat quam pereat* was implicitly recognized as a pertinent basis of decision in multi-state no less than in domestic law. The decision was not without precedent on the issue of usury;[10] nor is it without analogies in the conflict of laws. Where the relations of the transaction to two or more states are in fairly even balance, the law sustaining the transaction has been applied in the case of trusts[11] and of the formalities of wills (with the aid of the direction contained in the Uniform Wills Act, Foreign Executed),[12] less avowedly in the case of bills and notes,[13] and perhaps in the case of the form of execution of a power of appointment.[14]

There are, of course, dangers in this approach to conflicts problems. The *Seeman* opinion itself was careful to point out that the relation of the transaction to the more favorable state must be created in good faith. A merely colorable relation, as by the otherwise purposeless routing of documents into such a state, would not suffice.[15] It has been suggested that this need of examining the transaction for evidence of good faith makes this approach less satisfactory than the more orthodox place-of-making rule.[16] It may be doubted, however, whether the

[10] Miller v. Tiffany, 1 Wall. 298 (U.S. 1864); see Junction R.R. v. Bank of Ashland, 12 Wall. 226, 229 (U.S. 1871).

[11] *Compare* Shannon v. Irving Trust Co., 275 N.Y. 95, 9 N.E.2d 792 (1937) (upholding an *inter vivos* trust under the law of the settlor's domicil, which he had designated as governing), *with* Hutchison v. Ross, 262 N.Y. 381, 187 N.E. 65 (1933) (upholding an *inter vivos* trust under the law of the place of creation and administration). On testamentary trusts in New York, see LAND, TRUSTS IN THE CONFLICT OF LAWS 73-75 (1940).

[12] Estate of Marshland, 142 Misc. 230, 254 N.Y. Supp. 293 (Surr. Ct. 1931), applying UNIFORM WILLS ACT, FOREIGN EXECUTED § 1; *cf.* MODEL EXECUTION OF WILLS ACT § 7.

[13] See Note, 55 HARV. L. REV. 1181 (1942).

[14] See Sewall v. Wilmer, 132 Mass. 131, 137 (1882): "As to the form of executing the power, it would seem that a will executed in the form authorized by the law of either State [domicil of the donor or donee of the power] would be sufficient."

[15] *Cf.* Horning v. District of Columbia, 254 U.S. 135 (1920).

[16] See 2 BEALE, CONFLICT OF LAWS 1244-45 (1935). And compare NUSSBAUM, PRINCIPLES OF PRIVATE INTERNATIONAL LAW 182 (1943): "The Conflict law of usury has been developed in a peculiar way by the American courts."

latter rule, as exemplified in the diverse yet plausible treatments it received at the hands of Judge Mack and Judge Manton, would have established a more certain or predictable or evasion-proof rule of law than that sponsored by the Supreme Court in the *Seeman* case. The more serious objection, and one which, as Chief Justice Stone would have been the first to acknowledge, prevents this approach from being a universal solvent, is that it places on the court at the forum the responsibility of weighing in its own scales the competing policies of the interested states. This is indeed a dangerous jurisdiction if no further standards of judgment are available than that an activity should be upheld wherever reasonably possible. This standard has diminishing relevance as one moves away from the realm of consensual or commercial transactions. Even in that realm, the danger is that the judge may be encouraged to indulge a general preference for a permissive rather than a prohibitory rule, or for common rather than statutory law. Having been attuned to the themes of nineteenth-century philosophy, he may prefer to march to the familiar strains of Herbert Spencer rather than to the cacophonies, shall we say, of the New York legislature.

There are, to be sure, several ameliorating factors. The choice of the more favorable law is confined to those situations where the relations to several states are fairly equally distributed. Moreover, the choice does not differ radically from the problem of judicial decision in many purely internal controversies; judges must choose starting points for legal reasoning, must consider when to construe statutes narrowly and when broadly, must weigh the interest in security of transactions against the interest in protection of a group subject to duress, must, in short, own, and preferably own up to, a philosophic content in their decisions. There is no reason why the judicial process should become measurably simpler when a controversy touches and concerns more states than one. There is, finally, a means of resolution which does not leave so much to the independent judgment of the tribunal, and which has proved fruitful in domestic cases. Statutes, by reason of their pattern or their prevalence, may evidence a legal climate of opinion which makes less oppressive the responsibility of the judge in choosing between two inferences from a statute or between two possible rules of law.[17] A similar resort may be made in multi-state cases. If one of the competing laws is archaic and isolated in the context of the laws of the federal union, it may not unreasonably have to yield to the more prevalent and progressive law, other factors of choice being roughly equal. A married woman's disability to make a contract, imbedded in the law of one state, may be carried away by the current if contact is made with the main stream in another state. Perhaps one of the functions of conflict-of-laws decisions is to serve as growing pains for the law of a state, at all events in a federation such as our own.

When all this has been said, however, it remains true that the method of choice illustrated by the *Seeman* case — a choice by the forum between the policies of the competing laws — is to be adopted with caution and in default of a method which would harmonize or more objectively weigh the policies and interests involved. Such a method, more comfortable for the forum, requires a closer analysis of the several laws. It can be illustrated by two variations of the *Seeman* case and by an opinion of Chief Justice Stone.

Suppose, in the *Seeman* case, that the laws of the two states had been reversed, so that the agreement would have been valid under the internal law of New York, the borrower's state, and invalid under the internal law of Pennsylvania, the lender's state. Here a closer view of the two laws from the standpoint of the interests and policies of the two states suggests that the conflict may be only superficial and can be dissipated.

[17] See Pound, *Common Law and Legislation* 21 HARV. L. REV. 383, 406-07 (1908); Landis, *Statutes and the Sources of Law* in HARVARD LEGAL ESSAYS 213 (1934); Frankfurter, J., in Keifer & Keifer v. RFC, 306 U.S. 381, 389 (1939). This general attitude toward statutes had the support of Chief Justice Stone. See his address, *The Common Law in the United States* 50 HARV. L. REV. 4, 13-14 (1936).

The invalidating law of Pennsylvania may fairly be regarded as designed to protect Pennsylvania borrowers; New York borrowers, on the other hand, are not given that kind of protection by their own internal law. In a transaction which weaves back and forth between the states, a weighing of the interest of each would point toward an accommodation by sustaining the transaction, placing on the New York borrower no burden that he would have escaped had he dealt at home, while giving the Pennsylvania lender the benefit of the agreement which he would have lacked had he too dealt at home, but which there seems no sufficient reason to deny him in the interest of protecting the other party, at least if the transaction was not so obnoxious to the policy of the lender's state as to be made a criminal offense. If one of the great ends of the law is the harmonizing of interests, a system of conflict of laws may make a greater contribution to that end by such an examination of the policies of the competing laws—what Pillet calls *leur but social*[18]—than by a rule of thumb which fixes more or less mechanically on one state as the "place of making."

A second means of harmonizing by looking more closely at the competing laws may be found by examining not merely the policy but the conflict-of-laws delimitation of each law. If, for example, the internal laws of New York and Pennsylvania were the same as in the *Seeman* case, but if New York had itself adopted a conflicts rule like that announced by the Supreme Court, the clash of laws might be found by the forum to be illusory. In fact, the New York Court of Appeals, a few months after the *Seeman* decision, and citing it with approval,

---

[18] PILLET, PRINCIPES DE DROIT INTERNATIONAL PRIVÉ 265-300 (1903); PILLET ET NIBOYET, MANUEL DE DROIT INTERNATIONAL PRIVÉ 363-68 (1924). Pillet's doctrine has been severely criticized. See 3 BEALE, CONFLICT OF LAWS 1942-48 (1935); WOLFF, PRIVATE INTERNATIONAL LAW 41 (1945); *cf.* 1 RABEL, CONFLICT OF LAWS 9-10, 14 (1945). The criticism is sound in that Pillet overgeneralized by classifying types of laws as either territorial or "permanent" (following the person), thus developing in substance a more sophisticated version of the statutist theory of the fourteenth century. But the idea of *le but social* as an aid in choice of law need not be coupled with a rigid system of classification and can, it is believed, be a fruitful concept in the conflict of laws.

did establish for usury cases a conflicts rule substantially like that of the Supreme Court.[19] Had that New York case been on the books at the time of the *Seeman* case, the task of the federal courts could have been lightened, provided they were willing to hazard the reproach of adopting a technique bearing some resemblance to the renvoi. An examination of the whole law of New York, including its choice-of-law rules on the specific issue of usury, would then have dissolved the apparent conflict.[20]

What is here suggested by way of reconciling the interests of the states does indeed have some similarity to the renvoi, in that the conflict-of-laws reference of another state is taken into account; but those criticisms which have been justly leveled at the renvoi are not pertinent here. The renvoi, as usually conceived, may be a circuitous device for arriving at an application of the law of the forum, or at best it may be an endeavor to reach a uniform result with a foreign state. The former version, of course, is marked by a parochialism that is the antithesis of the spirit of the conflict of laws. The latter version is too apt to pursue uniformity as a will-o'-the-wisp. It assumes that the foreign state has no similar enlightened conflicts rule, for if it did, an endless oscillation would result between the two, or at least a cycle of references to be broken at some arbitrary chosen number of references. Moreover, if the foreign state were the forum and hence the starting point for the cycle, and were to adopt precisely the same numerical reference as a stopping point, the outcome would be quite different. And even if uniformity with a hypothetical decision in a foreign forum could be achieved, its desirability might well depend on whether the foreign state would have been a more natural and anticipated forum than the actual one. The final objection to

[19] Westchester Mortgage Co. v. Grand Rapids & I.R.R., 246 N.Y. 194, 158 N.E. 70 (1927).

[20] On the dissolving of apparent conflicts, see the valuable article by Sohn, *New Bases for Solution of Conflict of Laws Problems* 55 HARV. L. REV. 978 (1942).

renvoi in its classic form is that, in the interest of a doubtful goal of uniformity, it requires the forum to recant its own conflicts rule in favor of that of the foreign state on the identical issue, and thus tends to retard the development in the forum of more appropriate principles governing choice of law to which the forum can adhere with inner conviction. The reference to the conflicts rule of New York suggested here, however, is a tentative reference in the interest of possibly dissolving a superficial conflict between the states; it leads to no endless series of references; and it does not require the forum to surrender its choice-of-law rule for that of another state on the same subject, but rather to explore for a special rule in the foreign state which is applicable to the precise subsidiary issue in the case. If that special rule were embodied in a statutory provision of the foreign state, the statute would doubtless be accepted as the proper delimitation of the foreign rule of law. The circumstance that the delimitation is to be found in conflict-of-laws decisions may perhaps make it more difficult to apprehend, but should not negative its relevance.[21]

[21] See Griswold, *Renvoi Revisited* 51 HARV. L. REV. 1165 (1938), discussing approvingly a number of instances of unacknowledged renvoi, some of which would be justified on the reasoning above. But the much-controverted case of *University of Chicago v. Dater* seems to be an example of objectionable use of renvoi in the interest of supposed uniformity. 277 Mich. 658, 270 N.W. 175 (1936); *cf.* Griswold, *supra* at 1207-08. A Michigan married woman executed a note there, a mortgage was placed on Illinois land, and the lender advanced the money in Illinois. By the internal law of Michigan, the borrower lacked capacity; by the internal law of Illinois, she was capable. The Michigan court looked to the "place of making," Illinois, found that its conflicts rule would regard Michigan as the place of making, and so Michigan law was applied and the borrower held not liable. The result may be sound, not because it promotes uniformity (what result if Illinois were to adopt Michigan's technique, and why look to uniformity with the less probable forum, Illinois?), but because it so happens that the domicil may be justified in giving a married woman immunity on her note, under its policy, where the other interested state would apparently do the same. The difference in the two uses of renvoi is made clear when a case transposing the domicil is supposed. Hypothetical uniformity would again lead the Michigan court to hold the borrower not liable; but there seems less reason for this result in the case supposed, where neither the primary conflicts rule of the forum (Michigan) nor the internal law of the domicil (Illinois) would confer such an immunity. See also pp. 198-199 *infra*.

This excursus on the harmonizing of interests[22] will serve to introduce Chief Justice Stone's opinions in the workmen's compensation cases, particularly his concurring opinion in *Bradford Electric Light Co. v. Clapper.*[23] The case came up from the federal district court for New Hampshire, to which it had been removed from the state court. An employee suffered injuries on his job in New Hampshire; he was a Vermont resident, his employer was a Vermont corporation, and the employment contract had been entered into in Vermont. He sued under the employers' liability provisions of the New Hampshire compensation law; the Vermont statute contained no option to bring a civil suit, and provided that its compensation provisions were to be exclusive unless formally disclaimed; neither party had filed a disclaimer. In the Supreme Court Mr. Justice Brandeis, writing the prevailing opinion, took the position that the federal court in New Hampshire was bound by the full faith and credit clause to give effect to the statute of Vermont as a defense to the action. He pointed out that, since the statute was set up defensively, failure to apply it would subject the company to an irremediable liability and not simply remit the plaintiff to another forum. Mr. Justice Stone, concurring specially and applying that principle of decision known to lawyers as judicial parsimony and to philosophers as Occam's razor, would have placed the result on the narrow ground that, so far as appeared, the New Hampshire courts would have given effect to the Vermont provision as a matter of conflict of laws without the compulsion of the Constitution. This stress on the New Hampshire conflicts rule would of course be required today of a federal court in New Hampshire in a diversity case;[24] but at the time of the *Clapper* case the federal court, like the federal court in the *Seeman* case, had a certain independence

---

[22] On the general theory of interests in jurisprudence, see the extensive bibliography in POUND, OUTLINES OF LECTURES ON JURISPRUDENCE 95-114 (5th ed. 1943).

[23] 286 U.S. 145, 163 (1932).

[24] Klaxon Co. v. Stentor Electric Mfg. Co., 313 U.S. 487 (1941).

of the state conflicts rules and could be regarded as essentially the court of a third state, so that Mr. Justice Stone's opinion is of significance in its insistence on dissipating a conflict, if possible, by resort to the foreign conflicts rules. If by the self-limitation of a foreign rule an accommodation is disclosed, there is good reason to accept it; there is no need to be more Roman than the Romans.

Where, however, such an accommodation is not disclosed, the problem of choice of law becomes more acute. Subsequent workmen's compensation cases posed this problem on the constitutional level—that is, they called for decision of the question what a state court might legitimately do, not what it should preferably do as a matter of choice of law within a permissible latitude under the Constitution. Nevertheless, the opinions for the Court by Mr. Justice Stone are suggestive of an approach in conflicts cases generally. *Alaska Packers Association v. Industrial Accident Commission of California*[25] brought to the Court a judgment of the Supreme Court of California upholding an award of the compensation commission of that state for an injury occurring in Alaska. The contract of employment had been made in California, where the employer did business; the employee was a nonresident alien. The judgment was affirmed as against the contention that it violated the due process and full faith and credit clauses in applying the California law rather than the Alaska law, which purported to have exclusive application to injuries occurring in the course of employment there. No reconciliation was possible, in view of California's refusal to apply the Alaska statute in this state of facts. The opinion of Mr. Justice Stone deals with the problem not in terms of a classification of workmen's compensation cases as tort or contract claims referable to some generalized rule for the law applicable to the one or the other, but in terms of the interests of the respective states. From the point of view of due process, the facts disclosed clearly enough the interest of California in providing a legislative remedy:

[25] 294 U.S. 532 (1935).

The meagre facts disclosed by the record suggest a practice of employing workers in California for seasonal occupation in Alaska, under such conditions as to make it improbable that the employees injured in the course of their employment in Alaska would be able to apply for compensation there. It was necessary for them to return to California in order to receive their full wages. They would be accompanied by their fellow workers, who would normally be the witnesses required to establish the fact of the injury and its nature. The probability is slight that injured workmen, once returned to California, would be able to retrace their steps to Alaska, and there successfully prosecute their claims for compensation. Without a remedy in California, they would be remediless, and there was the danger that they might become public charges, both matters of grave public concern to the state.[26]

The question remained whether California was not obligated, by the full faith and credit clause, to prescribe the Alaska remedy rather than its own. The question was particularly acute because the Alaska statute, providing for suit in a court of general jurisdiction, was, unlike most compensation statutes, enforceable in the courts of other states. Mr. Justice Stone elaborated what he had adumbrated in the *Clapper* case, the paradox that would result if the full faith and credit clause were enforced automatically to require each state to apply the "exclusive" act of the other and to forbid it to apply its own. Short of this, the clause would require the Supreme Court to choose, on the constitutional level, the single applicable law. While in result the *Alaska Packers* case, like the *Clapper* case, applied the law of the place of contracting, Mr. Justice Stone was careful to embrace the *Clapper* opinion with a proper degree of aloofness, for it would have foreclosed, in the converse case, the application by the state of injury of its own law. Instead, he emphasized again the interest of California, asserting that "the conflict is to be resolved, not by giving automatic effect to the full faith and credit clause, compelling the courts of each state to subordinate its own statutes to those of the

---

[26] *Id.* at 542.

other, but by appraising the governmental interests of each jurisdiction, and turning the scale of decision according to their weight."[27]

The compensation cases come full circle in *Pacific Employers Insurance Co. v. Industrial Accident Commission*,[28] which also arose in California and in which the California court again applied its own compensation law. Now, however, that law was applied to a claim for an injury in California suffered by an employee there temporarily on business for his employer, a corporation formed in Massachusetts and having its head office there, and which had there entered into the employment contract. Mr. Justice Stone's opinion put the *Clapper* case on the ground stressed in his separate opinion in that case — that the place of injury, New Hampshire, had not indicated that it would decline to recognize the statute of the place of employment as exclusive. California, less self-effacing, left no scope for such a resolution of the conflict; nevertheless, its action was sustained. Within limits, there is room for assertiveness as well as reticence in the family of our states. What those limits are must be determined by appraising the interests of the states. After observing that full faith and credit to the Massachusetts statute would mean remitting the injured employee to Massachusetts for the administrative remedy which it provides, Mr. Justice Stone summarized: "Although Massachusetts has an interest in safeguarding the compensation of Massachusetts employees while temporarily abroad in the course of their employment, and may adopt that policy for itself, that could hardly be thought to support an application of the full faith and credit clause which would override the constitutional authority of another state to legislate for the bodily safety and economic protection of employees injured within it. Few matters could be deemed more appropriately the concern of the state in which the injury occurs or more completely within its power."[29]

[27] *Id.* at 547.
[28] 306 U.S. 493 (1939).
[29] *Id.* at 503.

The constitutional latitude thus afforded the states by virtue of their respective interests is not, of course, necessarily the measure of what may be desirable as a choice of law by either state, any more than the point at which a state may constitutionally curb picketing is necessarily the soundest limit on picketing as a matter of labor law. But the criteria found useful by Mr. Justice Stone for constitutional pruposes do at least furnish a helpful point of departure for conflicts cases.

Their usefulness may be tested by supposing a familiar state of facts.[30] A husband and wife, residents of state *A*, are injured in state *B* through the husband's negligent driving of a car in which the wife is a passenger, in circumstances that would establish his liability to an ordinary guest. State *B*, however, has a rule of no liability on the part of one spouse to the other for negligently-caused injury. The wife brings suit against her husband in state *A*. The traditional conflicts rule, referring the issue of liability to the *lex loci delicti*, would lead to a judgment for the defendant. A conflicts rule having as its immediate objective the reaching to a uniform result irrespective of the forum might take the analysis further and seek to ascertain whether the courts of state *B* would apply their rule to non-resident spouses. If the courts of *B* would not, a judgment for the plaintiff would be permitted in state *A*. But if the courts of *B* would apply their domestic rule to nonresidents, presumably the courts of *A* would direct judgment for the defendant. This approach, as was suggested earlier, presupposes that the conflicts rule of *B* is static, that *B* would not itself be persuaded to look to the conflicts rule of *A*, and that for some reason uniformity with the result in *B*, a hypothetical and no more appropriate forum, is the decisive objective. The approach which emphasizes the interests involved would carry the analysis still further. If state *B* would not apply its domestic rule to this bi-state situation, state *A* will not do so, not because of uniformity but because the apparent conflict of interests has

---

[30] For a weighing of interests of the states as a guide to conflicts problems in the limitation of carriers' liability, see Note 54 HARV. L. REV. 663 (1941).

been dissolved. If state B would apply its domestic rule, the conflict is inescapable and is to be resolved by considering the competing policies more closely. If the purpose of the rule in B is to close its courts to actions at law between spouses because of the danger of collusion, state A may well conclude that the policy will not control in its own courts, where the triers of fact are regularly entrusted with the responsibility of deciding similar controversies; and state A may so conclude even though state B would have dismissed the suit on the "merits" and not simply without prejudice to trial in another jurisdiction. If the purpose of the rule in B appears to be the prevention of domestic discord, state A may well conclude that the policy of B must yield to that of the parties' domicil, which in that regard has the more relevant interest.

A more difficult case would be presented if the laws of A and B were reversed, so that there was liability under the domestic law of B, the place of injury, and not under the domestic law of A, the domicil. A court in A might find that the conflicts rule of state B referred the matter to the law of the domicil, in which case no liability would be created. If state B did not do so, the interest of B might not necessarily have to yield to that of the domicil, for the place of injury may have an interest in the financial accountability of the defendant in relation to expenses incurred in B, particularly in view of the widespread use of liability insurance, and the policy of state A might be recognized as attenuated and anachronistic and properly to be limited to domestic occurrences in the event of such a clash of interests. This is admittedly only an arguable, not a clearly indicated, solution. At all events, it should not be a mark of intellectual dishonesty to choose the law of one state when it imposes liability and not when it imposes no liability; its competitive position may be stronger in the one case than in the other, when the interests of the states are compared. And if the fact that a judge-made rule of law is deemed anachronistic is one element inducing a court to limit its application in a conflicts case, that too may be a function of Conflict of Laws as an organ of progress in the law. Advances are often more readily undertaken in two steps than in one, and the first step may conveniently be the competitive conflicts case. When the art of military advance was described by Marshal Foch in terms of the movement of a parrot in his cage, he was describing the art of legal advance as well: grasp and pause, grasp and pause.[31]

Of course, the interests of the states will not always be vivid or the implicit policies clear. It may become necessary to fall back on a rule looking to the law of the state having the greatest connection with the facts or on a rule of thumb for a generalized class of cases. Nevertheless, the approach to these problems by way of attempting to harmonize and to weigh the respective interests of the states in the light of the policies sought to be subserved has at least the merit of putting meaningful questions as to the objectives of Conflict of Laws. And here as elsewhere, we shall be more likely to get the right answers when we have learned to ask the right questions.

The workmen's compensation cases have left great latitude to the states in choice of law. The Court is reluctant to rule that a statute of one state precludes application of the statute of another. But when a judgment of a court is brought into the courts of another state, the atmosphere changes into one of enforced hospitality. Partly the difference lies in the opportunity theretofore given for reversing the judgment on direct review and the policy of putting an end to litigation; it would be intolerable if states were free to indulge the human propensity described by Pope: " 'Tis with our judgments as our watches, none Go just alike, yet each believes his own." Partly the

---

[31] *But cf.* Mertz v. Mertz, 271 N.Y. 466, 474, 3 N.E.2d 597, 600 (1936), applying the New York judicial rule prohibiting husband-wife suits for personal injuries to an accident in Connecticut: "Even then the courts should not transform an anachrony into an anomaly ... " The rule was abrogated by the legislature the following year. N.Y. Laws 1937, ch. 669, N.Y. DOMESTIC RELATIONS LAW § 57. Perhaps another maxim of both law and warfare is that things must grow worse before they grow better.

difference may be due to the relatively more settled doctrines of merger, bar and res judicata, as compared with the overlapping reach of statutes in a mobile society. Partly the difference is traceable, as Chief Justice Stone has maintained, to the different treatment accorded judgments and statutes in the acts of Congress carrying out the full faith and credit clause:

> The mandatory force of the full faith and credit clause as defined by this Court may be, in some degree not yet fully defined, expanded or contracted by Congress. Much of the confusion and procedural deficiencies which the constitutional provision alone has not avoided may be remedied by legislation . . . The play which has been afforded for the recognition of local public policy in cases where there is called in question only a statute of another state, as to the effect of which Congress has not legislated, compared with the more restricted scope for local policy where there is a judicial proceeding, as to which Congress has legislated, suggests the Congressional power.[32]

It was Mr. Justice Stone's opinion in *Milwaukee County v. M. E. White Co.*[33] that put a quietus on the notion that a judgment of one state need not be enforced if compulsory enforcement of the underlying claim could not have been demanded. Assuming for purposes of the case that a revenue claim of one state need not be entertained by another, the opinion nevertheless imposes a duty of enforcement when the claim is reduced to judgment. This contribution to sound judicial administration in a federal system and to the balancing of the public budgets came only a little over a year after the *Restatement of Conflict of Laws* had declared the contrary. Section 443, setting forth the non-enforcement of foreign judgments for money which reflect a claim in furtherance of the "governmental interests" of the foreign state, offered this illustration: "In state X, A, an administrator, is ordered to pay $1,000 by way of an inheritance tax on the estate. X sues A in

---

[32] See Yarborough v. Yarborough, 290 U.S. 202, 215 n.2 (1933) (dissenting opinion).

[33] 296 U.S. 268 (1935).

state Y on the judgment for the amount of the tax. The suit will be dismissed."[34]

There are, to be sure, important qualifications on the enforcement or recognition of judgments of sister states. A judgment may be denied effect because it undertakes to settle too extensively the unrepresented interests of other states or the unrepresented interests of other persons.

In Mr. Justice Stone's opinion, the recognition of a decree for support in *Yarborough v. Yarborough* [35] was improper on the first of these grounds. A Georgia decree in a divorce action, fixing the husband's liability for support of a minor daughter, which was unalterable under Georgia law, was held to bar a suit a year later in South Carolina, to which the daughter's residence had meanwhile been moved, seeking an increased allowance out of the father's property there on the basis of present need. The Court's opinion, by Mr. Justice Brandeis, relies on the full faith and credit clause, although it reserves the question whether South Carolina would have the power it claimed were the father himself domiciled there. As failure to recognize the statute of another state in the *Clapper* case would result in irremediable liability, not merely the remitting to another forum, so here failure to recognize the prior decree would impose an additional obligation on the defendant. Mr. Justice Stone, joined by Mr. Justice Cardozo, stressed rather the projection of the Georgia decree into the realm of South Carolina's newly-acquired concern for the support of an inhabitant. Full faith and credit, in their view, "does not command that the obligations attached to a status, because once appropriately imposed by one state, shall be forever placed beyond the control of every other state, without regard to the interest in it and the power of control which the other may later acquire.[36]

[34] The illustration suggests also the troublesome problem of binding an administrator in one state by a judgment against him in another, in view of historic conceptions of the separateness of the administrations. See RESTATEMENT, CONFLICT OF LAWS (1934) § 510; *cf.* Brown v. Fletcher's Estate, 210 U.S. 82 (1908). *But cf.* Carpenter v. Strange, 141 U.S. 87 (1891).

[35] 290 U.S. 202 (1933).

[36] *Id.* at 219 (dissenting opinion).

Several streams of thought which have thus far been traced coalesced in *Magnolia Petroleum Co. v. Hunt*.[37] Chief Justice Stone had carried the day for freedom of choice in workmen's compensation; he had protested against subordinating the interest of the domicil of a minor even to a judgement; but he had shown in the *Milwaukee County* case that only very exceptional reasons of local policy would suffice to justify non-recognition of a judgment. What would be his position when, after a workmen's compensation claim was reduced to an award in the state where the injury occurred, the employee sought to obtain an award under the compensation law of the state where the contract was entered into? Such was the thorny problem in the *Magnolia* case, which produced a five-to-four decision and four opinions. The *Restatement of Conflict of Laws* had dealt with the problem in a way which commended itself to the Louisiana courts, where the *Magnolia* case arose. Section 403 of the *Restatement* provides: "Award already had under the Workmen's Compensation Act of another state will not bar a proceeding under an applicable Act, but the amount paid on a prior award in another state will be credited on the second award." Having breached the redoubt of the *Restatement* in the *Milwaukee County* case, Chief Justice Stone was perhaps emboldened to do so again, though in a more doubtful cause. The employee, after accepting some payments from the Texas insurer and filing a claim with the Texas Industrial Accident Board, attempted to withdraw the claim, but the Board set the case for hearing and proceeded to render an award, which became final. Meanwhile the employee began suit in a Louisiana court under the compensation law of that state. On the facts, there were disputed issues as to the effect of the attempted withdrawal and the effect in Texas of an award as a bar to another proceeding. Assuming that the Board's retention of jurisdiction raised no constitutional question and that under Texas law an award is a bar, the major question remained as to the power of Louisiana to render judgment under its law for a

[37] 320 U.S. 430 (1943). For a balanced discussion, see Cheatham, *Res Judicata and the Full Faith and Credit Clause* 44 COLUM. L. REV. 330 (1944).

greater sum, crediting amounts received under the other award. Meeting a rather broad argument of the dissenters that the Constitution does not compel a state to adopt any particular rule about splitting a cause of action, Chief Justice Stone essayed a broad answer. To him the question was essentially the same as that presented when any tort claimant seeks to disregard a judgment and sue in another state, claiming under a more favorable law. In such a case, of course, "it has never been thought that an actionable personal injury gives rise to as many causes of action as there are states whose laws will permit a suit to recover for the injury or that despite the full faith and credit clause the injured person, more than one entitled to recover for breach of contract, could go from state to state to recover in each damages or compensation for his injury."[38] Consequently, a judgment in a transitory action cannot be avoided on the theory that suit elsewhere is on a different "cause of action." The forum's choice of law is simply one of the legal issues in the case. But the difference between a transitory cause of action and a workmen's compensation claim was perhaps deserving of greater attention in the opinion. The tribunals of one state are not competent to adjudge claims under another law which must be administratively presented. The incapacity of the tribunal would seem to differ substantially from its function in choosing the applicable law, so far as concerns the effect of its judgment elsewhere. If a state statute, by providing that the bringing of a proceeding for an award shall bar any other claim, could not have precluded a claim in another state, it is difficult to appreciate why an award itself should have greater effect, where the tribunals of the state making it could not have considered the other claim. To say this is not quite to answer the question in the *Magnolia* case, for there the Louisiana law was subject to judicial, not administrative enforcement, and conceivably might have founded a suit in Texas; but such a suit could not have been brought before the tribunal actually invoked in Texas, the

[38] 320 U.S. at 445.

Accident Board, and hence the precise issue was perhaps whether the tribunals of Texas, judicial as well as administrative, should be taken into account, or only the particular tribunal rendering the award, to determine whether the award was tantamount to the resolution of a choice of law or the bringing of the proceeding tantamount to an election of remedies.

As precedent, Chief Justice Stone relied heavily on a decision holding that a determination by an Iowa court that a railroad employee was engaged in intrastate commerce is conclusive in an action brought under the Federal Employers' Liability Act in another state.[39] But the two acts were mutually exclusive in their scope, unlike the Texas and Louisiana laws; and from a holding that a determination of the character of commerce by a court having jurisdiction to enforce both acts is res judicata it need not follow that an award is a bar to another action which the first tribunal could not have entertained. Whether Congress could legislate under the full faith and credit clause to restore the practice adopted by the Louisiana courts and others is, to say the least, doubtful. The constitutional power to "prescribe the manner in which such acts, records, and proceedings shall be proved, and the effect thereof"[40] may well be thought to support legislation enlarging the compulsory area of full faith and credit beyond the bounds set by the present statute, as Mr. Justice Stone broadly hinted on more than one occasion;[41] but legislation withdrawing from the compulsory area what the Court has held is encompassed by the constitutional mandate may stand on a different footing.[42]

[39] Chicago, R. I. & P. Ry. v. Schendel, 270 U.S. 611 (1926).

[40] U.S. CONST. ART. IV, § 1.

[41] See Yarborough v. Yarborough, 290 U.S. 202, 215 n.2 (1933); Alaska Packers Ass'n v. Industrial Accident Comm'n of California, 294 U.S. 532, 546-47 (1935).

[42] Cf. Powell, And Repent at Leisure 58 HARV. L. REV. 930, 1011-12 (1945). But cf. Corwin, The Full Faith and Credit Clause 81 U. OF PA. L. REV. 371, 388 (1933). There is perhaps an analogy in the field of intergovernmental tax relations. So far as state taxation of federal instrumentalities is concerned, Congress may waive an immunity or, in the borderland area, extend immunity

From the standpoint of the possibility of correction, a nicely balanced question of full faith and credit might therefore more appropriately be decided against compulsory effect than in favor of it.

When we turn to Chief Justice Stone's treatment of the interests of unrepresented parties in cases of judgments, another interesting lineage of ideas is encountered. A non-conflicts case, *Hansberry v. Lee*,[43] was germinal. Suit was brought in an Illinois court by certain landowners to restrain the defendants, who were Negroes, from occupying land subject to a restrictive agreement of which they had notice. The defendants asserted that the agreement had never become effective by its terms because owners of ninety-five per cent of the frontage had not signed it. The complainants replied that that issue was concluded by the decree in an earlier so-called class suit, which had been brought by representatives of owners seeking to enforce the agreement, against named defendants. The present defendants, the Supreme Court held, were not represented by the earlier plaintiffs or by the earlier defendants; as to the latter, "it does not appear that their interest in defeating the contract outweighed their interest in establishing its validity."[44] The decree of the Illinois court in the second proceeding, holding the present defendants bound, was a denial of due process of law.

---

under the necessary-and-proper clause; hence constitutional decisions here are corrigible. See Cleveland v. United States, 323 U.S. 329, 333 (1945); Smith v. Davis, 323 U.S. 111, 114, 115 (1944). In the case of federal taxation of state instrumentalities, Congress may of course grant immunity where it has been denied, but may not curtail an immunity declared by the Court; hence, where judgment is poised, it may be better statesmanship for a court to deny immunity. Under the full faith and credit clause, it would seem that the function confided to Congress is that of promoting and not curtailing the extra-territorial recognition of state judgments and public acts.

A corrective through reciprocal state legislation is, however, possible. Since the effect in Louisiana of a Texas award depends on the effect given it in Texas, the latter state could, and might be induced to, untie the hands of Louisiana by enacting reciprocal legislation providing that an award shall not be an acquittance of liability under the law of the other state.

[43] 311 U.S. 32 (1940).
[44] *Id.* at 46.

At the following term, the issue of the effect of a judgment on absent persons came up in a conflict-of-laws case, and in a very different setting. *Riley v. New York Trust Co.*[45] is one phase of the hitherto intractable problem of multiple inheritance taxes based on conflicting determinations of domicil. Georgia executors and a New York administrator with the will annexed laid claim in Delaware to shares of stock owned by the decedent in a Delaware corporation. The New York administrator had been appointed on motion of the state tax commission and the decedent's husband. The administrator's claim was resisted by the Georgia executors and beneficiaries under the will, who set up a decree of a Georgia court admitting the will to probate and finding the decedent's domicil to have been there; the New York representative was not a party to the Georgia proceedings. In interpleader proceedings instituted by the corporation whose stock was thus claimed, the Delaware court found the decedent's domicil to have been in New York and so ordered a transfer of the shares to the New York representative. In affirming this decision, the opinion of the Supreme Court considered at some length the Georgia law relating to the effect of a decree of probate. Chief Justice Stone, in a concurring opinion, citing the *Hansberry* case, which was not referred to by the majority, regarded it as sufficient for decision that Georgia could not conclude the possible interest of the New York representative in the shares without having effected his participation or representation in the proceedings. Otherwise, he pointed out, it would be an easy matter to bar claims for taxes by probate proceedings in one state in which only the beneficiaries were represented. It has been suggested by Professor Chafee[46] that the case indicates a means of escape from multiple taxation based on conflicting findings as to domicil. The suggestion is that by bringing the executor and administrators before the court in an interpleader proceeding,

[45] 315 U.S. 343 (1942).
[46] See Chafee, *Broadening the Second Stage of Federal Interpleader* 56 HARV. L. REV. 929, 974-75 (1943).

they would be bound by the single finding, the property in the control of the court would be assets for which only the successful representative would be accountable, and when the estate is thus "cut down" in the other states there is "that much less" for each of those states to tax. If Chief Justice Stone's approach is followed, the success of this plan would depend not so much on general concepts of situs or privity as on a realistic view of the adequacy of representation accorded to the interested taxing authorities by virtue of the participation of the personal representatives, including an examination of the circumstances of their appointment and the adversary nature of the contest over domicil.

At the same term as the *Riley* case, the problem of representation in another forum arose in still another form. A policyholder in what was denominated a mutual company was sued in Georgia, his residence, on an assessment imposed in insolvency proceedings in New York, the state of incorporation. The Georgia courts, observing that the place of making the contract did not appear, applied Georgia law to determine whether the defendant was in substance a member of a mutual-benefit association or simply a contract creditor of the company, and concluded, contrary to the determination by New York, that it was the latter and hence was not subject to the assessment. This decision was sustained in *Pink v. A.A.A. Highway Express, Inc.*,[47] Chief Justice Stone writing the opinion. While not remarkable in its holding that the assessment against an absent policyholder was not res judicata on the issue of membership, the decision does countenance a notable latitude in choice of law on that issue. If choice of law in commercial transactions is to be subjected to some extent to the unifying force of the full faith and credit clause, there could scarcely be a more appropriate matter for such treatment than the relation of a policyholder to his company, for which it might well be obligatory to look to the law of the chartering state. That this was not required indicates that the attitude of tolerance displayed in

[47] 314 U.S. 201 (1941), *rehearing denied,* 314 U.S. 716 (1942).

the workmen's compensation cases is a more general one, and that, save in cases where the forum applies a law having no plausible connection with the events,[48] its choice will not be vetoed by the Supreme Court.[49]

Recently the passivity of the Supreme Court in this field has been challenged by Mr. Justice Jackson. In an important address, he recalled the historic function of the full faith and credit clause as an integrating force in our federalism.[50] "It was placed foremost among those measures," he said, "which would guard the new political and economic union against the disintegrating influence of provincialism in jurisprudence, but without aggrandizement of federal power at the expense of the states."[51] Lamenting the feeble and halting way in which this federal ideal has been pursued in the conflicts decisions of the Supreme Court, Mr. Justice Jackson drew a depressing picture; "Indeed, I think it difficult to point to any field in which the Court has more completely demonstrated or more candidly confessed the lack of guiding standards of a legal character than in trying to determine what choice of law is required by the Constitution."[52]

This is, of course, a reproach at the trend for which Chief Justice Stone was the leading spokesman. Finding in the full

[48] *Cf.* Home Ins. Co. v. Dick, 281 U.S. 397 (1930).

[49] The opinions of Chief Justice Stone on jurisdiction to tax are outside the scope of this paper. It may simply be observed that in finding no due-process objections to multiple taxation of intangibles, he draws heavily on the connections with several states by virtue of principles of conflict of laws. *E.g.,* Graves v. Schmidlapp, 315 U.S. 657 (1942); Curry v. McCanless, 307 U.S. 357 (1939). Perhaps his insistence on a distinction, for purposes of multiple taxation, between tangibles and intangibles is a reflection of the distinction in the conflicts field; compare his separate opinion in Pearson v. McGraw, 308 U.S. 313, 319 (1939). Conflict-of-laws principles also colored his views on national power in international commercial transactions. He was less ready than a majority of the Court to find these principles superseded by executive agreement, or by legislation of Congress. United States v. Pink, 315 U.S. 203 (1942); Guaranty Trust Co. v. Henwood, 307 U.S. 247 (1939).

[50] See Jackson, *Full Faith and Credit — The Lawyer's Clause of the Constitution* 45 COLUM. L. REV. 1 (1945).

[51] *Id.* at 17.

[52] *Id.* at 16.

faith and credit clause an undeveloped resource for a more
closely-knit federalism, without the "aggrandizement of federal
power," Mr. Justice Jackson is much closer to the philosophy of
Mr. Justice Brandeis, whose conflict-of-laws opinions are to be
read most illuminatingly from this point of view. Perhaps the
most ambitious application of the full faith and credit clause
was made in his opinion for the Court in *John Hancock Mutual
Life Insurance Co. v. Yates.*[53] There it was held reversible error
for the courts of Georgia, the insured's domicil at death, to
permit the introduction of evidence that a misstatement in the
insured's application had been inserted by the insurance agent,
where decisions in New York, the place of making of the
contract, had construed a New York statute as precluding
consideration of anything outside the application and policy.
The opinions of Mr. Justice Brandeis in the *Clapper* case,
invoking the full faith and credit clause to preclude recovery
under a workmen's compensation law, and in the *Yarborough*
case, to preclude a claim for additional support, both eliciting
protest from Mr. Justice Stone, have been noticed. It is perhaps
worth remarking, at a time when the indicia of "liberalism" of
judges are a fashionable subject of discussion, that the opinions
of Mr. Justice Brandeis in these three cases denied the claims,
almost literally, of a widow, an orphan, and a workingman.
Quite evidently his concern as a judge in these constitutional
cases was with distribution of powers rather than distribution
of goods. But to revert to the main theme, it may be doubted
whether even the resourcefulness of Mr. Justice Brandeis
would have been equal to the task of working out satisfactory
adjustments of competing interests by means of decisions under
the full faith and credit clause. Indeeed, he was to be found
resisting the effort to compel the rights of an insured and the
company under a defaulted policy on which loans had been
made to be resolved, in the name of the Constitution, by an

[53] 299 U.S. 178 (1936).

almost fantastic search for the "place of making" in a complex series of interstate transactions.[54]

Some support for absolutes that will reduce conflicts problems to manageable proportions for Supreme Court review may be thought to be deducible from opinions of Mr. Justice Holmes. But it would be a mistake so to take them. In the first place, the absolutes were generally made to serve as bulwarks for sustaining, not overturning, state decisions. The climactic statement that "the Constitution and the first principles of legal thinking allow the law of the place where a contract is made to determine the validity and the consequences of the act"[55] becomes somewhat anticlimactic when stress is put on "allow" and when it is observed that the action of the state court was sustained. Moreover, when Mr. Justice Holmes had to deal with contract cases in the conflict of laws his common-law instinct for the particular was not deadened by the opiate of an aphorism. When he was faced with the issue of a married woman's liability on a contract which she was legally capable of making by the internal law of the place of making but incapable of making by the law of her domicil, where she was sued, he recognized the interest of the domicil, "first principles" notwithstanding.[56] A Massachusetts case which had applied the law of the place of making in similar circumstances went, he asserted, "to the verge of the law."[57] And when, on the Massachusetts court, he dealt with an oral agreement to make a will, valid where entered into but invalid in Massachusetts, which was the decedent's domicil and the forum, he likewise found that the place-of-making rule must yeild to the more relevant interest of Massachusetts.[58] Finally, it may be ventured that on occasion his absolutes ascribed

[54] New York Life Ins. Co. v. Dodge, 246 U.S. 357, 377 (1918) (dissenting opinion).

[55] Mutual Life Ins. Co. v. Liebing, 259 U.S. 209, 214 (1922).

[56] Union Trust Co. v. Grosman, 245 U.S. 412 (1918).

[57] *Id.* at 417, referring to Milliken v. Pratt, 125 Mass. 374, 383 (1878).

[58] Emery v. Burbank, 163 Mass. 326, 39 N.E. 1026 (1895).

power to a state that might better have been limited. The sweeping formula that "Alabama is sole mistress of the devolution of Alabama land by descent."[59] rooted deeply enough in the incidents of feudalism, sufficed to allow that state to deny effect to adoption proceedings in another state, even though similar proceedings in Alabama would have established a basis for inheritance. The element of discrimination in Alabama's favors as mistress of her land might well have called for the corrective of the full faith and credit clause as applied to the judicial adoption proceedings of another state.[60]

The upshot is, or is meant to be, that problems of choice of law have not lent themselves to satisfactory solution as constitutional questions, and that in their nature they cannot be expected to. The first half of this statement is not disputed by Mr. Justice Jackson. Speaking of the Supreme Court, he confesses, "I have not paid any exaggerated tribute to its performance thus far in this complex field."[61] The second half of the statement brings us back to our starting point. If the task of Conflict of Laws is to understand, harmonize, and weigh competing interests in multistate events, and if the desideratum of uniformity will be approached most satisfactorily by evolving rules that deliberately seek these objectives, then we seem to be hardly ready for a set of precepts imposed in the process of Supreme Court decision as fixed canons of constitutional law. If we eschew an enforced uniformity and pursue these objectives, we may find that our canons need much more analysis and that in particular fields the constructive work of achieving uniformity is more appropriately a legislative than a judicial task.[62] In

[59] Hood v. McGehee, 237 U.S. 611, 615 (1915).

[60] A similar neglect of the question of discrimination may be noted in Mr. Justice Holmes' separate opinion in Fall v. Eastin, 215 U.S. 1, 14-15 (1909).

[61] Jackson, *supra* note 50, at 26.

[62] It may be asked whether the federal courts are to have any share in the development of the subject, in the light of Klaxon Co. v. Stentor Electric Mfg. Co., 313 U.S. 487 (1941). One appropriate field would be cases of federal interpleader, in which the venue of the federal court should not control the choice of law through conformity with state conflicts rules of the forum. The decision in Griffin v. McCoach, 313 U.S. 498 (1941), applying the doctrine of

the field of contracts, for example, the interests of the states involved may not be the same for contracts of insurance, contracts to make a will, and contracts of sale at a market place. Moreover, the question of what may be broadly termed validity may comprehend quite different interests in issues of the capacity of a married woman, the limitation of carriers' liability, and the efficacy of a seal. If the influence of Chief Justice Stone is to be more than the negative one of toleration by the Supreme Court, it will make itself felt in a surer sense that uniformity must be preceded by wisdom, and wisdom by an understanding of objectives and a realization that in both objectives and method conflict of laws is not the least subtle and complex phase of the law. If that counsel is heeded, we may hope, with patient diligence, to achieve some singularly good results while avoiding some uniformly bad ones.

---

the *Erie* case to federal interpleader, was a defensible application of the Rules of Decision Act; but an amendment to the interpleader legislation would be desirable to permit the federal courts to formulate uniform conflicts rules in interpleader and so minimize the choice of a particular federal court as the forum. A second appropriate field would be cases in which state law is made relevant by federal law but the federal law gives no directions for conflict-of-laws questions; certain issues in taxation and bankruptcy, and governmental obligations, are examples. See, *e.g.,* Royal Indemnity Co. v. United States, 313 U.S. 289, 297 (1941); United States v. Guaranty Trust Co., 293 U.S. 340, 345-46 (1934), as explained in Clearfield Trust Co. v. United States, 318 U.S. 363, 367 (1943); *cf. In re* American Fuel & Power Co., 151 F.2d 470 (6th Cir. 1945), *affirmed sub nom.* Vanston Bondholders Protective Committee v. Green, 329 U.S. 156 (1946).

12 Mr. Justice Black and the
Judicial Function

The performance of the Supreme Court in the 1920's and early 1930's has had a decisive effect on our thinking about the process of constitutional adjudication. Just as there is nothing like a depression to stir and sharpen the sensibilities of economists, a constitutional crisis is a powerful, if painful, awakener of thought about the proper role of judges in maintaining our constitutional order. The sorry record of judicial negatives on social legislation, over the protests of the most respected members of the Court, forced us to come to terms with the problem of judicial review.

Different minds, repelled alike by the excesses of the Court, nevertheless responded in different ways. Some were profoundly confirmed in the view that in a democratic society the judges must defer to the more representative organs of government, save where the infringement of the fundamental charter was beyond peradventure clear. Justice Black, ascending the Bench after participating in the debates in the Senate on behalf of President Roosevelt's Court reorganization plan, drew a different moral from the experience through which we had passed. For him the lesson was that the judges lose the way when they put glosses on the Constitution, that they are safe, and the people secure, only when they follow the man-

Published in 14 U.C.L.A.L. Rev. 467 (1967), on the occasion of the thirtieth anniversary of Mr. Justice Black's appointment to the Court, and reprinted by permission.

dates of the Framers in their full and natural meaning, so that the powers granted are not constricted and the guarantees prescribed are not cabined, cribbed and confined.

A few years after assuming office, Justice Black wrote, in words that have been reiterated throughout his opinions: "Constitutional interpretation should involve more than dialectics. The great principles of liberty written in the Bill of Rights cannot safely be treated as imprisoned in walls of formal logic built upon vague abstractions found in the United States Reports."[1] If the impassioned warning against subtle dialectics carries an echo of Jefferson's anathema on the judges as miners and sappers, it also sets up a resounding harmony—to form an unaccustomed trio—with Chief Justice Marshall:

Powerful and ingenious minds, taking, as postulates, that the powers expressly granted to the government of the Union are to be contracted, by construction, into the narrowest possible compass, and that the original powers of the States are retained, if any possible construction will retain them, may, by a course of well digested, but refined and metaphysical reasoning, founded on these premises, explain away the Constitution of our country and leave it, a magnificent structure, indeed, to look at, but totally unfit for use.[2]

The governing canon of constitutional interpretation for Justice Black may be said to be natural meaning in contrast to natural law. The process has been facilitated, of course, by treating the relatively open-ended guarantees of the fourteenth amendment as incorporating the more specific provisions of the Bill of Rights. The issues raised by the theory of incorporation have often been canvassed and require no more than a bare mention here: Does the due process clause of the fourteenth amendment incorporate the similar clause in the fifth, and if so does this open up a wider ambit, procedural or substantive, than the specific guarantees themselves; is each and every

---

[1] Feldman v. United States, 322 U.S. 487, 499 (1944) (dissenting opinion).
[2] Gibbons v. Ogden, 22 U.S. (9 Wheat.) 1, 222 (1824).

guarantee transferred literally against the states, including a right to jury trial in common law actions involving more than twenty dollars; when a guarantee is thus incorporated, are all its peripheral features similarly transferred, so that the one is a mirror image of the other? The last question may call for a closer separation than was heretofore necessary between the constitutional component of a decision under the original Bill of Rights and a judicial gloss pursuant to the supervisory power over the administration of the federal courts. Indeeed, Justice Black was for some time unable to agree that the exclusionary rule of evidence; established as a corollary of the search-and-seizure clause, was binding on the states, since it could not be derived from the text of the fourteenth amendment; when he came to concur in this application of the exclusionary rule, it was only with the aid of the self-incrimination clause of the fifth amendment.[3]

The consequences of Justice Black's insistence on natural meaning are twofold in relation to the Bill of Rights and the fourteenth amendment. In the first place, the rights enumerated will receive extremely generous protection, as may be seen in Justice Black's position that obscenity is no more a legitimate exception to the first amendment than is, say, political extremism. Whether in his view the immunity of speech is always absolute and unqualified will be considered presently. The second and complementary consequence is that certain interests pressing for constitutional sanctuary will be denied that shelter if they are not fairly referable to the constitutional text. The integrity of Justice Black's philosophy of judicial review was demonstrated vividly when, in the Connecticut birth-control case, he found it impossible to recognize privacy as a constitutional right.[4] His dissent puzzled and confounded those observers who had simply been counting judicial votes and ignoring judicial opinions. For the usual agreement

[3] *Compare* Mapp v. Ohio, 367 U.S. 643, 661 (1961) (concurring opinion), *with* Wolf v. Colorado, 338 U.S. 25, 39 (1949) (concurring opinion).
[4] Griswold v. Connecticut, 381 U.S. 479, 507 (1965) (dissenting opinion).

in result between Justice Black and a number of his colleagues could not conceal a difference in approach, one that could and did become decisive. Only those forecasters, unhappily all too fashionable, who reduce judicial positions to the binary system of the computer should have been astonished at the cleavage. As far back as *Adamson v. California,*[5] Justice Black made it clear that the Bill of Rights sets limits as well as horizons for him, while others on the Court were unwilling to make this commitment and chose to regard the Bill of Rights as furnishing a minimal, not a preemptive, content to the fourteenth amendment.[6] At this point Justice Black's position merges into that of judicial self-restraint, and it is not as out of character as it might at first seem that he has elected to quote from a contemporary *locus classicus* of that philosophy, Learned Hand's *The Bill of Rights.*[7]

The coherence and integrity of Justice Black's judicial philosophy are reflected as well in its application to constitutional sectors outside the Bill of Rights. The commerce clause empowers Congress to regulate; it does not, in his view, authorize the courts to do so. In this characteristically plain and plain-spoken way he sets himself against the tide, which has been running steadily since *Gibbons v. Ogden,*[8] that moves the courts to adjudge state laws invalid as undue burdens on commerce, without benefit of congressional action. Here Justice Black finds himself allied (another unlikely trio) with Kent and Taney.[9] And yet the abstention based on literalness is not unqualified, for he acknowledges a judicial power to rule against the enforcement of state laws that "discriminate" against

[5] 332 U.S. 46, 68 (1947) (dissenting opinion).

[6] Compare the views of Justices Murphy and Rutledge, *id.* at 124 (dissenting opinion).

[7] See Griswold v. Connecticut, 381 U.S. 479, 526 (1965) (dissenting opinion), quoting L. HAND, THE BILL OF RIGHTS (1958).

[8] 22 U.S. (9 Wheat.) 1 (1824).

[9] See Morgan v. Virginia, 328 U.S. 373, 386 (1946) (Black, J., concurring); Pennsylvania v. Wheeling Bridge Co., 54 U.S. (13 How.) 518, 579 (1852) (Taney, C.J., dissenting); Livingston v. Van Ingen, 9 Johns R. 507 (N.Y. Ct. Err. 1812) (Kent, C.J.).

interstate commerce; this power, however, he would prefer to ascribe to the equal protection clause.[10] Determining what is a discrimination, as distinguished from an undue burden, may of course present a difficult question of characterization. New York's milk price law, which required milk from out of state to bear the same minimum cost as in-state milk, he regarded as discriminatory, although from one point of view the scheme simply equalized the cost position of the two classes of sellers.[11] How he would regard a compensating use tax that similarly neutralizes an advantage held by out-of-state suppliers is not entirely clear; presumably he would sensibly avoid the question of discrimination by sustaining sales and use taxes indiscriminately, without resorting to the constitutional distinctions between the two that have led to the adoption of the compensating use tax with its possibly discriminatory credit for a local sales tax.[12]

The obligation of contract clause has also tested Justice Black's philosophy, since the terms of the clause ("pass any law impairing the obligation of contracts") are quite as absolute as those of the first amendment. He has found himself standing alone in applying the clause to a law setting a time limit on a defaulting purchaser-mortgagor's contractual privilege of reinstatement.[13] At the same time, not every statutory alteration of a contractual obligation has moved him to raise the constitutional bar.[14] Here, as in the field of state regulation of commerce, there are resources available to blunt the sharp edge of the constitutional text.

But it is in the field of the Bill of Rights, and particularly the first amendment, that Justice Black's view of judicial responsi-

---

[10] See, e.g., H.P. Hood & Sons v. Du Mond, 336 U.S. 525, 545 (1949) (dissenting opinion).

[11] See id. at 555, explaining Baldwin v. Seelig, 294 U.S. 511 (1935).

[12] Cf. McLeod v. Dilworth Co., 322 U.S. 327, 332 (1944) (dissenting opinion).

[13] El Paso v. Simmons, 379 U.S. 497, 517 (1965) (dissenting opinion).

[14] In Wood v. Lovett, 313 U.S. 362, 372 (1941) (dissenting opinion), he took the position that "distressed landowners" could be restored to their property under a law which altered the rights of purchasers at a tax sale.

bility and restraint has had the fullest measure of application. The first amendment, he has said repeatedly, contains no ifs, buts, or whereases; its command is absolute.[15] And in fact the roster of immunities that flows from this interpretation is a formidable one: obscenity,[16] libel (private as well as political),[17] "subversive" publications or associations,[18] and contempt of court by publication.[19] Still, on a closer view, the absolutes are not quite so unqualified as they may appear, any more than in the areas of commerce and contract. The uneasy question keeps intruding: may it not be as true of the Bill of Rights as of the Rule Against Perpetuities, that although you can put it in a nutshell, you will find it difficult to keep it there? Once you recognize that freedom of speech cannot be taken in a colloquially literal sense—no one would immunize speechmaking in the Senate Gallery—some meta-textual standards are inescapable.

Justice Black himself has set up differentiating categories for judging abridgments of speech. He has stoutly rejected either a clear and present danger test or a so-called "balancing" test (an unfortunate concept at best, as it seems to set a right against a countervailing public interest, whereas the real problem is to define or delimit—not the same as to limit—the right itself). His own formulation is a distinction between measures that "directly" and those that "indirectly" limit speech. In *Barenblatt v. United States*,[20] his deeply felt dissent treated as a direct infringement, and therefore ipso facto invalid, an effort by a House committee to compel a witness to answer questions concerning his membership in the Communist Party or

[15] See, *e.g.*, Barenblatt v. United States, 360 U.S. 109, 134 (1959) (dissenting opinion); Beauharnais v. Illinois, 343 U.S. 250, 267 (1952) (dissenting opinion); *Justice Black and First Amendment "Absolutes": A Public Interview,* 37 N.Y.U.L. REV. 549, 553 (1962).

[16] Ginzburg v. United States, 383 U.S. 463, 476 (1966) (dissenting opinion).

[17] New York Times Co. v. Sullivan, 376 U.S. 254, 293 (1964) (concurring opinion). See also 37 N.Y.U.L. REV., *supra* note 15, at 557.

[18] Dennis v. United States, 341 U.S. 494, 579 (1951) (dissenting opinion).

[19] Bridges v. California, 314 U.S. 252 (1941).

[20] 360 U.S. 109 (1959).

affiliated organizations. He contrasted a law prohibiting the distribution of handbills, as applied to political or religious tracts; such a prohibition is an "indirect" regulation of speech and may properly be judged by a balancing test, taking account of the public interest served by the law, the feasibility of less drastic measures, and the availability of alternative methods of proselytizing. Another example of indirect abridgment is a law requiring handbills to contain the name and address of a sponsor.[21] If there is a legitimate public interest in identifying the source of defamatory matter, he observed, that end could be achieved by a law less sweeping and indiscriminate in its coverage. And he has similarly classified as an indirect abridgment a law requiring teachers to disclose all their organizational affiliations.[22] These are all cases where the balancing test, as accepted by Justice Black, should lead and did in fact lead to a holding of unconstitutionality. In other cases, however, the regulation of speech may pass muster even in Justice Black's view, as in the application of the antitrust laws to verbal appeals on behalf of a boycott that would itself violate those laws.[23]

Several observations suggest themselves at this point. It is somewhat surprising that Justice Black should espouse a test that involves a constitutional dichotomy of direct and indirect. In the field of national power over matters affecting commerce it proved to be so artificial and eventually discredited a criterion that one might hesitate long before reviving it in the vital area of the first amendment. In the hands of a less sensitive judge than Justice Black the test could yield results that by his standards would be quite perverse. Control over the distribution of handbills might be thought to be a more "direct" limitation on speech than questioning a witness about his affiliations. The latter will cast a pall over political association

---

[21] Talley v. California, 362 U.S. 60 (1960).

[22] Shelton v. Tucker, 364 U.S. 479 (1960), as explained in Griswold v. Connecticut, 381 U.S. 479, 516 (1965) (dissenting opinion).

[23] Giboney v. Empire Storage & Ice Co., 336 U.S. 490 (1949).

(itself a constitutional right that is derivative), and so in turn repress political discussion; in a certain sense the abridgment may appear to be indirect, as substandard wages were held to have an indirect effect on commerce, and strikes a direct effect, when that criterion held sway.

Actually the categories that Justice Black has set up seem more complex than the direct-indirect classification would indicate. There are factors of the purposiveness of the measure in relation to the control of expression, the generality or selectivity of its impact in the realm of ideas, and its focus on the content of utterance or on its time, place, or manner. In his own hands his formulation has had the immense power of simplicity; one cannot help wondering whether it can be commended to others with confidence that its simplicity will not be. merely formal or mechanical, and with assurance that it will yield similarly perceptive, sure-minded judgments. It is all no doubt a question of congenial ways of thinking. Some minds, whether legal or scientific, are more comfortable with formal simplicities, resolving underlying complexities intuitively. Such minds are often the minds of the masters. Others need to be fortified by a more explicit and detailed framework of analysis.

There is a certain irony in raising the question of the adaptability of Justice Black's formulation to other minds. The motivation animating his approach is undoubtedly the conviction that judges ought to have the benefit and work under the constraint of firm and easily apprehended constitutional standards, to minimize the vagrant propensities and biases of the thousands of judges, trial and appellate, who, over time, are called on to administer our constitutional order. "Flexible" standards are to Justice Black not flexible; they are "mush." [24] The biases become no more respectable, the mush no more palatable, when they offer themselves as principles of "natural law." Thus there is irony, too, in the fact that this judge, whom

[24] See 37 N.Y.U.L. REV., *supra* note 15, at 562.

many would wish to honor as preeminently creative, would repel any such tribute as a reproach, a total misunderstanding and repudiation of his conception of the judge's role.

There is more than a touch of Jeremy Bentham in Justice Black, a Bentham with an unmistakably American accent. The intense energies of both are engaged by zeal to reform the laws, to cleanse away its excrescences, to exhibit law as a burnished instrument of popular will, not as the patina of judges' gloss. For Bentham the enemy was the common law, fastening itself on the statutes; for Justice Black it is judge-made law as an encrustation on the Constitution. Bentham was so repelled by Blackstone's panegyrics that he was impelled to a lifetime reforming crusade; and Justice Black would surely echo Jefferson's scathing dismissal of the "honeyed Mansfieldism of Blackstone." The animadversions of Bentham on the common law of his day could find a place in Justice Black's on the constitutional interpretation of his day: "The arrangements supposed to be made by the other branch [commonlaw judges] ... may stand distinguished by the appellations of unreal, not really existing, imaginary, fictitious, spurious, judgemade, law." [25] Or this, on natural law: "A defect this to which all books must almost unavoidably be liable, which take for their subject the pretended Law of Nature, an obscure phantom, which in the imaginations of those who go in chase of it points sometimes to manners, sometimes to laws, sometimes to what is, sometimes to what it ought to be." [26]

How are we to account, in the end, for the profound impression that Justice Black has made on the public law of our time? He is without doubt the most influential of the many strong figures who have sat during the thirty years that have passed in his Justiceship. He has exhibited to a singular degree an intense moral commitment, concentrated through the focus of an unwavering vision, and brought to bear with immense

[25] 9 BENTHAM, WORKS 8 (Bowring ed. 1843).
[26] BENTHAM, INTRODUCTION TO THE PRINCIPLES OF MORALS AND LEGISLATION, ch. 17, § 27 (Lafleur ed. 1948).

prowess. One thinks of Justice Brandeis' confident formula for achievement: brains, rectitude, singleness of purpose, and time. One thinks, too, of an integrity like Brandeis', which is faithful to principle when on occasion that fidelity has to be set above a more comfortable result. Both have met the confrontation unflinchingly: Brandeis voting against his sponsor, President Wilson, in the removal-from-office case, and later in support of President Hoover's authority to proceed with the appointment of a Federal Power Commissioner over the belated protest of the Progressive majority in the Senate;[27] Black ordering President Truman to return the seized steel plants to the custody of their owners, denying that there is any class of publications that can be suppressed as obscene, and finding himself unable to strike down an anti-birth-control law that he found unspeakably obnoxious.[28]

The cumulative moral force of Justice Black has grown prodigious. Happily, it continues unabated, in the service of an undimmed vision.

---

[27] See Myers v. United States, 272 U.S. 52, 240 (1926) (dissenting opinion); United States v. Smith, 286 U.S. 6 (1932).

[28] See Youngstown Sheet & Tube Co. v. Sawyer, 343 U.S. 579 (1952); Ginzburg v. United States, 383 U.S. 463, 476 (1966) (dissenting opinion); Griswold v. Connecticut, 381 U.S. 479, 516 (1965) (dissenting opinion).

13 Federal-State Relations in the Opinions of Judge Magruder

Our system of parallel state and federal courts places the federal judge in a position of peculiar delicacy and presents him with problems of special complexity. To the usual task of administering justice under law is added a new dimension of substance and procedure, which it is not wholly fanciful to compare with the complexities of modern poetry, where the verse presents concurrent levels of allusion and intersecting planes of meaning. The virtuoso qualities of a judge are nowhere better revealed than in his treatment of the themes of federalism in the setting of litigation. Calvert Magruder would surely disclaim any pretensions to virtuosity as a judge; his own gifts would be the last to escape his talent for understatement. And yet his two decades on the bench have given us many arresting examples of his judicial powers in this area of federal-state relations—his powers, above all, of analysis, exposition, and accommodation.

The opinions can be conveniently arranged in three groups: choice of federal or state law, actions under the civil rights acts, and habeas corpus for state prisoners.

Judge Magruder's appointment to the bench followed closely upon the Copernican revolution in the relation between state and federal law in the federal courts which occurred in 1938 with the decision in *Erie R. R. v. Tomkins*[1] and the promulga-

---

Reprinted from 72 HARV. L. REV. 1204 (1959).
[1] 304 U.S. 64 (1938).

tion of the Federal Rules of Civil procedure. It fell to Judge Magruder as early as 1940 to grapple in a single case with two of the most perplexing questions raised by the *Erie* decision: Should the burden of proof and the conflict of laws in relation thereto be classified as "substance" or as "procedure" in a diversity-of-citizenship case in a federal court?

It will be useful to recall the facts of *Sampson v. Channell*.[2] An action was brought in the federal district court for Massachusetts to recover damages for injuries sustained in an automobile collision in Maine. Jurisdiction rested on diversity of citizenship. The district judge charged, over the plaintiff's objection, that the burden of proof was on the plaintiff to establish his freedom from contributory negligence, in accordance with the law of Maine. The law of Massachusetts would have placed the burden of proof on the defendant to show contributory negligence. The jury found the plaintiff guilty of contributory negligence and returned a verdict for the defendant. On appeal, the judgment was reversed, with an extensive and path-breaking opinion by Judge Magruder.

At the risk of blunting the analytical edge of the opinion, it can be summed up briefly. Taking up first the question whether burden of proof is governed as a matter of procedure by the Federal Rules (in which case Rule 8(c), placing the burden of pleading on the defendant, would presumably be controlling) or as a matter of substance by state law under the *Erie* decision, the opinion assigns the issue to the latter category, primarily because the outcome of the case may be materially affected by the burden of proof, in the sense of burden of persuasion. Referring to the *Erie* decision, Judge Magruder observed, "The opinion in that case sets forth as a moving consideration of policy that it is unfair and unseemly to have the outcome of litigation substantially affected by the fortuitous existence of diversity of citizenship."[3] Turning then to the question of choice of state law as a federal or state issue, the opinion

---

[2] 110 F.2d 754 (1st Cir.), *cert. denied,* 310 U.S. 650 (1940).
[3] *Id.* at 756.

assigns this too to the state category. A federal court should apply the conflict-of-laws rule of the forum, as it "sits as a court coordinate with the Massachusetts state courts to apply the Massachusetts law in diversity of citizenship cases."[4] A Massachusetts court would apply its own rule on burden of proof as part of the *lex fori*; this choice of law is not unconstitutional; and the federal court should therefore do likewise. This result, as Judge Magruder acknowledged, has a certain element of paradox: Having determined that burden of proof is a matter of substance and hence is to be governed by state law, the federal court is led by the state conflicts rule to characterize the issue as procedural. But the analysis presents only a "surface incongruity,"[5] since the two characterizations are made for different purposes.

The decision in *Sampson v. Channell* seemed to offer an appropriate occasion for review by the Supreme Court. The bearing of the *Erie* case in these circumstances had not been authoritatively determined by that Court; and indeed in the court of appeals one judge announced his concurrence only in the result, and the third judge dissented without opinion. And yet certiorari, when applied for, was denied.[6] Not until a similar case came up from the Third Circuit did the Supreme Court deal with the problem, and then it vindicated the position of Judge Magruder.[7]

At this point it may not be amiss to recount two tributes to *Sampson v. Channell* from rather disparate sources. The first comes from a student, who ventured the judgment that Judge Magruder's opinion was the best judicial opinion he had read in his three years at law school. When asked to explain his standard of preeminence, he answered simply that this opinion lent itself most beautifully of all to abstracting. One might concur in the conclusion without endorsing the criterion. The second tribute is that of a member of the Supreme Court, no

[4] *Id.* at 761.
[5] *Id.* at 762.
[6] 310 U.S. 650 (1940).
[7] Klaxon Co. v. Stentor Elec. Mfg. Co., 313 U.S. 487 (1941).

longer in service, who remarked that he had voted to deny certiorari in the case because he felt that the Court would not produce an opinion as excellent as Judge Magruder's. This is a ground for denying certiorari not to be discovered in the Rules of the Supreme Court. Perhaps that Court might have adopted, *mutatis mutandis,* the course recently suggested by Judge Magruder himself for the review of decisions of a lower court: "And if the district court has written a careful and full opinion, with which we agree, and which we feel unable to improve upon, we should affirm on the opinion of the court below."[8]

In all candor, nonetheless, it must be admitted that not all commentators have been as appreciative of *Sampson v. Channell* as were the student and the Justice. Against its reasoning, and that of the Supreme Court in succeeding cases, powerful arguments, indeed polemics, have been directed.[9] Disclaiming the concurrence of the Supreme Court as proof positive of the rightness of the decision, Judge Magruder has taken wry cognizance of the criticism: "If the conclusion reached in that case is as wrong and as unfortunate as I understand they now say it is in the class on federal jurisdiction at Harvard Law School, assuming I was competent to write a persuasive opinion the other way, who knows but that I might have succeeded in persuading even the Supreme Court to take that view, in a matter which, after all, they had never focused on before." [10] But the Judge made it clear that he remained impenitent; and so it becomes relevant to examine the competing arguments.

The rule for burden of persuasion is part of the policy of the system of law governing liability rather than of the system governing the conduct of trials. The rule is not neutral on the issue of allocation of loss; to place the burden on the claimant or the defendant reflects a weighting for or against the defense

---

[8] Magruder, *The Trials and Tribulations of an Intermediate Appellate Court,* 44 CORNELL L.Q. 1, 3 (1958).

[9] See, *e.g.,* HART & WECHSLER, THE FEDERAL COURTS AND THE FEDERAL SYSTEM 633-36 (1953).

[10] Magruder, *supra* note 8, at 6.

of contributory negligence itself. The rule more nearly resembles a statute of limitations built into a statutory cause of action, than a rule on joinder of causes of action, whose policy is predominantly aimed at the economy and efficiency of litigation.

It may readily be conceded that there is no constitutional compulsion to treat the burden of proof in this way. The issue lies in a twilight zone where Congress could validly prescribe a uniform federal rule if it concluded that the difficulty of ascertaining the burden-of-proof rules of the several states, together with their marginal importance as part of the rules governing conduct or liability, outweighed the value of treating them as adhering to the "substantive" law. But, it is argued, if there is thus no constitutional compulsion, and if we are to take seriously the passage in the opinion in *Erie v. Tompkins* invoking the unconstitutionality of a general federal common law[11] as a necessary ground for overruling *Swift v. Tyson*,[12] must we not then conclude as a matter of logic that *Erie v. Tompkins* is inapplicable? I do not think so. Given the decision in *Erie v. Tompkins*, with its constitutional underpinning, the problem of its implications and peripheral applications presents a new issue. With so much removed from the scope of federal common law, the question of what remains there, in the guise of "procedure," is to be viewed in a new focus. Is it worthwhile to preserve a given matter, such as burden of proof, for a federal rule, even if permissible, when the major rules to which it is attached have been withdrawn (for constitutional reasons, as it happens) from the federal ambit? After *Erie v. Tompkins* the unconstitutionality of a given application of the concept "procedure" is a sufficient, but not a necessary, condition for attaching the "substantive" label. An equally sufficient reason may be that, on balance, it is not worthwhile to retain a special federal auxiliary rule when

---

[11] 304 U.S. at 77-78: "If only a question of statutory construction were involved, we should not be prepared to abandon a doctrine so widely applied throughout nearly a century. But the unconstitutionality of the course pursued has now been made clear and compels us to do so."

[12] 41 U.S. (16 Pet.) 1 (1842).

the major conduct-directing and liability-determining rules are themselves no longer within federal control. In the law, too, the hair generally follows the hide.

It is necessary to turn now to the more subtle question of conflict of laws. Against Judge Magruder's position there has been leveled a battery of arguments which are surely provocative and sometimes plausible. It will be convenient to speak first of conflict of laws in general and finally of conflict of laws in relation to the burden of proof.

As with the burden of proof itself, it may be conceded that conflict of laws lies in a twilight zone where either classification would be constitutional. It is a matter traditionally for the forum to decide which state has the closest connection with the transaction or event and to proceed to apply the law of that state; this decision is revocable, so to speak, only when the forum decides to employ some version of renvoi by looking to the conflict-of-laws rules of another state. Judge Magruder's approach commits the federal court, in cases involving state "substantive" law, to a kind of transmissive renvoi, through the conflict-of-laws rules of the state in which the federal court is sitting. Though this may not be constitutionally compelled, that consideration, for reasons already suggested, should not be decisive against this result. But other considerations are advanced and must be dealt with.

It is argued, in the first place, that the philosophy of diversity jurisdiction implies a federal conflict of laws to guard against parochialism in the choice-of-laws rules of a state. Unless this control is retained by the federal courts, the argument runs, there is little point in the retention of diversity jurisdiction itself.

It is true that this philosophy of diversity jurisdiction has been greatly undermined by the overruling of *Swift v. Tyson*. Protection of the outsider against local bias *may* have been furthered by federal common-law rules of liability for railroad, telegraph, and insurance companies. With this system abandoned, however, protection of the outsider is hardly to be achieved by supplanting state with federal conflict-of-laws rules. The bias to be feared in state choice of law is excessive application of the law of the forum. The correlation is weak between this bias and a bias against nonresidents. Whether a local rule of law happens to favor or disfavor the nonresident litigant is a matter of chance. If a local conflict-of-laws rule is actually nonneutral in respect of nonresidents, the remedy should lie rather in review by the Supreme Court under the equal-protection clause, giving protection to the nonresident whether the case arises in a state or a federal court. If a sound system of conflict of laws is so central to a properly working federalism that it ought to be a federal responsibility — a position which has much to commend it — the end can best be achieved by Supreme Court review under the due-process and full-faith-and-credit clauses. This course would have a double advantage: It would not depend on the circumstances of diversity jurisdiction, and it would give the Court an opportunity to approach the task on a selective basis, by taking appellate jurisdiction over those issues of choice of law which are most in need of authoritative uniform resolution.

It is argued, second, that the essential vice of *Swift v. Tyson* was not that the outcome of a case might turn on the choice of forum,[13] but that antecedent conduct was subjected to the hazard of conflicting rules of law. This objection has been overcome by *Erie v. Tompkins* in cases in which there is no problem of choice of state law; it could be alleviated even in the case of multi-state transactions if there were a predictable conflict-of-laws rule that could be relied on to the extent that the parties could count on a federal forum.

To this it should be said that there is some exaggeration in the emphasis on the relation of *Swift v. Tyson* to advance

[13] Judge Magruder himself has acknowledged that the goal of uniformity between state and federal forums is not an infallible guide in the application of the *Erie* doctrine; if it were, many of the Federal Rules of Civil Procedure would have to give way in diversity cases. D'Onofrio Constr. Co. v. Recon Co., 255 F.2d 904 (1st Cir. 1958). To the same effect, see Byrd v. Blue Ridge Rural Elec. Coop., 356 U.S. 525, 536-39 (1958).

planning of conduct. In cases of negligence, for example, this factor is much less relevant than in consensual transactions; and in important planned transactions the parties may obviate the conflict-of-laws problem by contractual provision for the applicable law, which if reasonable would presumably be respected by either a state or a federal court. In any event, the likelihood of a federal forum can hardly be foretold with any assurance, in view of the variables between the time of the transaction and of suit: the amount in controversy, the alignment of the parties as plaintiff or defendant, on which may depend the removability of the case, and the coincidence of a federal conflicts rule with the self-interest of a party who is entitled to remove.

To be sure, a federal conflicts rule does not present quite the same objection as a federal rule of tort or contract; in the former case there will be at least a reference to some state law as the ultimate ground of liability. But conflict-of-laws rules are themselves important pointers toward liability, and in default of some compelling reason for federal autonomy in this one phase of the conduct-regulating or liability-determining regime of law, conflicts rules ought to be treated as part of the substratum of non-federal law applied in diversity cases. Although conflicts rules are not as integral a part of the policy of the underlying law as is burden of proof, the function of those rules in selecting the applicable law sets them apart from rules of practice governing the conduct and management of litigation.

Third, it is argued that a state conflicts rule means the rule of the state in which the federal court is sitting, and this gives an artificial significance and effect to the venue of the federal action. It is no longer as accurate as it once was to equate a federal district court with a court of the state. The transfer-of-venue provision of the Judicial Code[14] suggests the beginning of a new

[14] 28 U.S.C. § 1404(a) (1952): "For the convenience of parties and witnesses, in the interest of justice, a district court may transfer any civil action to any other district or division where it might have been brought."

conception of the federal district courts as parts of a self-contained national system within which litigation is to be distributed on grounds of convenience. In interpleader, moreover, process extends throughout the country, and suit may be brought in the place of residence of any claimant.[15] If nationwide service is extended generally to other civil actions, with a wide choice of districts in which to sue, the attempt to bring about conformity with the courts of the forum state becomes more and more irrelevant.

If we had in fact reached this stage of federal jurisdiction, I would agree that conformity to local conflicts rules should be reconsidered. Indeed, I have suggested elsewhere that it be abandoned now for federal interpleader,[16] since by hypothesis no state court is likely to have been a possible forum, and the real danger of forum-shopping is between federal districts rather than between state and federal courts; in this kind of litigation a uniform federal conflicts rule would serve the anti-forum-shopping policy better than the rule of *Sampson v. Channell*. But this is still an exceptional jurisdiction. Even the transfer provisions of the Judicial Code are not comparable to interpleader; since they help center litigation in a district which is apt to have a closer connection with the cause of action than the one originally chosen by the plaintiff, there is all the more reason for adhering to the rule of *Sampson v. Channell,* applying the conflicts rules of the state to which the case has been transferred.*

---

[15] 28 U.S.C. § 1397 (1952).

[16] Freund, *Chief Justice Stone and the Conflict of Laws,* 59 HARV. L. REV. 1210, 1236 n.62 (1946). A valuable recent discussion of the rationale of the *Erie* doctrine will be found in Hill, *The Erie Doctrine and the Constitution,* 53 Nw. U.L. REV. 427, 541 (1958).

*The Supreme Court has in fact followed the rule of *Sampson v. Channell* in transfer cases, but has opted for the conflicts rules of the transferor rather than the transferee state. Van Dusen v. Barrack, 376 U.S. 612 (1964). The choice was evidently prompted by the fear that otherwise defendants would be encouraged to seek transfer for the purpose of affecting the outcome of the case. On the other hand, the Court's rule may inhibit the allowance of a meritorious transfer because of the difficulty the transferee court might experience in

The point just made, that *Sampson v. Channell* is the more persuasive as the state of the forum has greater connection with the events of the case, can be turned into a final argument against the actual decision. Federal conflicts rules are eschewed because there is no federal *lex causae*, and yet a state conflicts rule is followed which leads to the burden-of-proof rule of Massachusetts although that state likewise does not provide the *lex causae*. Moreover, from the point of view of the goal of a uniform rule of decision irrespective of the choice of a forum, *Sampson v. Channell* does not afford the optimum result. If the action had been brought in a state court in Maine, the burden of proof would have rested on the plaintiff (under a conflicts rule pointing either to the *lex fori* or the *lex causae).* In Massachusetts, it rested on the defendant. Under *Sampson v. Channell,* the federal court in each state would follow the rule of that state, making for two chances out of four that the burden of proof would rest on the plaintiff, and the same chances that it would rest on the defendant. If, however, the federal courts were to adopt a conflicts rule of their own which characterized burden of proof as a matter of substance in the conflict-of-laws sense, the burden would rest on the plaintiff in the state and federal courts of Maine and the federal court in Massachusetts, making the odds three to one in favor of the likelihood of that result.

The answer to this line of argument is in part that the assumptions of available alternative forums may be unrealistic, in view of the requirements of jurisdiction and venue. More basically, the answer reverts to a philosophy of federalism, of

---

determining the conflicts rule of the transferor state. In any event, the suggestion in the text above may stand as an argument for adopting the "whole law," including the conflicts rules, of the transferee state if the transferor state had negligible connection with the facts of the case; this result could be reached by renvoi from the transferor state if its courts had indicated in other cases that it would so apply the conflicts rules of the state having the clearly predominant interest.

abstention from devising federal judge-made law as an append-age to state law, of leaving problems of conflict of state laws in a federal system to be worked out by the Supreme Court and Congress without regard to the happenstance of diversity juris-diction in a given case.

This philosophy, which may seem to prescribe a passive role for federal district courts, has its active side as well, which is shown in the converse case: a federal statutory scheme which has to be provided with peripheral rules of law. It is notewor-thy that Judge Magruder has given us a leading opinion on each of these aspects of federal-state relations. The counterpart of *Sampson v. Channell* is *O'Brien v. Western Union Tel. Co.*,[17] decided later the same year. The company accepted and dis-patched to Father Coughlin a telegram containing defamatory references to the plaintiff, who was a candidate for the Senate and Vice-Presidency in 1936 on the Union ticket, which Father Coughlin headed. In an action brought in the federal court for Massachusetts, the plaintiff requested, and the court rejected, a charge that the company was not privileged in transmitting and delivering the message. On appeal from a judgment for the defendant, the court of appeals considered the source of the applicable rules for the duties and liabilities of the telegraph company. The Communications Act provided only, in section 202 (a), that it was unlawful to make any unjust or unreasona-ble discrimination in charges, practices, or services.[18] From this provision Judge Magruder inferred that the duty to accept and transmit defamatory messages must be subject to a uniform rule, necessarily to be fashioned by a kind of common law of the statute. Stressing the practical needs of the business, Judge Magruder concluded that a privilege existed greater than that which the sender might have. The significance of the opinion lies in its frank readiness to mold a federal law of defamation in a limited area, and in the sweep of its rationale. Earlier cases had applied *Swift v. Tyson* to interstate communications problems, in the interest of a uniform law in the federal courts.

[17] 113 F.2d 539 (1st Cir. 1940).
[18] 48 Stat. 1070 (1934), 47 U.S.C. § 202(a) (1952).

Judge Magruder's opinion does not rest on the role of the judiciary in diversity cases. Rather, it provides a basis for a uniform national rule of law, binding on state and federal courts alike, where the operative legal policies are federal in origin. Though the result is 180 degrees removed from *Sampson v. Channell,* Judge Magruder was steering faithfully by the same stars.

The Court of Appeals for the First Circuit has not escaped the invitation to constitutional lawmaking provided by those ubiquitous litigants, the Watchtower Bible and Tract Society, Inc., and its members, Jehovah's Witnesses. But Judge Magruder has with great courtesy kept the acceptance of the invitation to a minimum.

The first occasion was presented in *City of Manchester v. Leiby,*[19] in which the Society had sought to enjoin the enforcement of a municipal ordinance requiring bootblacks and sellers of newspapers and magazines on the public streets to obtain a badge, to be issued by the superintendent of schools, who was to keep a record of the name and age of each recipient. The Witnesses refused to apply for badges as a condition of distributing their pamphlets at five cents a copy on the streets of Manchester. Pointing out that there was no indication of any censorship or discretion to withhold a badge on the ground of impropriety of the literature to be disseminated, Judge Magruder announced a policy of abstention: "If, conceivably, the ordinance might be given an interpretation of broader sweep and more doubtful constitutionality, the notable and altogether proper reluctance of federal courts to issue injunctions against state and city officials, restraining their enforcement of criminal laws and ordinances, would lead us to adopt the most innocent interpretation until the state courts have ruled otherwise, or at least until the local officials have proceeded to act on an interpretation which brings the law or ordinance in conflict with constitutional guarantees."[20]

[19] 117 F.2d 661 (1st Cir.), *cert. denied,* 313 U.S. 562 (1941).
[20] *Id.* at 665.

There was a characteristically sympathetic appreciation of the position of the unsuccessful plaintiffs:

The mandate of Jehovah to teach and preach the gospel is interpreted by the plaintiffs as a command, upon pain of everlasting destruction, to sell the gospel message on the streets of Manchester at five cents a copy without applying for the badge or permit required by the ordinance. From the plaintiffs' point of view they face a painful dilemma in this conflict between the call of conscience and the demands of man-made law. The possibility of such conflict is, for the most part, fortunately eliminated by the guarantees of the First and Fourteenth Amendments. But not altogether... The civil authority can never concede the extreme claim that police regulations of general application not directed against any sect or creed — however widely the regulations may be accepted as being reasonable and proper — are constitutionally inapplicable to persons who sincerely believe the observance of them to be "an insult to Almighty God." See Cardozo, J., in Hamilton v. Regents, 293 U.S. 245, 268...[21]

Citing the requirement of a permit for sacramental wine under the National Prohibition Act, and of a license for the sacrament of marriage, the opinion concludes that in the circumstances the requirement of a permit is not a transgression of religious liberty.

The Manchester ordinance raised implicitly a number of questions of interpretation: Would it be applicable to adults as well as to minors, to religious proselyters as well as to secular newsboys? If the ordinance had been of more doubtful validity the court might well have held the case pending a determination of the issues of construction in the state courts. A more doubtful constitutional problem did arise in a later Jehovah's Witnesses case, this one challenging an ordinance of the town of Haverhill, which prohibited the use of the streets for selling any article except newspapers unless authorized by a special permit. It will be seen that this regulation went beyond a uniform requirement of identification and was vulnerable to

[21] *Id.* at 666.

the objection that no standards were prescribed for the granting or denial of permission to sell religious tracts on the streets. In *Hannan v. City of Haverhill*,[22] however, the relation between God and Caesar yielded place to that between federal and state courts. The case reached the court of appeals on review of a denial of a temporary injunction sought by the Witnesses, some of whom had been arrested, prosecuted, and fined in a state court for violations of the ordinance. In this posture of the case, Judge Magruder found it possible to decline to decide "a doubtful question" of constitutional law. An appeal from the convictions to the Supreme Judicial Court would preserve the constitutional issue, and all that the federal appellate court had to decide, and did decide, at this juncture was that the district court did not abuse its discretion in denying a temporary injunction.

It is worth noting that in due course the Supreme Judicial Court did pass upon the Haverhill ordinance, construing it, in the light of constitutional limitations, not to apply to noncommercial distributors like Jehovah's Witnesses.[23] It is true not only of desegregation, one suspects, and not only in Virginia, that in the control of local authorities it is most effective for the federal court to do the hinting and the state court the hitting. At least this is so where there is as responsible a state tribunal as the Supreme Judicial Court of Massachusetts.

A different set of problems was raised by a series of cases in which damages were sought against state officials under the Civil Rights Act, section 1983 of title 42 of the *United States Code*:[24] "Every person who, under color of any statute, ordinance, regulation, custom, or usage of any State or Territory, subjects, or causes to be subjected, any citizen of the United States or other person within the jurisdiction thereof to the

---

[22] 120 F.2d 87 (1st Cir.), *cert. denied,* 314 U.S. 641 (1941).

[23] Commonwealth v. Akmakjian, 316 Mass. 97, 55 N.E.2d 6 (1944); *cf.* Commonwealth v. Pascone, 308 Mass. 591, 33 N.E.2d 522, *cert. denied,* 314 U.S. 641 (1941).

[24] Rev. Stat. § 1979 (1875), 42 U.S.C. § 1983 (1952).

deprivation of any rights, priviliges, or immunities secured by the Constitution and laws, shall be liable to the party injured in an action at law, suit in equity, or other proper proceeding for redress."

An action for damages against a public official is the epitome of the Rule of Law as expounded by Dicey in his classic formulation.[25] And yet this image of the liability of public servants as if they were private wrongdoers has never been an accurate depiction of the actual law. Absolute immunities and qualified privileges have honeycombed the fabric of liability.[26] The extraordinary remedies of habeas corpus and injunction may, in fact, be more readily available than an action for damages. In this area it would seem almost that no action at law will lie where there is an adequate remedy in equity. Be that as it may, the problem for the federal court is whether the immunities and privileges of the common law are to be read as a gloss on the unqualified language of the Civil Rights Acts.

In *Cobb v. City of Malden*,[27] a group of public-school teachers brought an action for an injunction and damages against the city, the mayor, and members of the board of aldermen and city council, alleging a conspiracy to bring about a referendum to reject a proposed appropriation by the school committee for

[25] DICEY, LAW OF THE CONSTITUTION 193-94 (9th ed. 1950). For a striking recent illustration of Dicey's principle, see Roncarelli v. Duplessis, [1959] 16 D.L.R.2d 689 (Can. Sup. Ct.), holding the Premier of Quebec liable in the amount of $33,123.53 for arbitrarily ordering the manager of the provincial liquor commission to cancel the liquor license of the plaintiff, an active member of Jehovah's Witnesses.

[26] See KEIR & LAWSON, CASES IN CONSTITUTIONAL LAW 199-204 (4th ed. 1954). It is interesting to recall how many of the great English cases on the liberty of the subject have arisen as actions for damages, from Entick v. Carrington, 19 St. Tr. 1030 (1765), on search and seizure, to Liversidge v. Anderson, [1942] A.C. 206, on preventive detention. It is tempting to suggest that certain decisions in favor of the defendant officer, like the *Liversidge* case itself, may have been affected by this risk of personal liability for damages; but it is necessary to remember also the readiness with which Parliament has traditionally passed acts of indemnity. See CARR, CONCERNING ENGLISH ADMINISTRATIVE LAW 67-70 (1941).

[27] 202 F.2d 701 (1st Cir. 1953).

teachers' salaries. Such a rejection, it was alleged, would constitute an impairment of the obligation of contract. While affirming a dismissal of the action against the city, the court of appeals ordered the complaint retained as against the individual defendants. It is difficult to see how nondefamatory political propaganda directed to the electorate could constitute an actionable wrong by virtue of the unconstitutionality of the decision which might be taken by the electorate. Judge Magruder concurred specially. The Supreme Court had held that members of a state legislature enjoy under the Civil Rights Acts the absolute immunity conferred by the common law in respect of their official functions.[28] Judge Magruder, relying on the principle of qualified privilege for members of a subordinate lawmaking body in cases of defamation, concluded that the plaintiffs could recover in theory if they established that the defendants "realized that they were subjecting plaintiffs to harm by an unconstitutional impairment of the obligations of their contracts with the City." But, he added with blunt candor, "I don't suppose for a moment that plaintiffs will be able to establish what it is necessary for them to show in order to recover damages... There is ample procedure under state law by which plaintiffs' substantive rights under their alleged contracts may be vindicated in the state courts. I cannot escape the feeling that this case does not belong in the federal courts."[29]

The utmost frankness in facing this riddle of the Civil Rights Acts marked Judge Magruder's opinion in *Francis v. Lyman*.[30] The plaintiff had been released from confinement as a defective delinquent by reason of the state court's decision that the commitment proceedings were lacking in procedural due process. There followed an action in the federal court for damages against the state trial judge, the commissioners of correction, the members of the parole board, and the superintendents of the state farm and the reformatory where the plaintiff had been

[28] Tenney v. Brandhove, 341 U.S. 367 (1951).
[29] 202 F.2d at 707.
[30] 216 F.2d 583 (1st Cir. 1954).

confined. Certain of the defendants were ordered dismissed from the action without great difficulty: the judge because of his absolute immunity, the commissioners of correction and the parole board because they had no authority to release the plaintiff on the ground of the invalidity of the commitment proceedings. There remained the actual custodians who held the plaintiff in confinement. "We do not pretend," said Judge Magruder, "that it is easy to explain why these two defendants are not liable in damages within the coverage of the federal tort liability imposed by the Civil Rights Act."[31] There would no doubt be a privilege at common law to hold a prisoner pursuant to a judicial order for which the judge himself enjoyed immunity; but there is no perfect correlation between common-law privileges and responsibility under the Civil Rights Acts, as shown by redress for denial of voting rights on racial grounds. Damages have been recognized as proper even when the public officials have acted in the belief that they were carrying out their duties in a constitutional manner; in *Smith v. Allwright*[32] the complaint was sustained even though it was necessary to overrule a Supreme Court precedent on which the voting officials could reasonably have relied. *Francis v. Lyman* might possibly have been differentiated as a case of monetary damages pure and simple; since the plaintiff had already been released and the statute under which he had been committed declared wanting in due process, a judgment would have had no utility in coercing state officials to conform to federal constitutional requirements.[33] Neither this nor any similar distinction was essayed by Judge Magruder. He contented himself with the reflection that in the area of racial discrimination, the immediate target of the Civil Rights Acts, the legislation could be given more intensive application than in areas opened up by the evolution of the fourteenth amendment as judicially

[31] *Id.* at 586.
[32] 321 U.S. 649 (1944).
[33] See Note, 68 HARV. L. REV. 1229, 1233 (1955).

construed. In the latter areas some circumspection is called for in applying the terms of the Civil Rights Acts:

When courts come to deal with a statute phrased in terms of such vague generality, they are faced with two possible alternatives: (1) They may give effect to the statute in its literal wording, and thus reach results so bizarre and startling that the legislative body would probably be shocked into the prompt passage of amendatory legislation. This seems to be the approach which the Third Circuit intended to take in its opinion in Picking v. Pennsylvania R.R. Co., 1945, 151 F. 2d 240. (2) The courts may refuse to regard the statute as an isolated phenomenon, sticking out like a sore thumb if given a strict, literal application; and upon the contrary may conceive it to be their duty, in applying the statutory language, to fit the statute as harmoniously as may be into the familiar and generally accepted legal background, and to confine its application, within reason, to those situations which might possibly have had the approval of the Congress if it had specifically adverted to the particular cases, bearing in mind the basic purposes which gave rise to the legislation in the first place. . .

From the trend of decisions applying this particular statute, we think it no longer appropriate for this court to proceed in accordance with the first of the above alternatives.[34]

No aspect of the federal judge's authority calls more imperatively for a finely disciplined temperament than does the task of collateral review of state convictions through habeas corpus. It is an extraordinary jurisdiction, demanding vigilance without aggressiveness, moderation without abnegation. The terms of the jurisdiction are set by section 2254 of title 28:

An application for a writ of habeas corpus in behalf of a person in custody pursuant to the judgment of a State court shall not be granted unless it appears that the applicant has exhausted the remedies available in the courts of the State, or that there is either an absence of available State corrective process or the existence of circumstances rendering such process ineffective to protect the rights of the prisoner.

An applicant shall not be deemed to have exhausted the remedies

[34] 216 F.2d at 587.

available in the courts of the State, within the meaning of this section, if he has the right under the law of the State to raise, by any available procedure, the question presented.

The qualities of mind which Judge Magruder has brought to these clashing interests of public order and individual rights, of state authority and federal oversight, can best be seen by examining the cases in ascending order of intervention. In *McGarty v. O'Brien*,[35] the petitioner sought habeas corpus on the ground that the state had denied him funds to employ psychiatrists for the defense, as requested by his state-appointed counsel in a capital case. Two psychiatrists designated by the Department of Mental Health under the so-called Briggs law[36] had rendered a report unfavorable to the defendant. Affirming a denial of the petition, Judge Magruder observed that the psychiatrists were not partisans of the prosecution, and that neither their impartiality or qualifications nor the thoroughness of their examination was challenged.[37]

A more difficult question was presented by an allegation of the knowing use of perjured testimony. *Coggins v. O'Brien*[38] was a habeas corpus case brought after the same claim had been made in a state court on a motion for new trial, which was denied after a hearing but without findings or opinion; the order was affirmed on appeal and certiorari was denied. The district court dismissed the petition, and the court of appeals

---

[35] 188 F.2d 151 (1st Cir.), *cert. denied*, 341 U.S. 928 (1951). See also Soulia v. O'Brien, 188 F.2d 233 (1st Cir.), *cert. denied*, 341 U.S. 928 (1951), in which a prisoner convicted of murder petitioned for habeas corpus on the ground that the state had introduced a knowingly false report of a ballistics expert. The district court heard evidence and denied the petition on the facts; the court of appeals affirmed.

[36] MASS. GEN. LAWS ANN. ch. 123, § 100A (1958).

[37] Mr. Justice Frankfurter has pointed out the advance made by the Briggs law over the older system of partisan experts. The quality of the Briggs law examination, he observed, is such that the report of the nonpartisan experts generally controls even when the defendant elects to employ his own psychiatrists. FRANKFURTER, OF LAW AND MEN 89-90 (1956) (testimony before the Royal Commission on Capital Punishment, July 21, 1950).

[38] 188 F.2d 130 (1st Cir. 1951).

affirmed. Judge Magruder, in a concurring opinion, analyzed the duty of a federal court in these circumstances. On the one hand, denial of certiorari is to be given no weight against the petitioner. Nor is it enough that a full hearing in the state court was afforded on the post-conviction claim; in taking this position Judge Magruder rejected what he understood to be the view of the Second Circuit.[39] On the other hand, the prisoner is not entitled to an independent federal hearing if it appears, as it did here, that the state court found on adequate evidence that there had not been a knowing use of perjured testimony. Judge Ford, dissenting, concluded that the state judge had applied a state rule of law requiring a showing that the perjured testimony was probably decisive with the jury in reaching the verdict of guilty. Without disagreeing on the inadequacy of such a legal test for federal constitutional purposes, Judge Magruder was prepared to give the benefit of the doubt to the state judge on an issue involving an established rule of federal constitutional law.

Abstention can be final or provisional. Only provisional abstention was approved in *Buchanan v. O'Brien*,[40] where the prisoner claimed that denial of the appointment of counsel had prejudiced his defense in a case which carried the possibility of life imprisonment, a sentence actually imposed. The prisoner had applied first for habeas corpus and then for a writ of error in the state court; both applications were denied by a single justice of the Supreme Judicial Court. Owing to the defendant's failure to give notice to the Attorney General of exceptions filed to the orders, final judgment was entered against the defendant. The federal district court denied the petition without prejudice, and the court of appeals affirmed in an opinion by Judge Magruder which reflected some anxiety and a readiness to stand by for further proceedings: "After some hesitation, we have come to the conclusion that the district court committed

[39] See Schechtman v. Foster, 172 F.2d 339 (2d Cir. 1949), *cert. denied,* 339 U.S. 924 (1950).
[40] 181 F.2d 601 (1st Cir. 1950).

no error in denying the petition without prejudice, leaving petitioner to the expedient of filing in the Supreme Judicial Court another petition for a writ of error."[41] The court would not assume that the state court would apply res judicata to successive applications for writ of error, or would fail to afford review because of financial inability to prepay the costs of preparing and printing the record for review. The petitioner did in fact file a writ of error before a single justice, on which he again appeared *pro se,* although appearances by two attorneys were entered. After a hearing the justice, taking account of the principles of due process governing the right to counsel, found that the defendant had not been overreached or misled in his defense and that the trial judge had safeguarded his rights. The defendant filed exceptions before the full bench, and after notice of estimated expenses for printing the record he filed a motion for extension of time to pay costs and later a motion to proceed in forma pauperis. This motion was denied.[42]

The *Buchanan* case points up two deficiencies in state procedure which are not only troublesome from the standpoint of due process but are sources of vexation in relations with the federal courts — the failure to adopt a flat rule making counsel available to indigent criminal defendants, and the inflexibility of printing requirements for the record on appeal. Happily both these trouble spots have been alleviated by the Supreme Judicial Court. There has been added to the Rules the following provision: "Where in these rules there is a reference to printing, the record may be prepared in such other manner as may

[41] *Id.* at 605.

[42] Buchanan v. Commonwealth, Law No. 51306, Sup. Jud. Ct. for Suffolk County, June 27, 1952. The single justice stated: "I find that the petitioner took the stand freely and voluntarily and was not induced to do so by misrepresentation or coercion. The petitioner concedes that he testified to his having participated in the robbery of which he was charged and that the testimony was the truth. I find that that testimony was not obtained in violation of the petitioner's privilege against self-incrimination." For assistance in locating this record I am indebted to my friend Herbert P. Gleason, Esq., of the Massachusetts bar.

be ordered by the full court or a justice." And in 1958 a new Rule was adopted requiring counsel for indigent defendants in felony cases.[43]

But we have run ahead of our story. It remains to speak of three cases in which the federal court of appeals took a more active role on habeas corpus. In *O'Brien v. Lindsey*,[44] the defendant, after conviction, sought a writ of error on fourteenth amendment grounds, which was denied by a single justice of the Supreme Judicial Court, and no petition was filed with the full bench because of the defendant's lack of funds to pay the estimated cost ($375) of printing the record. A motion to be allowed to proceed on the original record was denied by the single justice. The constitutional claim was that the defendant had tried to secure the services of a lawyer from the Voluntary Defenders Committee, that in fact a lawyer had appeared for him but had not had time to familiarize himself with the case and had been denied a continuance. The federal district court granted habeas corpus. The court of appeals, agreeing with the district court that the state justice had evidently regarded the case mistakenly as raising a question of right to appointment of counsel rather than effective representation, nevertheless directed that a more moderate course be taken. Instead of issuing the writ, the court directed that the case be retained on its docket, with a suggestion to the prisoner that he proceed forthwith in an effort to have his bill of exceptions entered and heard in the Supreme Judicial Court. Judge Magruder was not prepared to assume that the full bench lacked power to afford review on a typewritten record, especially since the liberalizing amendment to the Rule on printing had already been adopted. The subsequent history of the case is interesting. The full bench did grant a writ of error and reversed the conviction for denial of an opportunity to counsel to seek a continuance owing

[43] On printing, see MASS. SUP. JUD. CT. (FULL CT. PRACTICE) R. 10; on right to counsel, see MASS. SUP. JUD. CT. (GEN.) R. 10.

[44] 204 F.2d 359 (1st Cir. 1953).

to "an unfortunate combination of circumstances." [45] Thereafter, its watchful waiting ended, the court of appeals discharged the writ of habeas corpus whose execution it had stayed.[46]

In two cases the writ was actually issued. *Melanson v. O'Brien*[47] presented the claim of denial of an opportunity to employ counsel. The prisoner asked the district attorney how he might secure a postponement in order to obtain counsel and was told, with more rhyme than reason, that no postponement was possible because "jail cases had to be tried before bail cases." After conviction, motions for a new trial and writ of error were denied, and ultimately certiorari was denied by the Supreme Court. The federal district court, erroneously viewing the case as a problem of *Betts v. Brady*,[48] denied habeas corpus, but the court of appeals reversed. Finally, in *Robbins v. Green*,[49] the court was moved not only to affirm the granting of the writ but to express its sentiments on the limits of forebearance. The case arose in Maine, and involved a trial without adequate opportunity to consult with counsel and a sentence imposed in counsel's absence. After unsuccessful efforts to secure habeas corpus and review in the state appellate courts because of financial inability to prepare a bill of exceptions, Judge Clifford in the federal district court granted habeas corpus. The warden contended in the the district court that the proper state remedy was writ of error; on appeal he conceded that this would not open up errors outside the record, but argued that a writ of error coram nobis was the proper course, though acknowledging that it had never been used in Maine to secure release from confinement pursuant to a void judgment of conviction. "There comes a point," Judge Magruder said, "where federal judges in discharge of their present statutory duty are obliged to give a

[45] Lindsey v. Commonwealth, 331 Mass. 1, 5, 116 N.E.2d 691, 693 (1954). The facts as found differed slightly from the findings of the federal district court.
[46] 210 F.2d 953 (1st Cir. 1954).
[47] 191 F.2d 963 (1st Cir. 1951).
[48] 316 U.S. 455 (1942).
[49] 218 F.2d 192 (1st Cir. 1954).

hearing to a convicted state prisoner petitioning for a writ of habeas corpus, however delicate and distasteful this duty may be—otherwise the petitioner may justifiably have the impression that he is being treated to a grand 'run around' between the state and federal courts. We think such a point was reached in this case."[50]

This series of habeas corpus cases places in a strong light the characteristic qualities of Judge Magruder's opinions in the whole area of federal-state relations: painstaking care, close analysis, utter candor, courtesy, forbearance, strength husbanded for the decisive occasion. It is not too much to say that in these qualities he stands as an exemplar, unself-consciously to be sure, for judges as well as others who are called upon to play a statesmanlike role in the troubled conflicts of authority that beset a federal union.

---

[50] *Id.* at 195. Judge Magruder stated: "It is of course conceivable that some time in the future the Supreme Judicial Court of Maine may revive the ancient common law writ of error *coram nobis* and hold that it is an available procedure for challenging the validity of a judgment of conviction under circumstances like the present case." *Id.* at 194-95. Subsequently the Supreme Judicial Court of Maine did revive the writ of error coram nobis. Dwyer v. State, 151 Me. 382, 120 A.2d 276 (1956). In its opinion the court said: "The U.S. Supreme Court has pointed out many times that there should be a post conviction procedure within the various states which will be broad enough to cover all deprivations of constitutional rights under the Federal Constitution, and it is well to note that a writ of error *coram nobis* has been accepted by the U. S. Supreme Court as an appropriate post conviction remedy. Hysler v. Florida, 315 U.S. 411 ... Maine takes pride in attempting to carry out the old maxim that 'for every wrong there is a remedy.'" *Id.* at 388, 395, 120 A.2d at 280, 283.

14   Judge Learned Hand

Learned Hand was born to be a judge. Not that his vocation was ordained by inheritance, by the circumstances that his father and his grandfather wore the robe and his cousin and he were to share for many years that extraordinary bench of the Second Circuit. ("Quote Learned and follow Gus" was Justice Jackson's even-handed advice to the bar when they met to honor the cousins.) Nor is it that Learned Hand was unfitted for callings of another kind. A student of James and Santayana, his speculative bent might have found fulfillment as a critical philosopher. His gift of tautly sustained eloquence could have been given scope as an essayist. The passionate and playful side of his nature, which so delighted his friends—in extra-judicial gatherings he loved to put an antic disposition on—might have been disciplined in another way for the stage. The poetry and precision of his mind might even have led him to become, as in moments of self-doubt he insisted he would want to be in another incarnation, an atomic physicist.

And yet who can doubt, reading his beautifully wrought opinions and sensing the aesthetic satisfaction that comes from the final mastery of almost intractable materials, that nature meant him for a judge? One is reminded of the Frenchman's comment on Lord Mansfield: "Il s'amuse de juger." Humane, scrupulous, resourceful, searching, he sought to find principles of order that would compose the anarchy of human experience without suppressing the vitality of diversity and disarray. He

Published in Harv. L. Record, September 21, 1961, on the occasion of the death of Judge Hand, and reprinted by permission.

had the artist's touch, and it is not surprising that in his skeptical world of values craftsmanship stood very near the summit. Speaking on the occasion of his eightieth birthday he said:

Win or lose, the day will come when "the great globe itself, yea, all which it inherit, shall dissolve and ... leave not a rack behind"; and on that day it can be said of each of us: "Thou thy worldly task hast done, home art gone, and ta'en thy wages." That is the nature of all things; though, little as we may like to acknowledge it, it is irrelevant to their value and their significance; for permanence as such has neither value nor significance. All that will then matter will be all that matters now; and what matters now is what are the wages we do take home. Those are what we choose to make them; we can fix our pay; the splendor and the tragedy of life lie just in that. Values are ultimate, they admit of no reduction below themselves; you may prefer Dante to Shakespeare, or claret to champagne; but that ends it. Nevertheless, I believe you will agree to put among the most precious and dependable of our satisfactions the joy of craftsmanship. In that I include all efforts to impose upon the outside world an invention of our own: to embody an idea in what I shall ask your leave to call an artifact. It is not important what form that may take; it may be in clay, in bronze, in paint or pencil, in a musical score or in words; it may even be in sport; it may be in the mastery or exercise of a profession; it may be in a well-balanced nature, like Aristotle's "Great-Souled" man; or it may be in redeeming the world. It is enough that we set to mould the motley stuff of life into some form of our own choosing; when we do, the performance is itself the wage.

It is not surprising that Learned Hand was a judge's judge, an lawyer's judge, a student's judge. Within the profession, as John Morley said of Mill, to respect him became a mark of one's self-respect. His distinction in no way derived from judicial heroics. Quietly and firmly he molded the law in such specialties as admiralty, patents, and unfair competition. One cannot recall his ever holding an act of Congress unconstitutional, though opportunities were not wanting in his more than fifty years of judging. He did, to be sure, rule in the Schechter case that the labor provisions of the N.R.A. were invalid, but the noteworthy aspect of that decision was that he did not pronounce a doom on the Act as a whole and in fact he sustained the trade-practice regulations that were later overturned by the Supreme Court. In World War I he protected the radical monthly, *The Masses,* from suppression under the Espionage Act (and was reversed on appeal), but construction of the Act and not its unconstitutionality as applied was the basis of decision. And in World War II he wrote a much-controverted opinion sustaining the validity of the Smith Act. The philosophy of his Holmes lectures on the Bill of Rights is indeed reflected in his decisions.

His judicial credo—to use too formal a term for what was essentially a mood—was expressed in a letter to the senior judge of another circuit, marking the latter's twenty-five years of judicial service: "In this quarter century how much the whole character of the job has changed! You and I do not accept those changes; we believe that judges are to be the means of carrying forward the continuity of political institutions, not of making them over. Let us be loyal to that conviction, confident that, if the show is to go along at all, our duty will in the end seem as important as even that of those who seek to rebuild this world nearer to their heart's desire."

Coming from someone less sensitive, such a conception of the judge's station and its duties might be taken as an apologia for the wooden and pedestrian. But for Judge Hand, to be detached was not to be aloof. Rather, I believe, he meant to prescribe for judges something of the counsel which Matthew Arnold offered for literary critics: that they do two things, enter sympathetically into the experience of a work of art and then withdraw. Substitute for a work of art another form of human experience, whether it be a contract, a collision, or an act of the legislature, and the counsel is not inapt. To remain immersed is to run the risk of becoming bemused and sentimental; to remain aloof is to court the danger of obtuseness and pedantry. The judge, like the critic, must perceive the peril that lies in pursuing one virtue alone.

The more remarkable appreciation of Learned Hand is that which has come for this supreme craftsman from outside his own profession. It is as if, amid the jarring clamors of the zealots of the world, there has emerged wistful admiration for the voice of moderation, a clinging faith that perhaps the qualities of the gifted judge are not irrelevant to the troubles of our time; a hope that beneath the raucous slogans of the partisans a sensitive ear may listen for undertones of common speech; an awareness that civilization, like the legal order, is not to be nurtured arduously for all by uprooting it conveniently for some. This ampler legacy from a life in the law may be but dimly seen, yet is somehow perceived.

And so I venture to think that Judge Hand's impress, deeply cast upon the law, is, in the mysterious ways of thought and feeling, trembling on much else besides.

Index of Cases

General Index